April 2024

Cold War Kids

Cold War Kids

POLITICS AND CHILDHOOD IN

POSTWAR AMERICA, 1945–1960

Marilyn Irvin Holt

 University Press of Kansas

To Cathy, Teresa, David, and Joel,

my baby boomer sisters and brothers

© 2014 by the University Press of Kansas

Published by the University Press of Kansas (Lawrence, Kansas 66045), which was organized by the Kansas Board of Regents and is operated and funded by Emporia State University, Fort Hays State University, Kansas State University, Pittsburg State University, the University of Kansas, and Wichita State University.

Library of Congress Cataloging-in-Publication Data

Holt, Marilyn Irvin, 1949–
Cold War kids : politics and childhood in postwar America, 1945–1960 /
Marilyn Irvin Holt.
pages cm
Includes bibliographical references and index.
ISBN 978-0-7006-1964-1 (hardback)
1. Child welfare—United States—History—20th century.
2. United States—Social policy—20th century. I. Title.
HV741.H566 2014
362.70973'09045—dc23
2013048670

British Library Cataloguing-in-Publication Data is available.

Printed in the United States of America

10 9 8 7 6 5 4 3 2 1

The paper used in this publication is recycled and contains 30 percent postconsumer waste. It is acid free and meets the minimum requirements of the American National Standard for Permanence of Paper for Printed Library Materials z39.48–1992.

CONTENTS

ILLUSTRATIONS

ACKNOWLEDGMENTS

For their invaluable assistance and many helpful suggestions, I offer sincere thanks to the archivists and photoarchivists at the Eisenhower Presidential Library and the Truman Presidential Library. Particularly, I want to thank Mark Corriston (now retired from the National Archives Central Plains Region) for pointing me toward an important set of records and David Haight (now retired from the Eisenhower Presidential Library) for his enthusiastic support for my use of the White House Conference on Children and Youth collection. I also want to thank staff at the Library of Congress, Kansas State Historical Society, Marquette University, and Nebraska Children's Home Society for their help in locating and providing images for this publication. Lastly, a special thank you to readers of this manuscript; their comments and suggestions were greatly appreciated.

Introduction

In 1909, President Theodore Roosevelt sponsored the first national conference concerned with America's youth, bringing together the country's most prominent leaders in social reform and child welfare. Such an event seems unremarkable today. After all, in present-day America, it is generally assumed that political leaders and presidential administrations will take an interest in issues related to children and teenagers. It is taken for granted that any number of federal agencies and programs will affect youngsters' lives. This, however, has not always been the case. In the not-so-distant past, presidents and lawmakers paid scant attention to any issue related to children and childhood, and with the exception of a few programs for specific child populations, federal agencies and bureaus were not in the business of evaluating childhood experiences or responding to the needs of children.

That began to change early in the twentieth century when Roosevelt's White House conference led to creation of the U.S. Children's Bureau in 1912. The bureau, which conducted studies used to support proposed legislation and which developed health-care programs for mothers and children, was the federal government's first recognition of "not merely the rights of children, but also the need to create a permanent agency to at least study, if not protect them."[1] Child welfare was an accepted function of the state. In the years that followed, other presidents held White House conferences on children while Congress took unprecedented steps to enact a handful of laws that addressed child labor, provided grants-in-aid to dependent children, and funded health-care services for the poor and marginalized. In each case, legislation was narrowly structured to include only particular segments of the population deemed to be the most socially and economically dependent. These incremental policy developments only affected specifically defined groups. Middle- and upper-class children may have benefited by the very fact that the government recognized children as a presence, but they were not the intended targets.

This approach continued into the postwar years, but it was joined, and sometimes pushed aside, when monumental events such as introduction of the Salk vaccine or the Soviet launch of *Sputnik* produced a federal response that included all children. Reaction to a periodic crisis or issue did not open a floodgate of sweeping mandates or rapidly enlarge the federal government's role. Nonetheless, the mid-twentieth century was a turning point in state-to-federal relations and in increased federal action directly affecting children and teenagers. This set the postwar era apart from earlier decades, making the immediate years after World War II a distinct period in the history of children.

Nevertheless, in studies of children and childhood after World War II, the late 1940s and the decade of the 1950s receive short shrift. Scholars skim past those years on their way to the 1960s and beyond. While some policy analysis appears in such volumes as *Reinventing American Childhood after World War II* and in *Children, Families, and Government*, the immediate postwar years are not the focus. Studies of childhood history have approached the subject of government policies from various angles. Judith Sealander's *The Failed Century of the Child*, for instance, studies specific examples of state programs and their failure to deliver on their promises, while Kriste Lindenmeyer's *"A Right to Childhood"* considers government involvement from the federal side, examining the shortcomings and achievements of the U.S. Children's Bureau. These volumes— like broader narratives such as Steven Mintz's history of American childhood and Julia Mickenberg's analysis of the Left's influence on children's literature—present the postwar period as a small part of a larger story. The dearth of in-depth study and analysis is largely a result of the perception that the late 1940s and the 1950s were, in the words of one writer, a time of "stagnation." From that point of view, the time was simply an unremarkable era, bracketed between the Progressive/New Deal programs before World War II and the explosion of federal mandates that began in the 1960s under President Lyndon Johnson's Great Society.[2]

This characterization is misleading. A closer look reveals a pivotal period in which the federal government's role in issues related to America's youth was hotly debated, periodically challenged, sometimes championed, and slowly expanded. By definition, politics is the act of influencing or guiding government policies, and those components of political action are readily apparent in the postwar era. Activism in the forms of national conferences sponsored by the White House and federal agencies, rigorous congressional debates and hearings, and presidents' active involvement contributed to a national discourse. Politicians, policymakers, and the public talked about a myriad of topics that ranged from the benefits of physical fitness to foodstuffs contaminated by radioactivity to the dangers of comic books. Some of these discussions produced tangible legislative action or social policies. These, in turn, impacted the growing-up experiences of millions of youngsters. At other times, lawmakers considered and then rejected any course of action, providing instructive blueprints for limiting government's reach into childhood.

The political narrative and public discussion were driven by many forces. Television, urbanization, divorce, working women, and social integration were just a few. Some pressing issues, such as the immediate postwar housing crisis and its impact on families, reflected temporary problems and then faded into the background with time, but most of the issues affecting children were long-lived. Desegregation was a drawn-out process, and there was simply no easy fix for poverty or delinquency or child dependency. In that context, readers will find many of the topics as relevant today as they were almost fifty years ago. Some of the language and debates for or against certain courses of action sound eerily familiar, particularly when lawmakers and the public voiced opinions and offered solutions regarding aid to education, health care, and juvenile delinquency.

This volume examines the ways in which governmental entities and the postwar administrations of Presidents Truman and Eisenhower reacted to special problems and needs associated with children and teenagers. It considers the ways in which the federal government, against the backdrop of a Cold War mentality, became more involved in aspects of health, education, and welfare. And it looks at the baby boom as a phenomenon that shaped American thought and a societal acceptance of the argument that *all* children, not just the poorest and neediest, deserved their government's attention.

This study begins with the 1950 and 1960 White House Conferences on Children and Youth as a framework for discussing childhood policy and children's experience in relation to population shifts, suburbia, divorce and family stability, working mothers, and the influence of television. The chapters that follow provide an in-depth look at education, at the government policies and congressional actions affecting the child/teenage population of orphans, foster children, and juvenile delinquents, and at the multifaceted issues of health care. In conclusion, the final chapter considers the levels at which the federal government was involved in child-related issues and programs by the end of the 1950s and how that informed later legislation.

In order to talk about the postwar period, defined here as the years from 1945 to 1960, it must be said that despite the nostalgia often attached to those years, it was a time of tensions and conflicts. These were the years of the Korean War, the Berlin Airlift, the Soviet Union's iron fisted control of Eastern Europe, the partition of Palestine and the creation of Israel, and the economic revitalization of war-ravaged Europe under the Marshall Plan. Americans worried about foreign instabilities and the international spread of communism. At home, they sought domestic tranquility and prosperity, and minority groups, most visibly African Americans, felt that their wartime service on the home front and in the military had earned them the right to better treatment and an end to segregation.

With the Great Depression behind them and World War II finished and won, Americans talked about returning to routines of everyday life. Although periods of economic recession and inflation occurred after the war, there was a sense of great possibilities. The shift from wartime industry to a consumer economy brought more material goods to market, and a new prosperity meant that more families could afford the bounty. Between 1940 and 1960 real wages increased by about 30 percent. The median family income rose from $3,083 to $5,657. Although the spread of prosperity did not touch everyone or every household, the middle class expanded. Surveys showed that the majority of Americans, across lines of race and ethnicity, considered themselves to be members of the middle class, if not in actual income, in outlook and self-confidence.[3]

More buying power and access to a larger quantity of material comforts were proof that personal finances and the national economy were on the upswing. Nevertheless, a fundamental element in a return to normal was marriage and parenthood. Observers of the time and scholars of today have drawn a correlation between the out-of-the-depression, postwar climate and Americans' enthusiasm for marriage and children. Americans began to marry at an earlier age, have more children per household, and equate stability with home and family.

The return to peacetime and normalcy on the home front impacted children, too. Just as returning servicemen and women had to readjust to civilian life, children had to adapt. Youngsters growing up during the war years fell into two categories—those who were old enough to remember a time when the country was not at war and younger children for whom war was the norm and peace was a new experience. During the war, children and teenagers did their "bit" on the home front. They took part in scrap drives, saved money for Bond drives, planted Victory Gardens, and signed on with the U.S. Crop Corps as Victory Farm Volunteers. They took jobs vacated by adults; they looked after younger siblings and shouldered a larger amount of home chores; they stepped in as leaders for Girl and Boy Scout troops, 4-H Clubs, and other youth organizations. Summing up the result, one girl wrote that the war turned "our life from Kids to 'Mini-Adults' with much responsibility."[4]

By war's end, 183,000 American children had lost fathers; untold others were without brothers or other close relatives. There were no concrete numbers for how many youngsters were placed into the care of relatives or orphanages while fathers were away and mothers worked, but there was data to show that juvenile delinquency was on the rise and that the substantial increase in employment of teenagers between the ages of fourteen and seventeen was enabled by lax enforcement of school attendance and child labor laws. The signs were troubling, but there was a general feeling that all would be righted with peacetime.[5]

As for war's impact on children, the adult world acknowledged that children were affected, but it preferred to emphasize the everyday, normal experiences of childhood and adolescence. In 1945, for example, *Life* magazine took this line during the months that the German war machine was collapsing and battles in the Pacific were at their most desperate. But, at home, *Life* portrayed kids as if they remained untouched by war news. One photographic essay pictured "Teen-Age Ballet," while another set out to prove that "Teen-age Boys Are Just the Same as They've Always Been," and seven covers that year (with accompanying articles inside) pictured children or older teenagers doing what kids were supposed to do—play basketball, attend school, romp with friends at a pajama party, or join a social club.[6]

America's national birth rate, which showed signs of an increase in the late 1930s, reversed to a downward trend during the war. Then, in May 1947, the U.S. Public Health Service reported a slight change. Although barely noticeable, there was an increase between August 1946 and May 1947. In the short term the numbers could be explained as the natural result of veterans returning home, reuniting with spouses, or getting married and starting families. Having children was an affirmation of life after the terrible destruction and loss of life during the war. Domestic life, including the addition of children to the home, suggested a desire for stability, anchored by the nuclear family. For the long term, however, the Public Health Service was not sure how to interpret its data, cautioning that there was "no way of telling whether the increase will continue."[7]

The increase not only continued, but multiplied the population beyond all predictions and expectations in the postwar years. Between 1946 and 1960, almost 60 million children were born in the United States. These baby boomers, as well as the adolescents and teenagers who were children during World War II, made up the first television generation. They were first to grow up in the atomic age. This group of youngsters witnessed the first orbiting satellite in space, and they were the first to not only see but experience the beginning of school desegregation in the nation's schools. And, family mobility meant that an increasing number of the boomer generation grew up in the suburbs.

The country was not prepared for the ways in which the astounding boom in babies, as well as the existing population of teenagers and younger children, strained the educational, welfare, and social systems of the country. It was against this backdrop of the baby boom and a society that regarded the teen years as a special phase of life with its own distinct culture and social problems that political discourse debated what role the federal government would take in the lives of children. Should it continue, as in the past, to narrowly confine its responses? Or, did changing circumstances demand more action? Congress, Presidents Truman and Eisenhower, federal agencies, and White House conferences and committees became part of the national discussion. In one way or another each entity examined the state of American childhood and adolescence as the country returned to a normal rhythm of peacetime and an anticipated era of prosperity.

The American Dream—the belief that social, educational, and financial advancement was possible for anyone—seemed within the grasp of more people. Not only parents, but society in general, expected a greater portion of American promise for young people. This meant modern schools and an adequate number of qualified teachers, nicer homes and neighborhoods, better and more accessible health care, and the chance for youngsters to explore and develop their personal interests and talents. Parents were primarily responsible for their children's daily lives and shaping their futures, but there seemed to be a general agreement that other adults in the local civic, educational, and church communities played supporting roles. And, as expectations rose for America's youth, parents and the public in general wondered if everything they wanted and imagined for children could be accomplished without the federal government taking a larger part to support their hopes. Were existing programs enough, or did circumstances call for additional legislation and funding?

It was a prickly question. On the one hand, some issues such as providing quality education or controlling juvenile delinquency often seemed too overwhelming and complex for communities or states to tackle on their own. Conversely, no one wanted the government to become a nursemaid to the country's children, either overstepping the bounds of parents' rights to rear children as they saw fit or treading on states' rights to control welfare and health-care programs, public education, and laws concerning such things as juvenile crime.

Before the war years, both the private sector and federal programs focused on the needs of the poor, the marginalized, and the dependent. They were the "luckless" children who most needed society's protection. In the postwar era, that focus remained. Aid to widows with children, health-care clinics for minority populations, and new education initiatives for the children of migrant workers were just a few of the projects. Nevertheless, a number of problems seemed so enormous and affected so many youngsters of all economic or social backgrounds, policymakers often began to consider America's youth as one collective group.

Every child had the right to a childhood that included enough to eat, health care, classroom instruction, protection under child labor laws, and a stable family life. This concept, first articulated in the late nineteenth century, was reinforced during the Progressive Era and post–World War I and New Deal years. Woodrow Wilson, for instance, talked about the rights of children; Herbert Hoover produced a "Child's Bill of Rights"; and well-known reformer Florence Kelley proclaimed that "a right to childhood follows from the existence of the Republic and must be guarded in order to guard its life." By the late 1940s, the idea of child rights was inculcated into the public psyche. While it went without saying that the poor and dependent needed society's help, there was a growing acceptance of the argument that children of the middle and upper social and economic classes should be added to the equation. They, too, deserved notice and support in a number of areas. The point was emphasized by planners for the 1950 White House Conference on Children and Youth. As the conference's executive committee struggled to find the right wording for its mission statement, it agreed to emphasize that the conference was about "the dignity and worth of every individual [child]."[8]

American society—not just the white mainstream society that traditionally drove the discussion, but the broad spectrum of ethnic and racial groups—believed that it had a stake in seeing that children and teenagers were intellectually, emotionally, and physically equipped for their personal futures and for their later roles as responsible citizens. They should be able to pursue individual talents and interests, while also being prepared to confront a very uncertain world that included nuclear weapons and the specter of spreading Communist ideology. The country's youth had the right to expect society to act on their behalf. As a result, the growing-up years of the baby boomers and teenagers of the era were influenced in innumerable ways by public discourse, political ideology, Cold War rhetoric, and the policies of presidential administrations.

Yet, anyone hoping to find extensive studies of domestic policies in the many available biographies and autobiographies of presidents and members of Congress will be disappointed. David McCullough's massive biography of Truman, for instance, devotes only eight of its over one thousand pages to the president's domestic agenda, referencing the postwar housing crisis, unemployment, and a national health insurance program. The same holds true for seemingly comprehensive Eisenhower biographies. In his work on the Eisenhower presidency, Stephen Ambrose considered only two domestic problems, the desegregation of Little Rock Central High School and the administration's reaction to *Sputnik*. This line of discussion is also found in more recent biographies such as the one by Jim Newton, which barely acknowledges Eisenhower's domestic challenges. An exception to the lack of in-depth domestic investigation, although it is not a full-scale study of the Eisenhower presidency, is David Nichols's volume on Eisenhower and civil rights.[9] Given the volatility of world events, it is perhaps understandable that historians and biographers have said comparatively little about domestic agendas and policies, including those that concerned children and teenagers. After all, it was a turbulent and uncertain time in foreign relations as one dangerous crisis after another erupted.

As for the postwar era in general, published works abound in the form of scholarly books, popular nonfiction, presidential studies, biographies, and memoirs. Among the diverse topics are the era's popular culture, the growth of suburbia, the Cold War, family life, and the status and roles of women. Elaine Tyler May's *Homeward Bound*, for example, connects postwar family life to the containment policies of the Cold War, while *Not June Cleaver*, edited by Joanne Meyerowitz, expounds on the diversity of postwar women. Lary May's edited collection of essays in *Recasting America* offers a perspective on the many influences that transformed American culture. Lizabeth Cohen's *A Consumers' Republic* considers the premise that mass consumption promoted prosperity and a more egalitarian society, and John Bradley's anthology, *Learning to Glow: A Nuclear Reader*, delves into first-person accounts of experiences and fears associated with the atomic age. These are, of course, just a sampling from among many publications that seek to describe, analyze, and better understand American culture and society immediately after World War II.[10]

Certainly, these volumes and studies include references to children and childhood experiences, particularly when the subject is family relationships, domesticity, and the roles of women, but the children are secondary to the primary thrust. A few volumes have concentrated on the baby boomers themselves, but the context has been either personal experiences or boomers' later impact on American culture. Among these are Tom Brokaw's *Boom!*, Victor D. Brooks's *Boomers*, Steve Gillon's *Boomer Nation*, and Landon Jones's *Great Expectations: America and the Baby Boom Generation*.[11]

This volume uses some of the voices of boomers and their older teenage counterparts. Ethnic, racial, economic, and geographical diversity is considered, as is the shared popular culture. This, however, is not intended as a study of reminiscences or an analysis of a generation and its later influences on American society. Rather, the narrative is an exploration of the relationship between the political landscape, cultural views of childhood, and the impact these had on the country's young. It uses the words of the presidents, congressional debates and investigations, the viewpoints of various members of Congress, studies and reports issued by the White House Conferences on Children and Youth, the White House Conference on Education, and presidential commissions dedicated to juvenile delinquency, physical fitness, and migratory labor. Included in the archival material consulted for this study are records that have not been used to any extent, if at all, by researchers. The Orphan Correspondence Files, for example, are in the holdings of the National Archives and Records Administration, but required a Freedom of Information Act review and release from the U.S. Department of State because the documents pertain to the adoption of European war orphans by American couples. And, while the extensive records for the White House Conferences on Children and Youth have been opened for years to researchers at the Eisenhower Presidential Library, the material has largely been overlooked.

Many and varied sources were used to construct the narrative. They provide a multifaceted view of the interplay between the private sector, social change, state initiatives, and the federal government. This is the story of what people said they wanted for their children. It is a study of society's expectations and how those were expressed and played out in the political arena. Whether lawmakers and presidents were prepared or wished it, this study argues that this period was a turning point for greater government involvement. When federal legislation and action are considered collectively, rather than as stand-alone events, they illustrate increased federal action in all aspects of childhood issues. Politics and public policies affected children's lives and their growing-up years. What was said about youngsters and what was done, or not done, on their behalf influenced what Americans at midcentury believed about childhood and about the part government at the federal level should play in the lives of children and teenagers.

White House Conferences on Children and Youth: The Public Discussion

"It is particularly important in today's troubled times that we continue to move ahead toward our basic objective—improving the well-being of our children."

—*President Harry S. Truman, June 20, 1950*

Truman was speaking to the men and women planning the 1950 White House Conference on Children and Youth, also known as the Midcentury Conference. Seven months later, in early December 1950, 6,000 conference participants crowded into the Armory in Washington, D.C. They came as representatives from all forty-eight states and the U.S. territories. They came from rural and urban backgrounds, from federal agencies and Congress, and as representatives of 460 national organizations that covered the gamut of religious, medical, educational, recreational, and industrial interests. Somewhat overwhelmed by the numbers, national committee chair and Federal Security Agency administrator Oscar R. Ewing wondered if, instead of this throng, more might be accomplished with fewer delegates concentrating on "one or more specific problems." At the same time, he realized that every state and territorial entity expected to be heard and that no organization wanted their particular constituencies or interests ignored. Participants came to Washington for the purpose of initiating a "detailed examination of all problems relating to children."[1]

The increasing child population, as well as a new emphasis on considering children of diverse social-economic backgrounds, gave participants more to talk about. They met in small groups according to their special expertise and interests. Some concentrated on research projects devoted to health care, education, and the influence of the mass media. Others studied laws affecting adoption, divorce, employment, institutionalization, and juvenile justice. A number of groups looked at community resources, as well as the subjects of discrimination, youth organizations, recreational outlets, social work methodologies, religious instruction, and church youth groups. As the topics explored in this chapter will show, discussions delved into such areas as adequate housing, the impact of television, family life and divorce, and working women.

Behind the scenes, months of preparations had gone into gathering information for the delegates' use. Data collected by state, territorial, and local organizations and agencies was submitted in reports that offered a picture of local and regional needs, effective programs, levels of funding, special local circumstances, and conditions among groups such as migrant workers and Native Americans. The U.S. Children's Bureau provided statistical data collected nationally, and the Interdepartmental Committee, established in 1948 to promote better communication between federal agencies and departments administering programs affecting children, contributed information.

The number and reach of these federal entities was somewhat surprising. The Department of Agriculture, for example, had allocated funds for 4-H youth programs since 1928 and ran the National School Lunch Program, which began in 1946. The Bureau of Indian Affairs was in charge of Indian-only schools and medical services; the Department of Defense was responsible for military dependents, both overseas and on stateside military bases; the Veterans Administration provided survivor benefits to widowed women and their children; and the Social Security Administration oversaw Aid to Dependent Children (ADC, later renamed Aid to Families with Dependent Children, AFDC). Obvious leaders of the Interdepartmental Committee were the U.S. Children's Bureau and the Department of Health, Education, and Welfare (HEW), established in 1953 as a cabinet-level agency to assume the functions of the Department of Education and most of those under the Roosevelt-created Federal Security Agency. By the time the second postwar White House Conference on Children and Youth met in 1960, the number of agencies associated with the Interdepartmental Committee stood at twenty-eight. From its input, conference participants had detailed information at their finger-

Among the 6,000 participants at the 1950 White House Conference on Children and Youth were members of the conference's Advisory Council for Youth Participation. Dwight D. Eisenhower Library

tips. How else would they know that during the 1947–1948 school year almost 78,000 one-room schoolhouses were still operational, that national infant mortality rates were dropping, or that in 1960 over 155,000 children of servicemen killed in World War II and Korea were eligible for aid through the War Orphans' Educational Assistance Act?[2]

The 1950 White House Conference on Children and Youth was the fifth in a succession of meetings that began in 1909 when activists and reformers in the national child welfare movement urged President Theodore Roosevelt to sponsor the first such conference. Reformers and child-care advocates came together in other federally sponsored meetings over the years, but the White House Conference was different. It had the power of the presidency behind it. Intended or not, the 1909 meeting (subtitled "Care of Dependent Children") laid the groundwork for future ones and for presidential involvement. The 1909 conference was followed by one in 1919 (subtitled "Standards of Child Welfare"); later meetings, federally funded beginning in 1930, convened on the decimal year until 1970 when the last officially titled "White House Conference on Children and Youth" occurred.

Detailed organization went into conference planning. For both the 1950 and 1960 meetings, there was a small executive committee, aided by a national committee with about 100 members. Some individuals such as child-rearing expert Benjamin Spock and social welfare leader Robert Earl Bondy were considered "musts" for the national committees and, as a rule, committee members were sought out for their expertise. Occasionally, however, a name triggered political opposition. One well-known psychologist, for instance, was dropped from consideration in 1960 because Senator Bourke B. Hickenlooper, a Republican representing Iowa, "violently objected" to the man as a liberal "New Deal Democrat." A congressman might block a potential participant, but he or she was just as likely to intercede on behalf of an individual or organization that wanted to serve on the national committee or attend the conference. Missouri's Senator Forrest C. Donnell, for example, put in a word for the president of the Reorganized Church of Jesus Christ of Latter Day Saints, which was headquartered in Truman's hometown of Independence, and members of the Democratic National Committee asked the White House in 1950 to consider a judge who, although a Republican, was "very liberal, and an exceptionally good man." Conferences were never completely free of partisan politics or conflicting political ideologies, but they did not dominate discussions or recommendations made in final reports. In fact, a chief concern of the executive and national committees was not political leanings but individuals and organizations that zealously advocated for one group of children at the expense of others. Conference goers had to be reminded that the meetings were about "all children," unlike prewar conferences where the greatest emphasis was directed toward the most economically and socially disadvantaged.[3]

At each conference, many issues such as alleviating poverty and fighting juvenile delinquency were staple topics. In that sense, meetings shared similarities, but each also reflected the distinctive nature of the period in which it occurred. The 1950 conference resonated with an urgency to make up for what had not been accomplished or had been allowed to fall by the wayside during the war years. In the face of military mobilization and the wartime culture at home, proposals and expectations advanced by the 1940 White House Conference on Children and Youth were overshadowed or put aside. To accommodate the need for home-front labor during the war, for example, states relaxed enforcement of compulsory school attendance laws, and officials at both the federal and state levels failed to vigorously enforce the Fair Labor Standards Act of 1938, which was designed to eliminate child labor in particularly dangerous working conditions. The result was a pressing sense of regaining lost ground when conference participants gauged current conditions and then identified emerging issues.

The world of 1950 was vastly different from that of 1940. The United States had emerged from World War II as a superpower with nuclear capability, facing off against the Soviet Union in a Cold War. When President Truman spoke of "today's troubled times," his mind was on the foreign troubles that faced the country. Just months before the White House conference convened, the president approved development of the hydrogen bomb as another weapon in America's arsenal, and many in the United States believed that the country was just a breath away from another war. International tensions escalated when North Korean troops crossed the 38th Parallel in June and Truman authorized sending U.S. troops as part of the United Nation's contingency to stop the invasion. There were troubled times at home, too. Senator Joseph McCarthy was on television and radio with claims of finding Communist sympathizers in and out of government, and Americans demanded that lawmakers address domestic issues that affected their everyday lives. Senator Hubert H. Humphrey, elected in 1948 as a Democrat from Minnesota, called it a time of "postwar and newwar [sic] angers and problems." He later wrote, "Letters from constituents reflected the craze. Do something about housing, do something about education, do something about unemployment, but cut taxes, slash expenditures, cut budgets, they said in obvious contradiction."[4]

Domestic issues and conflicts abroad were ever present in the minds of those concerned with the 1950 White House Conference on Children and Youth. Less obvious, or noticed, were reports that the child population was on the rise. While the conference was in its planning stages, the

U.S. Census Bureau was counting the population. During the late 1940s the U.S. Public Health Service noted a slight increase in the national birth rate, but it was not until the Census Bureau began issuing preliminary reports for the 1950 U.S. Census that Americans began to realize that the increasing number of children they saw in their own communities was a national trend. In 1950, the number of children under the age of fifteen stood at a startling 1.4 million, and there were over 363,000 young people between the ages of fifteen and nineteen in the United States. No one could have predicted in 1950 that growth in the child population would continue at an unprecedented rate, but the decade that followed witnessed the phenomenal "baby boom." Between 1946 and 1960, almost 60 million children were born in the United States.[5]

By their sheer numbers they, as well as teenagers of the postwar period, had the capacity to impact American culture and its institutions. Their behavior and their perceived needs influenced society's concept of childhood, as well as the formulation of public policies that affected them. Enormous expectations were invested in this group. Both parents and society in general projected the belief that these youngsters and teenagers would achieve more and have greater opportunities than any generation before them. The repeated message for children was that they lived in a country where they could grow up to be whatever they wanted, realizing any personal dream.

In a way, postwar expectations were a culmination of decades in which American society formed beliefs about childhood and the nature of children. In the 1800s perceptions evolved from defining childhood as a relatively short phase early in life to expanding the period of childhood into adolescence. Children were perceived as innocents and childhood as a time for emotional and intellectual development. In the ideal childhood, there was time to play, especially when games and playtime were adult-directed and structured. There were chores to be done, but no hard labor, and youngsters were to be nurtured in a child-centered family.

By the early twentieth century this attitude, perpetuated by the middle class, was firmly established. In fact, one commentator wrote in 1903 that "The Cult of the Child" reigned in the United States. Contemporaneously, Ellen Key proposed in *The Century of the Child* that in the twentieth century "all social arrangements and decisions would be based solely on an assessment of their impact on children." Key's charge to the citizens of the world came during a period of heightened activity among those involved in America's child welfare movement and at a time when the systematic application of the social sciences was touted as the modern way to cure the country's many social ills and inequities.[6]

Facing the future, and its demands, required progressive thinking in all things, including how society defined children and the elements that produced a nurtured childhood. The growing-up period called childhood expanded during the nineteenth century. By the end of World War I, adolescence, considered to be the period between puberty and the legal age of majority, was thought of as a developmental stage toward adulthood. No longer children, adolescents were not yet quite adults. In part this viewpoint became common because an increasing number of older adolescents lived at home for longer periods of time, attended secondary school, and entered the labor force at a later age. To accommodate that stage in life, the words "teenage" and "teenager" entered the vocabulary of twentieth-century Americans. Sometimes the words were used interchangeably with adolescent, but they took on their own meanings. "Teenage" first appeared in publication in the 1920s. "Teenager" became widely used in the 1940s when teens, too young for war duty but old enough for the home-front war effort and jobs, solidified a youth culture that was uniquely their own.

Traditionally, children and young people are defined by milestones associated with a certain age. These might be religious or cultural markers, but others are established by state laws—for instance, the age that a teenager can leave school or get married. While society generally divided youngsters into children, adolescents, or teenagers, the age at which youngsters passed from one stage to another could be rather nebulous. By the mid-twentieth century, the U.S. Children's Bureau established new definitions for its own purposes. Using data from the 1950 census, children and "youth" were placed into five categories: 0–4 years (preschool); 5–9 years (early school ages); 10–14 (middle school ages); 15–19 (latter school ages); and 20–24 (years at the threshold of adult working lives and/or marriage). The addition of an age category beyond the teen years indicated that young people attending college or vocational schools, serving in the military, beginning their married lives, and/or becoming parents were in a transitional phase between the teen years and full adulthood. This last category also suggested that American society felt some continuing responsibility for these young adults.[7]

In the postwar era, the everyday lives and experiences of children and teenagers were scrutinized by educators, child-rearing advisors, psychologists, medical personnel, child-welfare workers, and the popular press. The country had fought a war to protect itself and its young. Now that the war was won, adults faced the daunting task of ensuring that America's youth were not only nurtured but prepared to meet the challenges of a world that now included nuclear weapons and a Cold War environment that pitted the "free" world against communism.

Children and teenagers, as well as family life, became popular topics for magazines, newspaper columns, television and radio programs, child-rearing literature, and professional forums. No topic was too important or, it seemed, too trivial. In the popular press, hosting the perfect birthday party was treated as seriously as identifying warning signs in a child's physical development. Women's magazines and newspaper columns offered up advice, as did authoritative parenting books. There seemed no end to expert opinions on discipline, infant feeding, nutrition, home health care, or child psychology.

Advice was not limited to the care of young children. An increasing amount of literature was devoted to the subject of teenagers. Adults, parents or not, read commentaries and advice columns concerned with teenagers' preoccupation with cars, music, "teen town" dance clubs, and spending time on the phone. The power of words shaped society's view of children and teenagers. They were to be nurtured, educated, and allowed to explore their talents. At the same time, public discourse painted a gloomy picture of what might happen if parents, communities, and society in general failed in their vigilance and their responsibilities.

Since the late nineteenth century, reformers and child-welfare advocates championed school attendance and child labor laws, worked to reduce juvenile delinquency, and sought welfare reforms. They pushed at municipal and state governments to enact laws; less often they lobbied for federal statutes. After its creation, the U.S. Children's Bureau was regarded as the government's child advocate, although a number of federal departments and agencies operated child-related programs and early twentieth-century presidents of both political parties demonstrated interest in some aspects of problems affecting children. At midcentury, the federal role in shaping childhood experiences was small when compared to the impact of state and territorial laws and programs. The paradigm began to shift, however, after 1945. State and territorial entities, along with private-sector child advocates, regarded some issues as too enormous to be dealt with on local/state levels. Numerous problems were national, not localized or regional. Without giving up states' rights or local options, they wanted a greater federal presence in leadership, funding, and state-federal, public-private partnerships. No one wanted the federal presence to become too large, but recommendations coming out of the 1950 White House Conference clearly signaled a shift when the call went out for more federal involvement.

Slowly, public policy formed by Congress and presidential administrations increased, affecting childhood experiences and the public expectation for government's role. There were single-issue campaigns aimed at addressing specific problems, as well as activist-driven agendas in which youngsters were symbolic of social change or reform. Sometimes policymakers and lobbyists from the private sector were able to convince Congress that a vote against a proposed program such as the National School Lunch Program was a vote against children, but more often than not, much more was involved than the simple question of how youngsters benefited. America's young and issues directly affecting them were considered by Presidents Truman and Eisenhower, debated in congressional committees, analyzed in the reports of special commissions, and pored over in special conferences sponsored by the White House.

The 1950 White House Conference on Children and Youth, and the one that followed in 1960 (the "Golden Anniversary" meeting), were the most comprehensive in breadth of topics and in the number of public and private citizens to come together for the purpose of discussing America's youth. The conferences examined in detail the multifaceted state of childhood, adolescence, and the early post-teen years. They also suggested ways in which the private sector, states, and the federal government could act as partners. Working together these diverse entities could better identify pressing needs and hammer out solutions to what sometimes seemed insurmountable problems. The pronouncements, conclusions, and discussions that took place at the White House Conferences on Children and Youth were particularly instructive because participants studied and dissected the ways in which issues of the times impacted young peoples' lives. These meetings also solidified the cultural concept of children as beings with rights.

That children had rights was not a new, radical concept. For most of the twentieth century, the "inalienable rights" of America's children, articulated by President Woodrow Wilson in 1919, had been forming and coalescing. During the 1920s Herbert Hoover narrowly applied the concept to child health when, as director of the American Child Health Association, the organization published a "Child's Bill of Rights." Then at the 1930 White House Conference on Children and Youth, President Hoover added to the list of rights with a lengthy eighteen-point charter. The itemized points specified that children had the right to an education, health care, and nutritional food. They should rightly expect protection under child labor laws, and to the child "in conflict with society," the charter declared the "right to be dealt with intelligently as society's charge, not society's outcast." Although the chief concern was the most dependent and unfortunate, the 1930 charter did not make distinctions along lines of income or social standing. Subtly, the charter implied that society was obligated to acknowledge *all* children. No matter their situation, gender, ethnic or racial background, America's youth were entitled to certain considerations. Foremost, they should be able to expect that the nation in which they lived would act on their needs and enhance their growing-up years. By 1950, the idea of children's rights seemed to be taken for granted. When that year's White House Conference met, it drew up its own charter, a "Pledge to Children." This reiterated much of the 1930 language, adding, "We will respect your right to be yourself and . . . to understand the rights of others."[8]

The pursuit of happiness was not explicitly stated in the list of rights, but society accepted the idea that children should be happy. The culture of consumerism said that youngsters would be happy with more material things. Psychologists and child-rearing literature talked about bringing greater happiness into children's lives by relieving feelings of fear, guilt, and jealousy. Achieving happiness went hand-in-hand with self-expression. No longer was it desirable, even necessary, for youngsters to be reared with the expectation that they might have to defer personal hopes and interests. These were not the depression or war years. Self-denial was a thing of the past. Parenting experts, including Dr. Benjamin Spock, advised a child-centered approach. What once would have been punishable behavior was now explained as a child's normal exploration of his or her environment. If parents recognized misbehavior as a form of self-expression, it could be dealt with more easily and channeled into acceptable, productive conduct.[9]

Although there were many who considered some child-rearing advice too permissive, there was no doubt that the principles of child happiness and personal fulfillment had entered social thought and acceptance. Youngsters who were free to pursue their own interests and talents would contribute more to a democratic society and be greater assets to the country's future. This was largely the thinking of those participating in the White House Conferences on Children and Youth during the postwar era. In fact, "Individual Fulfillment in a Changing World" was the theme selected for the 1960 conference, but then scrapped because neither it nor any other phrase adequately captured the meeting's extensive agenda of topics.

Abandoned or adopted slogans were telling reflections of a particular place in time. Planners for the 1940 White House Conference on Children and Youth, for example, chose "Children in a Democracy." Although the depression of the 1930s took a toll on children and their families in innumerable ways, the conference theme proclaimed that America remained a democracy while Fascism and militarization were sweeping much of the world into war. Still, participants at the 1940 meeting felt that the country was at a crossroads, caught between the catastrophic circumstances of the Great Depression and the gathering clouds of military conflict. The conference's final report declared, "In the interest of child welfare, we must be on guard."[10]

Ten years later, in 1950, democracy and America's future were still very much on the minds of conference organizers. There was another type of war being waged—the Cold War—and Americans still needed to be "on guard" for their children. Not only should youngsters be physically protected from harm, they needed the emotional and psychological tools necessary to deal with the world as it was. In choosing a theme for the 1950 conference, organizers were influenced by President Truman's support for the National Mental Health Act of 1946, the act's creation of the National Institute of Mental Health, and the 1949 launch of "Mental Health Week" by a private organization, Mental Health America. Conference participants, it was decided, would approach all of the meeting's many topics from the viewpoint of psychological well-being. The conference's subtitle became "For Every Child a Fair Chance for a Healthy Personality."

Mental health and child development were discussed to some extent at both the 1930 and 1940 White House Conferences. As more was learned and disseminated about child psychiatry and early development, that information began to shape educational philosophies and child-rearing advice. Professionals gave more credence to psychology and the relationship between children and their home environments. Participants at both the 1930 and 1940 meetings agreed that "the family . . . [is] the greatest power in his [the child's] life for or against mental health." In 1950, however, conference participants were asked to move beyond the family unit and to consider community, educational, and religious environments. They were to analyze "what is needed, socially, economically, and psychologically to render an emotionally and intellectually sound generation."[11]

Whether conference goers were focused on race relations or adequate health care, community resources or recreational facilities, they prefaced the discussion by asking how mental health and emotional development were encouraged or adversely affected. Said one conference proposal:

Not only is it necessary that children have families and that they receive from their parents adequate food and clothing and shelter and instruction in our way of life; it is also necessary that these . . . be provided in a way that is psychologically sound. The same is true of all other services [i.e. education, medical treatment]. . . . various professions are discovering that the new findings in psychology, sociology, and physiology have important implications in their work . . . , and the general public regards them as matters of interest and concern.[12]

No aspect of childhood or the teenage years was to be ignored. At previous White House Conferences, a few new topics were added to those initially discussed in 1909, but the 1950 meeting substantially widened the field of subjects. Religious instruction and spiritual development, access to health care and schooling, ethnicity and race, work, leisure, and family relationships were studied and analyzed from every angle. The desired outcomes were identifying usable solutions and strategies that, once implemented, would enable youngsters to become emotionally sound "efficient workers, clear thinkers, [and] loyal citizens."[13] A nagging concern, however, was ensuring a healthy outlook in the face of crises around the globe and the threat of nuclear war. How did adults strike a balance between making children and teenagers feel safe while also warning them that their world could disintegrate in a flash of a bomb or be overwhelmed by Communist forces?

News reports were filled with stories of U.S.-Soviet tensions, Communist takeovers in China and Korea, and arrests of Soviet agents working in the United States. Commentators and politicians warned of Communist subversives and infiltration. Soon after the end of World War II, an article in *Life* magazine proclaimed that the Soviets had thirteen U.S. cities targeted for missile attacks that would initially kill 10 million. On television, youngsters saw newsreels of above-ground nuclear tests and simulated footage of what happened during an atomic blast. Through television, radio, and the popular press, they learned about bomb shelters being constructed and provisioned in home basements or backyards. During one televised interview a woman told reporters that even if her family's new shelter was never used for its intended purpose, it would "make a wonderful place for the children to play in."[14]

Considerable lines of newsprint, along with radio and television air time, were devoted to home shelters, although relatively few were actually built. Some families considered them a passing fad while many decided that if the worst happened, they would rather not live in a post-nuclear world. Other families turned existing space into a shelter. Said one boy of his parents' solution, "A corner of the basement was weekly stocked with Spam and stuff—a few candles and jugs of water." Pragmatically, shelter construction took money, and the government decided not to subsidize family shelters. Both Congress and the Federal

"We Stay in Safe Places" was one reminder of what to do in the event of a nuclear attack. Library of Congress

Civil Defense Administration rejected proposals for federally financed shelters, opting instead for "American-style ... self-help defense."[15]

Young people were unlikely to live in a house or apartment building with a bomb shelter or know anyone who did. Still, just the knowledge that they might be needed underscored the tenuous times, as did civil defense practices. In thousands of small towns and cities, preparedness exercises brought blaring sirens, alerts sounded over radio and television stations, and drills that rushed evacuees out of impact areas. In thousands of schools, youngsters watched the film short *Duck and Cover*. Produced by the U.S. Office of Civil Defense, the film calmly assured students that the unthinkable probably would never happen, but if it did, everyone needed to know the best ways to protect themselves. And, adults were reminded to be constantly vigilant. A disaster preparedness pamphlet distributed to local school districts, for instance, was illustrated with a mushroom-shaped cloud rising over a schoolhouse. The accompanying text warned that radioactive fallout would affect much larger areas than bombs' intended military and industrial targets. Rural schools, cautioned the pamphlet, were as much at risk as urban ones, and school administrators around the country were admonished to take civil defense and student preparedness seriously.[16]

Youngsters internalized the messages of doom. One baby boomer recalled, "Every Thursday night a passenger plane traveling from Denver to Dallas flew over our house. I knew what it was and where it was going, but I'd hear the engines and think, 'Is that the bomb?'" Another child of the 1950s later wrote of *Duck and Cover* and his elementary school's air raid practices: "I didn't know much, but I knew enough to know the probability of this protecting us against an atomic bomb was on the order of slim to none." And, on the subject of shelters, a boy said, "When I saw a brochure for a bomb shelter in the mail on the hall table, I couldn't sleep for three nights. Instead, I slept on the floor outside their [his parents'] bedroom. . . . I never did tell them why."[17]

Most parents were probably unaware of how the talk of bombs and Communists affected their children, and they did not assume, as do adults in the postmodern world, that youngsters were cognizant of life's unpleasant realities. The head-in-the-sand approach was aided and abetted by child-rearing advisors who explained ways to handle normal childhood fears of the dark or strange surroundings, but failed to talk about children's anxieties about more terrifying unknowns. Psychologists were, noted one historian, "strangely silent on the issue of the fear of atomic weapons." Some adults did remark, however, on a growing sense of "individual helplessness" observed among America's youth during the postwar years. This was articulated by a 1960 White House Conference youth participant: "I'm part of a generation that is faced with evidence daily that the H-bomb may drop tomorrow. We need something that tells us that life is worth something—has meaning."[18]

In the Cold War climate of the times, psychologically sound children and teenagers were essential to what Truman characterized as the "struggle between freedom and communist slavery." The United States had just emerged victorious from a world war, but the country faced new military threats from Communist countries and what many believed was an insidious infiltration of Communist sympathizers inside America. The Soviet Union tested its first atomic bomb in 1949. Alger Hiss was put on trial in 1950 for denying his association with a Communist agent, and in the same year Julius and Ethel Rosenberg were arrested and charged with committing espionage against the United States. Senator Joseph McCarthy was making his name synonymous with a "red scare" anti-Communist campaign, and American troops were fighting in Korea.

Wherever one looked, it seemed that communism was an imminent threat to the country and its children. If they were to save themselves and their democratic society, that generation needed the moral fiber that came from good mental health and emotional stability. Speaking to the 6,000 assembled for the White House Conference on Children and Youth, Truman said, "I believe the single most important thing our young people will need to meet this critical challenge in the years ahead is moral strength."[19]

To some degree, White House Conference discussions mirrored the times in which they occurred. At the 1950 gathering, for instance, delegates did not fully understand or appreciate the effects of migration to the new suburbs or to "boom" states where defense/military industries offered employment. Nor could they anticipate the baby boom and the

In the early 1950s, television was a novelty in American homes. In this New York City apartment, Father reads the paper while the children stare at a test pattern. Library of Congress

ways in which changing demographics would impact the ability of states and local communities to provide and maintain such services as schools and hospitals.

Also largely overlooked by the 1950 conference was television, its programs for children, and the medium's impact on learning and child development. After all, there were fewer than 100 commercial television stations in the country, and those were located in metropolitan areas. In Illinois, for instance, there were four stations, all in Chicago. In 1950 it was difficult to imagine that the number of stations would mushroom nationally and that 85 percent of all American households would have a television by the end of the decade.[20]

By 1960, however, television had White House Conference partici-pants talking and shaking their heads. What were children sprawled before the TV seeing and absorbing? Hugely popular with the younger set were *The Howdy Doody Show* with Buffalo Bob and the marionette Howdy Doody; *Watch Mr. Wizard*, which made science fun and understandable; *Ding Dong School* with the kind but firm Miss Frances; and *Captain Kangaroo* and his Treasure House. Saturday mornings were devoted to Westerns while early evening prime time offered *Lassie, Adventures of Rin Tin Tin*, and *The Wonderful World of Disney*. When youngsters got home after school on weekdays, they could tune in to *The Mickey Mouse Club*; teenagers had *American Bandstand* or local stations' versions of teen dance programs. Of course, youngsters watched other shows, too; the situation comedies, game and variety shows, and sports events watched by their parents. From a kid viewpoint, it seemed perfectly normal to see a children's program in the morning and then watch the wrestler Gorgeous George slam his opponents in the evening.

Television brought families and friends together when everyone gathered around the set for an evening of viewing. It informed with news programs and "specials" on weighty issues of the day, and it offered pure entertainment. Television also had huge potential as an educational tool. The right kind of programs could teach youngsters basic values of respect, cooperation, and teamwork. The medium could expand children's horizons and introduce them to places and people that most were unlikely to visit or meet in person. In hindsight, the Native American characters on Captain Kangaroo are embarrassing stereotypes, but at the time, their intent was to teach about other cultures. Television held great educational possibilities, but many parents, commentators, and educators felt that, even in its early stages, it was falling short. Impressionable children were being exposed to potentially damaging images and messages.

One of the chief complaints was the portrayal of violence. While it was true that the good guys always triumphed in Saturday-morning Westerns and that gun fights seldom resulted in deaths, some critics did not see exciting action but uncalled-for violence. An episode of *Hopalong Cassidy*, for instance, was taken to task for showing a gang of rustlers holding a "small crippled girl" hostage. Other commentators saw violence in the slapstick comedy of Howdy Doody and Captain Kangaroo. Children could be emotionally damaged in any number of ways, and it was not beyond the realm of possibility, warned some, that more youngsters would act out the violence they saw and become juvenile delinquents.

By 1960 when television was a common fixture in American households, participants at the 1960 White House Conference explored the influence of television violence on the young. As a reference point, they turned to the 1954 Senate Subcommittee to Investigate Juvenile Delinquency, which heard from television performers, network executives, and representatives from the National Association for Better Radio and Television. According to the latter, the "most objectionable" shows were *Captain Midnight*, *Dick Tracy*, and *Captain Video*. (Interestingly, each came to television because they were popular radio shows, comic book characters, or Saturday afternoon movie serials.) In his rebuttal to claims that these shows, and several others, fed antisocial behavior, ABC vice president Robert Hinckley was succinct: "Television is a very young industry, while juvenile delinquency is very, very old." The new medium would not become a scapegoat for a social problem that seemed to have no single cause or cure.[21]

Another common complaint lodged against television, unrelated to violence, was the commercialism attached to children's programming. Children and teenagers were bombarded with images of things they "had" to have. Even the best educational programs had commercial sponsors, and the family-oriented *Wonderful World of Disney* was criticized as nothing more than an extended commercial for the Disneyland theme park. There was some truth in that; Disneyland loomed large on the vacation wish list of thousands of boys and girls. Nevertheless, the accusations simply would not stick. The television show was too popular, and Disney movies were considered to be an art form of quality.

Experts in education, child psychology, and early childhood development were largely disappointed in television. It was not living up to its "educational potential." Neither were radio or motion pictures, for that matter, but television was the chief worry. At its very worst, it failed to provide positive messages of fair play, teamwork, and personal integrity. Instead, said the critics, it encouraged violence, materialism, passivity, and self-absorption. One solution was more noncommercial channels with educational programming. However, the Federal Communications Commission had licensed only eleven such stations by 1955, and only three of those—the ones in Madison, Wisconsin; Pittsburgh, Pennsylvania; and St. Louis, Missouri—were commended by the U.S. Children's Bureau for "outstanding" children's shows. Clearly, noncommercial television, which by the early 1960s consisted of fewer than sixty stations, was not in a position to draw the majority of viewers away from commercial stations. The answer, said critics, was to pressure the networks for more educational programming and less violent content. Ultimately, however, it was agreed that parents, who generally showed less consternation over what their children watched than child-rearing experts, were the ones responsible for their children's viewing habits.[22]

In the context of television and other elements of the popular culture, conference participants talked about young people as a general population. In other instances, however, children and teens were discussed in terms of race, religion, and economic and social circumstances. Within this framework, forums at the White House Conferences on Children and Youth separated and then subdivided youngsters into defined study populations. This was consistent with the approach taken at earlier White House Conferences. The final report of the 1940 "Children in a Democracy" White House Conference on Children and Youth, for instance, devoted an entire chapter to minority children. Much of it detailed the many ways in which African Americans, Filipinos, Mexicans, Chinese, Japanese, and Native Americans were deprived of social services and schooling.[23]

One noticeable difference between the 1940 report and discussions at the 1950 and 1960 conferences, however, was the interjection of civil rights and discrimination as an issue that was uniquely African American. Other minorities faced forms of discrimination, but their experiences became even less visible as African Americans marched, organized, and staged sit-ins. Looking back on the 1960 conference where younger representatives listed "the right of nonviolent resistance" as a "youth priority," one adult participant remarked that civil rights was "as significant as the discovery of the Salk vaccine and penicillin," but "we couldn't see it in 1960 enough, or clearly enough."[24] There was no way to predict the rapid cultural and social shifts taking place in the country as African Americans pushed for an equal place in all aspects of American life.

Aid to Dependent Children (ADC) programs offered a case study in discrimination and regional economic differences. In southern states, racial prejudice kept African American children from receiving ADC support, and when money was provided, it was far less than that available to children in other sections of the country. In Mississippi, which had the lowest national median income of $1,200, the average grant to a child was $6 a month; by comparison, in Illinois, where the median income was $3,500, the average monthly grant was just over $26.[25]

This was just one disparity among many. Although other minority children often faced similar problems, the focus of postwar conferences was Black America. Issues of discrimination, civil rights, and integration were hotly debated. The 1950 White House Conference report from President Truman's home state of Missouri called for an end to segregation because it produced "psychological insecurity" in children. Still, conference participants found it difficult, if not impossible, to find common ground. When it was suggested that the 1950 conference officially support wholesale integration, the recommendation was voted down. So, too, was the demand from younger delegates and the American Psychological Association that no future meetings or conferences be held in Washington, D.C., until the city completely integrated its restaurants and hotels. While those calls for equality were overruled, the Midcentury Conference aimed for an ideal, promising in its "Pledge to Children" that "we will work to rid ourselves of prejudice and discrimination, so that together we may achieve a truly democratic society." The conference was a microcosm of America. Some wanted to hold back the tides of change; others wished to usher in a new social order.[26]

During the ten years between the 1950 and 1960 conferences, there were advances in eliminating discrimination. Public facilities in the District of Columbia were integrated; the Supreme Court ruled "separate but equal" unconstitutional in *Brown v. Board of Education*; federal troops escorted black students into Little Rock's Central High; and civil rights demonstrations became a national occurrence. Reflecting these changes in America's social and cultural life, the 1960 conference expressed perceptively different attitudes from those voiced in 1950. There was little opposition to resolutions calling for an end to segregation in schools, housing, and employment. More than half the work groups demanded an end to discrimination and Jim Crow laws. Several voted to support sit-ins taking place at lunch counters in a number of cities. The teenage chairman of one work group announced that civil rights protesters would "not stand alone." To make the point, a number of youth delegates, described as "aggressively progressive" by one observer, used their free time to organize picket lines in support of sit-ins.[27]

Changes in the social fabric of America were reflected in the White House Conferences on Children and Youth. Also apparent were what one sociologist called "trends . . . typical of the decade." Housing, or the lack of it, was a good example of an issue that drew considerable attention in 1950, but far less notice in 1960 when adequate housing was not regarded as a national crisis but one that touched only specific groups. Most of these were marginalized, low-income families, including southern sharecroppers, Native Americans on reservations, residents of the Ozarks and Appalachians, and Latinos in urban barrios.[28]

In 1950, however, there was a national housing crisis that affected Americans across a broad spectrum of social, economic, and ethnic backgrounds and in all parts of the country. The public demanded that Congress and President Truman act to correct a postwar shortage that actually began in the 1930s. During the Great Depression there was little new home construction or modern improvements made to existing dwellings. Then, during the war years, building and modernization were a low priority when materials went to the war effort. By the time GIs began to come home, the problem could not be ignored. The dramatic rise in marriage and birth rates turned the housing crunch into a crisis. "More and more families are looking for a place to live," Republican Everett M. Dirksen told his Illinois constituents. "Every Congressman's desk is piled high with literature on the subject of housing. . . . Veterans recently discharged are writing Congressmen, clamoring for action." In Chicago alone at least 100,000 veterans were homeless, prompting the city to sell old streetcars for conversion into housing.[29]

Demand for homes and apartments in large urban centers, small towns, and even in farm communities consistently rose while owners of rental properties took advantage of the situation. Inflationary rents, which the Truman administration attempted to control with the 1947 Housing and Rent Act, and the scarcity of homes for purchase forced young families to live with relatives or share space with nonrelations. A reported 6 million families were "doubling up" with friends or relatives in 1947. Another 2 million, noted a 1948 congressional Joint Committee on Housing, wanted private housing but could find no accommodations other than those available in boarding houses, tourist cabins, or trailer parks.[30]

There was a general outcry for a national housing program that would meet the needs of families in every income group, in every type of community, but delegates at the 1950 White House Conference on Children and Youth were most concerned with those at the bottom of the social and economic ladder. Children in those households also deserved decent housing that, in turn, provided a nurturing, safe environment. It was recommended that the federal government help communities around the country build 800,000 low-rent housing units "at full speed." The conference also endorsed federal legislation aimed at urban redevelopment, slum clearance, and construction of "good quality" low-cost housing. The conference was in effect backing Truman who, as early as September 1945, promoted federal support for low-income housing and redevelopment of blighted urban areas.[31]

By 1949, construction and urban renewal were under way as a result of that year's Housing Act (expanded by the 1954 Housing Act that not only provided funding for new construction but for rehabilitation of deteriorating areas). The result in 1950 was 177 local housing projects opened to families of all races and religions. Nonetheless, progress was slow. Truman faced opposition from a coalition of Republicans and southern Democrats who once stood against Roosevelt's social reforms and now tried "to block his successor." They refused to support the 1949 bill, and the real estate lobby called it a step toward socialism. Although the goal of the 1949 Housing Act was to provide a "suitable living environment for every American family," it never lived up to the promise. Instead of the 810,000 new low-cost housing units planned for, only about 360,000 were built.[32]

Part of the difference between the ideal and the reality was not enough federal funding. However, resistance at state and local levels played a significant part. In California, for example, twenty out of thirty projects were defeated by anti–public housing campaigns. Some of these efforts were led by local citizens. Others were organized by realtors and devel-

An aerial view of Levittown, Pennsylvania, one of the famous postwar housing developments. Library of Congress

opers. Responding to the latter, Richard M. Nixon, at the time a U.S. senator representing California, tried unsuccessfully to block a $13 million federal construction contract in Los Angeles. Arguments that public housing held down real estate values or brought blight to otherwise stable communities meant that the working poor, often minorities, remained in substandard housing and neighborhoods, taking an emotional and physical toll on children. Bad housing, said one report, contributed to a breakdown in family unity, slowed child development, and encouraged juvenile delinquency. A number of social service programs existed for residents, but, said one teenager, "The agencies seem more like satellites around the [housing] project without ever touching the needs of the people there."[33]

The experience was quite different for youngsters whose parents were able to build or buy homes. Thousands of families were helped by the

Veterans Administration program of guaranteed mortgage insurance to returning GIs. The number of new housing starts soared, reaching a record high of 1.65 million in 1955. Although "the dream house shown in the movies, by the mass media, and on the subdivision circulars" did not represent the many types of housing that sheltered American families, the homes in new subdivisions and developing suburbs became stereotypical of the era. The suburbs themselves came to represent a changing trend in American life, accounting for more population growth during the 1950s than that found in the central cities they surrounded.[34]

Some real estate developers offered large homes on good-sized lots, but the suburbs became equated with the well-known Levittown model, the first large-scale style of housing development to use prefabrication techniques in construction. The tract homes were designed for young families. The basic Levitt house, for example, had two bedrooms, one bath, and was built on a slab. The Levitt Cape Cod, priced at just under $8,000 could be "all yours," said one ad, "for $58 [down]." House designs were limited and lot size standard.[35]

Nationally the Levitt technique, which began with the first Levittown on Long Island, New York, was replicated by other builders in other suburban developments. Duplication did not mean, however, that everyone applauded this form of homebuilding. There were those who denounced the housing for its numbing conformity. Lewis Mumford, known for his critiques on architecture, described the new suburbs as "a multitude of uniform, unidentifiable houses, lined up inflexibly . . . inhabited by people of the same class, the same income." Developers like William Levitt defended the overall design. In an article for *Good Housekeeping* magazine, he declared that "Houses are for people, not critics."[36]

Home buyers, often young couples, seemed to agree. For them, a new suburban home presented a chance for home ownership, and many explained their decision to relocate to the suburbs as a move to benefit their children. The youngsters seemed not to notice the cookie-cutter similarity between homes, and like children elsewhere, their playmates were from the "neighborhood." They played in neighbors' yards, in the street, and took advantage of organized activities such as scouting and Sunday school.

The sameness of the homes' exteriors in suburbia reflected the sameness of the people inside. The overwhelming majority were Caucasian. The most notable diversity was between being Catholic or Protestant. The new suburbs went a long way in solving the worst housing crunch the country had ever experienced, and as Lizabeth Cohen noted in her study of postwar consumerism, suburbia "promised to create a more egalitarian and democratic society as more Americans than ever before would own a stake in their communities." When a family from a Polish neighborhood in the city moved next door to a family that came from an Irish enclave or a family that claimed English roots, the new mix seemed to prove the promised outcome. On the other hand, minority families met resistance when they tried to move into neighborhoods where they were not wanted. Discrimination in housing was lessened in some places after the U.S. Supreme Court, in *Shelley v. Kraemer* (1948), declared restrictive covenants unenforceable and when the Federal Housing Authority and Home Finance Agency called on lending agencies in 1955 to approve loans for purchase and construction of homes by minorities. Nevertheless, redlining by banks, the realtor practice of racial steering, and segregation of public housing in some cities continued to limit accessibility to African Americans, Latinos, Asians, and Jews.[37]

Inside American homes, no matter the place or their occupants' heritage, a noticeable trend was emerging. Couples seemed determined to stay together. Except for a sharp rise in divorces in 1946 when returning servicemen and their wives found that they could not sustain their marriages in peacetime, the divorce rate began to decline. The number of divorces in 1947, for example, stood at approximately 450,000, down from the previous year's 613,000. "With all the risks inherent in marriage," mused *Parents Magazine* in 1948, "it is comforting that more than three quarters of all marriages stick."[38]

The stick-to-it-iveness of couples and a continuing decline in divorce rates was not, however, readily apparent when the White House Conference on Children and Youth met in 1950, and it was certainly not anticipated when the National Conference on Family Life convened in 1946. That conference, first suggested by the American Home Economics Association in 1944 to consider problems facing the modern American family, was attended by representatives from more than 100 national organizations.[39] Discussions dealt with such topics as "marriage courses" for high school and college students, couples' adjustment to parenthood, and marital compatibility. Also on the agenda was the subject of divorce, which was on the rise when the conference convened. Family Life delegates found the increase so disturbing that they urged President Truman to establish a presidential commission to study marriage and divorce laws. Family Life's goal was to make it more difficult for couples to end their marriages and turn more youngsters into children of divorce.

Truman approved the idea of a conference on the American family. There was no reason to do otherwise. He also appeared before Family Life conference delegates to deliver an "off-the-cuff speech," but he refused to do more. Truman rejected the idea of giving the meeting presidential sponsorship, and he refused to create a presidential commission to study the state of marriage and divorce in the United States. Although a number of government programs existed to help families and sustain them in times of destabilizing crises, neither the White House nor federal agencies would become embroiled in a public discussion on the subject of divorce. If states and territories decided to toughen their laws, as the Family Life conference suggested, that was up to them.[40]

In the late 1940s, statistical evidence suggested that divorces would increase, leaving more children to be raised in one-parent households, the products of the often-studied and much-decried "broken home." In fact, just the opposite happened. Married couples stayed together during the 1950s. In part, this was a result of the era's emphasis on home as a refuge and the nuclear family as an American ideal. But it also had to do with a collective attitude. Both men and women believed in marriage, were determined to make it work (even when it was unhappy), and often considered unmarried men and women as somehow flawed in personality and attitude.

Marriages could survive a great deal, including mothers taking jobs outside the home. Despite dire warnings about the effect on children and despite society's prevailing emphasis on domesticity, the number of women in the national workforce steadily rose during the 1950s. In 1958 a reported 22 million women were employed either full or part time. Of that number more than 16 million were, or had been, married, and more than 7 million of these women had children under the age of eighteen. Women with very young children were the least likely to seek outside employment while "older married women, once a small minority among women workers" became the largest group of employed females. According to Katherine Howard, administrator of Federal Civil Defense and one of 175 women to hold high-level positions in the Eisenhower administration, American women worked "in every category listed in the 1950 census."[41]

Family finances were one reason to work outside the home, but there were other factors. Women talked about having the money to purchase "extras" for the home. Some cited finding personal satisfaction, as well as having more options for employment. The decade was filled with contradictory messages about work and women's personal experiences. A well-known professor and expert in social work, for instance, wrote that married women who were comfortably supported by their husbands were moving "toward masculinity" when they left their children in the care of others and competed with men in the workplace. These women, said the author, did not "represent a common feminine pattern in this country."[42]

The social pressure represented in this sort of attitude, said Betty Friedan in *The Feminine Mystique*, led educated women like her to remain home as wives and mothers, rather than carve out professional careers. That was the experience of Friedan and many others, but it was not a singular one, shared by all women. Studies conducted during the 1950s found that many working women, including African Americans, who had to support their families would have preferred to be at home rather than in the labor force. The reality of working women was that there was a wide spectrum of circumstances that included not only the question of if women worked outside the home but why.[43]

The effect of working mothers on children received far less notice at the 1950 White House Conference on Children and Youth than at the 1960 meeting. The reason was simple. The number of working women significantly increased during the 1950s. Of the 16.6 million women in the labor force in March 1958, for instance, 7.5 million had children under the age of eighteen. This number was 80 percent higher than the 4.2 million in 1948. Speaking to the 1960 national White House Conference committee, President Eisenhower recognized that many women did not have the option to decide if they would work outside the home. He still wondered about the impact on children and family life. The topic produced spirited debate when conference workshops later met to discuss various aspects of the American family. Some participants argued that working mothers lived "richer, fuller lives." Others called them "irresponsible." Fathers were also faulted for a variety of perceived failings—"allowing" their wives to work, putting women in the position that they had to work, and taking over the mother's role when she was gone.[44]

Teenagers had their own perspectives on working mothers. Said one girl at the 1960 meeting, "My mother has always had to work and when we were children, my father and mother told us why and what we had to do and we did it. I think it is helping me become what I hope to become." As for the suggestion that working mothers inadvertently encouraged juvenile delinquency, the youth representatives were skeptical. Young people were responsible for their actions. This view was articulated by one young man. "I think that by the time a person is a teenager he has a responsibility for the way he behaves and if he knows his mother has to work he ought to be ashamed for becoming wild."[45]

Not everyone thought parents were doing a bad job, but there was a nagging concern among experts and commentators that no one knew the long-term outcome for children of working mothers or the emotional and physical price women paid. A number of authoritative experts, including Dr. Benjamin Spock, were reluctant to criticize working women too harshly. After all, some mothers had no choice but to work outside the home. "Usually," soothed Spock, "their children turn out all right." He was less sympathetic to women who could afford to stay home. His advice to them was that a "little extra money" and their personal satisfaction were "not so important" as their job of being mothers. While some experts and commentators suggested that children of working women were fortunate to have mothers who felt fulfilled, rather than frustrated, many others were quick to predict adverse effects on children. "The energy output required by trying to fill two jobs," said one study, "[made] mothers more irritable with their children." Many believed that it was not only the children, but women who suffered when they strayed from home and family. Oregon's White House Conference report, for instance, cited "a terrific increase in the sale of aspirin and whiskey" as proof that women invited "psychological hardship" when they tried to be both homemaker and wage earner.[46]

One hardship was the lack of day care. During the war years, centers operated near defense plants, but these served only about 10 percent of those needing day care. After the war ended, the continued funding of these centers was questioned. Mothers once employed in defense work were now expected to go home and look after their children there. This was, in fact, the argument made by Fritz G. Lanham, a Democrat from Texas, when he spoke from the House floor in 1945. Although Lanham sponsored the 1942 Community Facilities Act (better known as the Lanham Act), which provided, among other things, federal funds for day-care centers connected to defense plants, he considered the need over. If there were no centers, he further reasoned, women would likely give up their jobs, leaving room for returning GIs. Lanham had his way. In 1946, federally supported day care ended.[47]

Not considered in this decision was the ongoing expansion of defense industries and military bases during the Cold War years. To meet the demand for workers, women were once again needed, but it was difficult to recruit women with children. Local communities whose economic lives relied on defense plants asked the government to reinstitute federal aid for day care. Wichita, Kansas, for instance, was located near a military base and had a healthy aircraft industry with military contracts. What it lacked were adequate child-care programs that would encourage women to enter the workforce. The city turned to the government for help. The response from HEW, the U.S. Children's Bureau, and the U.S. Women's Bureau (under the U.S. Department of Labor) was not what the city hoped for, but it reflected the agencies' mandates, which typically conducted studies that sometimes laid the groundwork for future legislation. The study findings on the Wichita project, as well as those conducted where there were no defense or military installations, supported what working parents already knew. There was a substantial lack of day care and after-school programs in the United States. The need for these facilities increased, and by 1959, a reported 7 million youngsters under the age of twelve lived in households where mothers worked outside the home. Most of these children were cared for by relatives or private sitters. Only about one child out of every forty was in group care, and at least another 400,000 under the age of twelve looked after themselves and younger siblings.[48]

Both the U.S. Children's Bureau and U.S. Women's Bureau were prepared to document the problem and to push for more public awareness. Solutions, however, were left to local communities, industries, and the parents themselves. Stressing the importance of adequate child care, Katherine B. Oettinger, Children's Bureau chief, and Alice K. Leopold, assistant to the Secretary of Labor, issued a joint statement in 1959 stressing "community responsibility." Yet, "too frequently," the statement acknowledged, the needs of mothers and their children were not addressed by either private or governmental agencies.[49]

As for Washington politicians, there was largely silence. No matter their affiliations or philosophies, lawmakers preferred not to acknowledge that family dynamics were changing as more women entered the national workforce. To do so would have required that Congress do more than its 1954 approval of a tax deduction allowing families earning up to $4,500 per year to deduct $600 for child care from their income taxes.

Direct funding for child care was reintroduced in 1958 when Senator Jacob Javits, a Republican from New York, presented the Day Care Assistance Act. Although the Inter-City Committee for Day Care of Children (ICC) lobbied for passage and mobilized grassroots support, the bill was rejected. Child-care tax deductions were as far as lawmakers were willing to go, particularly when they knew that women, however maternal, did not vote as a bloc on child-centered issues and, therefore, would not launch a large-scale lobbying effort. Clearly, women did not share the same concerns. Nor did they project a united front that could influence politicians to give their attention to an issue or to sway their vote for legislation. This was a lesson that the Children's Bureau learned early on when some women's organizations wholeheartedly supported the bureau while others opposed it.[50]

In the instance of day-care centers, the federal response was to maintain a hands-off attitude. Federal agencies could collect statistics and publish reports. The U.S. Children's Bureau and U.S. Women's Bureau could cosponsor the 1960 National Conference on Day Care of Children. These activities did not mean, however, that federally funded day care was likely. The issue was loaded with controversy. To some, it smacked of state-run nurseries in the Soviet Union and its satellite countries. To others, it had the potential to weaken the nuclear family by helping women work outside the home.

In other child-related issues, there were, however, calls for action and robust activism toward improving the lives of children. A national spotlight turned on children and teenagers, partly because there were so many of them and partly because there was so much emotionally and materially invested in their futures. There was a keen cultural interest in everything to do with childhood and the teen years. Anyone likely to be part of a child's life—parents, relatives, teachers, clergy—had a responsibility. So, too, did the nation at large.

The country's "basic objective," said Truman, was "improving the well-being of our children." How to accomplish that was the driving force behind the myriad discussions, debates, and proclamations that emerged from the White House Conferences of the postwar era. And, as delegates left these conferences, they were urged to return to their organizations and local communities ready to turn talk into action. Dr. Dean W. Roberts, representing the American Public Health Association, for instance, arrived at the 1950 White House Conference a skeptic but left feeling that the meeting had accomplished much more than talk. In his estimation, it had clearly focused on the "importance of personality development in our society," offering concrete ways to improve the positive influences of educational, social, recreational, health-care, and religious institutions. Two participants at the 1960 conference were equally impressed, adding that the meeting had produced a "useful catalogue of unmet needs on which to base future programs," even if that meant more taxes and the "sacrifice of vested interests."[51]

Another conference participant, this one a teenager representing the youth of America, felt energized but somewhat overwhelmed with the task ahead. "We all hope," said the teen, "that when we go back home we'll be able to take what was done here and bring about the changes that are necessary." In some instances, changes came rather quickly, as when the 1950 conference stimulated local, regional, and federal agencies to create additional programs for migrant children. Sometimes, however, it might take many years to see any results. Prior to the 1919 White House conference, for example, only eight states had child welfare departments.

Danny Kaye (far right), a popular entertainer and dedicated UNICEF
spokesperson, led youth forums at the 1960 White House Conference on
Children and Youth. Dwight D. Eisenhower Library

Conference participants wanted to change that and set out to lobby state
legislatures, but it was not until the beginning of the 1950s that every
state (but not all U.S. territories) had such a department.[52]

Lawmakers at state and federal levels might not be inclined to follow
conference recommendations or bow to demands. The White House
Conferences on Children and Youth did, however, serve an important
purpose in the national discourse on children. The meetings involved
presidential administrations and federal agencies. They drew the attention of Congress and raised public awareness. News stories reported on
the meetings as they were taking place, and prior to the conference,
celebrities lent their names to media promotions. In 1960, for instance,
actors Walter Brennan, Robert Young, and Jane Wyatt appeared in televised public service announcements. Sports stars Jackie Robinson and

Mickey Mantle were asked to do the same, as were well-known personalities popular with young people—Roy Rogers, Dale Evans, Ricky Nelson, and Pat Boone. Entertainer Danny Kaye, a tireless worker for the United Nations International Children's Emergency Fund (UNICEF), agreed to serve as master of ceremonies for the opening of the 1960 conference if he could participate in the conference's youth meetings.[53]

Young people at White House Conferences were not unheard of. A "youth band" welcomed Herbert Hoover to the 1930 conference, and during the postwar meetings, a few hundred children and teenagers provided musical entertainment, including Navajo children performing traditional dances. An innovation of these later conferences, however, was inclusion of high school and college-age "youth representatives." Racially, ethnically, and geographically diverse, the young people were selected on recommendations from religious organizations, 4-H clubs, youth divisions of the YWCA and YMCA, and the National Scholarship and Service Fund for Negro Students. They arrived as members of state/territorial delegations and as members of the Advisory Committee on Youth Participation. Some were, noted one observer, "aggressively conservative," while others were moderate or liberal in their views.[54]

Seldom were young people able to step outside their adult-controlled environments and be actors in their own lives. Active engagement in the civil rights movement—integrating schools and lunch counters—was one example of youngsters moving to shape events, as was delinquent behavior, which brought an entirely different set of adult responses. White House Conferences offered another opportunity for young people to act on their own behalf. The youth representatives came together in work groups with adults and their peers. They tackled topics of family and peer relationships, community youth programs, job availability and training, educational opportunities, and the influence of spiritual values on behavior. Their views were acknowledged in conference recommendations, and more importantly, from the organizers' point of view, these young people were potential community and neighborhood activists for the betterment of young people's lives.

Conferences gave participants, who listened to speakers at assemblies and sat for days in deliberation with their work groups, ideas and strategies for dealing with their particular areas of concern. Delegates were willing to work in their local communities and at the state level to produce beneficial changes, but organizers realized that enthusiasm could lag over time. To revitalize participants and keep them thinking about their conference experience, the national committees kept working after conferences ended. At its follow-up meeting in 1952, the national committee was pleased to note that every state and territory had organized its own Committee for Children and Youth, and many state governors had called "Little White House Conferences," some of which drew over 1,000 people. A National Council of State Committees for Children and Youth was formed and established a working relationship with the Interdepartmental Committee of federal agencies. After the 1960 White House Conference on Children and Youth, a Council of National Organizations for Children and Youth was created. Serving approximately 400 individual child-service providers and state-based Committees for Children and Youth, the council also included the National Committee for Children and Youth. This committee acted as a liaison between federal agencies and local and state-based organizations; it sponsored conferences directed at identifiable populations such as rural youth or "unemployed, out-of-school" teenagers; and it prepared a mid-decade *Report to the Nation* in 1965 that analyzed which recommendations from the 1960 conference were showing results, identified emerging problems, and shelved once-acceptable solutions that time and changing circumstances made obsolete.[55]

There was fluidity to the conferences. An issue considered of paramount importance at one meeting could seem inconsequential at the next. Conferences were a lens to both long-standing problems and fleeting trends of the historical, political, and cultural period in which they occurred. Whether it was 1950 or 1960, however, conference delegates agreed that the federal government "must become a more effective partner" in the efforts to improve the lives of America's children and teenagers.[56]

No one advocated that government take over the parental role. And, it was not suggested that state governments and local communities wait to follow federal mandates, rather than initiate their own solutions to a problem. The federal government was, however, expected to take a larger role in leadership and, when necessary, put forth policies that were in the best interests of children and teenagers. How to do that was not always easy to decide. The presidents, Congresses, and government agencies did not necessarily agree on specific issues, but their decisions were both shaped and informed by what American culture at the time believed about childhood, by the belief that children had rights, and by an image of what life should be like for young people.

Education at Midcentury

"In this highly technical era, education has become as much a part of our system of defense as the Army, the Navy or the Air Force. We must have good schools, not only because of our ideals, but for survival."

—*Neil H. McElroy, Chairman, White House Conference on Education, November 28, 1955*

McElroy spoke for many who saw a strong link between school instruction and fighting the Cold War. Patriotism, literacy, skills in science and technology taught in the classroom would prepare youngsters to repel Communist influences. While Americans may have agreed that education had a role in winning the Cold War, this was an abstraction when compared to what parents and society said they believed about schooling and its importance in children's lives.

Education was part of the American Dream. Education opened doors to social and economic advancement. It introduced youngsters to ideas, skills, and avenues for personal expression. Each generation was expected to advance further in schooling than the one before. After a decade of economic depression and the war years of the 1940s, it seemed imperative in the postwar era that the upcoming generation have the opportunity to become the most educated in the nation's history. For that to happen, parents, educators, and communities were expected to join forces in an effort to provide the best possible classroom instruction.

Education was a cornerstone of childhood. By the mid-twentieth century, it was considered a basic right of children. In Washington, D.C., it was discussed and fought over more than any other child-related issue. Both major political parties referred to it in their national platforms.

When Truman ran for president in 1948, the Democratic platform endorsed federal aid to schools, insisting that a good education was "the right of every American child." The Democrats consistently supported this view in later elections. The Republican platform, on the other hand, evolved as problems facing America's schools continued to mount. The Republican platform said nothing about education in 1948; opposed federal aid in 1952; but by 1956, it advocated government-funded school construction. Education was a hot-button issue that shaped party doctrine and elicited political comment. Addressing the 1950 White House Conference on Children and Youth, President Truman, for instance, expounded upon the importance of supportive parents and good teachers in the early grades who set children on the path to becoming "useful and honorable citizens." This was his personal experience, as it was for his successor, Dwight D. Eisenhower, who did not elaborate on the qualities of any particular teacher but recalled one who suggested that he might "skip" ahead a grade. This, said Ike, was "not a tribute to my academic mastery . . . [but] simply recognition that I lived in a home where learning was put into practice." In both the Eisenhower and Truman boyhood homes, learning was valued and parents passed to their children a respect for education.[1]

Parental encouragement and good teachers were keys to learning. Were they enough, however, to overcome the many problems facing American education in the postwar years? There were not enough teachers, classrooms, or funds to support the increasing numbers of students. Adding to the complexity of finding solutions was the rhetoric of Cold War preparedness and the prospect of school desegregation. Public opinion, social commentators, and both Truman and Eisenhower agreed that federal involvement could alleviate some problems, but there was far less consensus on how government monies would be used or who would benefit. In fact, the question of federal aid was extremely divisive. Northern conservatives opposed government action if it meant an increased federal budget; states' rights advocates feared the loss of control, arguing that accepting aid would lead to school desegregation; the Catholic Church, through the National Catholic Welfare Conference, lobbied against school aid because parochial schools would be excluded; and some blocked federal support because parochial schools might benefit.

In May 1950 this California classroom, with students' desks pushed together, showed signs of the overcrowding that plagued the nation's schools during the postwar years. (Visiting officials at the back of the room include Pakistan's first prime minister Liaquat Ali Khan, who was touring the United States.) U.S. Department of State, Courtesy Harry S. Truman Library

The language used to discuss education underscored the country's cultural and religious divides, its prejudices and mistrusts.

Pragmatically, the most pressing issues were shortages of teachers and classroom space. These were exacerbated by an explosion of school-age children. Babies born during the first year of the wartime draft were ready for kindergarten in 1947, increasing the number of kindergartners by 10 percent over the previous year. This was just a hint of what was to come. During the 1950s, the number of children entering elementary school rose about 3 percent each year until, by the 1960–1961 school year, over 25 million children were in school.[2]

Although the baby boom had a greater impact on the country's elementary and secondary schools during the 1950s, problems were already apparent in the late 1940s. In observance of National Education Week in 1947, Truman noted: "Today American education is in the grip of a grave crisis. Our schools are compelled to offer education of inferior quality. Educationally, many millions of our children are underprivileged." The country needed more classrooms, teachers, updated equipment, and funding. In response, Truman made education a priority of his administration.[3]

In his 1946 State of the Union message, Truman recommended using federal grants to improve the nation's educational system "where improvement is most needed." However, school-aid legislation introduced during the 79th session of Congress failed, partly because lawmakers could not reach a consensus on whether federal aid should go to nonpublic schools. Undeterred, Truman returned to the 80th Congress with another funding request. This was also defeated. It was an election year, and in his acceptance speech at the 1948 Democratic convention, the president spoke of the crisis facing American education. He vowed to call Congress back into special session to deal with education, as well as inflation and the housing crunch. About two weeks after the Democratic convention, Truman made good on his promise, arguing before the special congressional session that the country could not afford to wait eight months for the 81st Congress to convene. "The present educational crisis" said Truman, was further impacted by an inflationary economy. "The children in our schools, and the men and women who teach there, have been made the victims of inflation." The president proposed a $300 million aid-to-education package. While Congress mulled it over, Truman went on the campaign trail, complaining that the House of Representatives was "roosting" on a bill passed by the Senate.[4]

Although Truman suggested that the fight over his aid package was drawn along party lines, such was not the case. New Mexico representative Georgia Lee Lusk, for instance, staunchly supported Truman's plan, but a fellow Democrat from North Carolina, Graham A. Barden, derailed the Senate-passed aid-to-education bill by sponsoring an amendment that set off a firestorm of controversy because it specifically denied any form of assistance to parochial schools. Another Democrat, Senator Harry Byrd of Virginia, called the bill, with or without parochial assistance, a "Pandora's box of expense." Other southern Democrats, as well as non-southern fiscal conservatives, agreed. If parochial schools needed improvement, the job fell to the Catholic Church, and if communities or states wanted to upgrade their schools they could allocate funds or raise taxes. Nor would lawmakers, including many Democrats, support Truman's proposal that schools in all states and territories be funded with revenues from off-shore oil drilling. As it turned out, Truman had only one success. As tensions with the Soviet Union intensified and military preparedness seemed imperative, Congress approved aid to school districts affected by population growth near military bases and booming defense industries.[5]

Throughout Truman's administration, and that of his successor Eisenhower, school construction and teacher shortages were persistent problems. Shortages began during the war when both men and women left the classroom for military service or to work in war-related jobs. As early as 1942, for instance, the shortage was estimated at between 50,000 and 68,000 vacancies. In peacetime, many who could have returned to teaching, did not. Although several factors contributed to the teacher shortage, including women deciding to stay home and raise families, it was widely believed that inadequate salaries were a major cause. In 1947 when the median family income was just over $3,000, half of the nation's teachers earned less than $2,000. By comparison, the 1947 median income for attorneys was $5,700 and just over $4,000 for steel and auto workers. While many districts increased teacher pay, the national picture remained bleak. By 1955, there were 140,000 unfilled teaching positions. It seemed that the only educators who wanted jobs and could not find them were "qualified Negro teachers" who lost their positions when black-only schools closed after *Brown v. Board of Education* began to enforce school desegregation in the latter half of the 1950s.[6]

Certainly, the number of displaced African American teachers could not begin to compensate for a nationwide shortage. To attract teachers, states reduced qualification requirements or lured older teachers out of retirement. Some districts raised salaries, including the "progressive" Long Island, New York, school featured in a 1952 issue of *Life*. In this particular Long Island district, teachers were "well paid," earning from three to seven thousand dollars a year. Some commentators suggested that more teachers could be found if the federal government exempted them from paying income tax. This would offset school districts' inability or reluctance to raise teacher salaries.[7]

Although there was some support for giving teachers a tax break, the proposal was never seriously considered. Instead, the government worked with educational organizations to spread the word that teachers were needed. The Department of Health, Education, and Welfare (HEW) produced televised public service announcements touting teaching as a career. If there was a positive result, it was long-term, having more influence on those who were still in school and unlikely to earn their teaching credentials for some time. Not until the late 1960s would teacher availability begin to realign the teacher to student ratio.

Fewer teachers meant larger classes, and the need for more classrooms translated into overcrowding. Like the teacher shortage, classroom space and new-school construction were problems that had brewed beneath the surface for years. During the depression of the 1930s, structure rehabilitation or new construction was a low priority, except where Works Progress Administration (WPA) projects did the job. Then, during the war years, material and labor went to the war effort. The exceptions were schools constructed, maintained, or operated through the Lanham Act of 1942, which provided federal aid to communities suddenly overwhelmed by an influx of workers in war production or military projects.

Portions of the Lanham Act were continued by the Truman administration through the 1946 Defense Area School Aid package. In 1950, this was replaced by the School Assistance to Federally Affected Areas Act, which was then extended under Eisenhower in 1953 as a necessity in the country's Cold War defense mobilization. Federal aid went to public schools impacted by families that moved to be near employment at new or expanding defense plants and military installations.

For many communities, funding could not come soon enough. Congressman Craig Hosmer, a California Republican whose district included fast-growing Los Angeles County, complained that federal funds were being held up by "administrative indecision" at the highest levels of government. It was of little concern to Hosmer that he was criticizing his own political party and president. The aid was needed desperately in an area where the aircraft industry contributed to a population increase of

48 percent between 1940 and 1950, and where the number of new residents was expected to rise. At least 200 other districts were also candidates for federal aid. Eventually, the money came. Nevada, for example, received $500,000 in 1955 for new school construction and almost $2 million in operating funds to offset the impact of "defense boom towns" that sprang up when the Nevada Proving Ground (later renamed the Nevada Nuclear Test Site) began to employ thousands and when an air base in the state became a training center for test pilots. Most school districts were not, however, close to defense plants or military bases. They did without federal funds. If they financed any construction it was with bond options or state monies. Because many districts did not expend the monies needed and because more children entered school each year, barely a dent was made in the need for more space. By 1955 over 200,000 additional classrooms were needed in the nation's schools.[8]

As communities tried to cope with overcrowded schools and too few teachers, both Truman and Eisenhower were cautious. They did not want to trample upon the tradition of a public education system based on local districts and the control of state boards of education. Ike made his position clear to both the general public and state officials on a number of occasions. Responding to a teacher who wrote the president about classroom shortages and antiquated equipment, Ike replied that the government could do very little when "some states" were strongly opposed to federal involvement. In another letter, sent to state and territorial governors in 1954, Eisenhower offered assurances "that the primary responsibility for meeting these problems must lie with the States and local communities, and that the Federal Government should strengthen not interfere with State administration of education."[9]

Local school boards hired teachers, paid their salaries, and purchased textbooks. State boards sometimes mandated specific textbooks, set the overall curriculum, and established standards for teacher certification. They inspected school buildings and evaluated districts for fire code and safety compliance. Custom and state laws also decided when and if schools were segregated by race. In Eisenhower's home state of Kansas, for example, legislation created a crazy quilt of integrated and segregated schools. Segregation was illegal in second-class cities (defined as having a population of at least 2,000), but it was allowed in first-class cities (a population of at least 15,000). However, the state's twelve first-class cities did not present a united front. One city never segregated its schools; two integrated all classrooms in 1952; and Topeka, famous for the landmark *Brown* case, operated segregated elementary schools but had an integrated high school. Segregation laws also varied from state to state, and there was little uniformity in how state boards operated. In fact, in 1955 when there were still only forty-eight states, four had no state boards of education and six others had only recently established them. When there were no state boards, local districts were autonomous.[10]

During the 1950s, school districts and state boards of education began to cut costs by consolidating several school districts into one. It was often a contentious issue. Rural neighborhoods and small towns clung to their schools because they were the heart of a community. Nevertheless, consolidation became a national trend. Between the school years of 1952 and 1955, the number of school districts in the nation fell by almost 12 percent. Included in that number were thousands of one-room-school districts. Still, not all one-room schoolhouses disappeared. By the mid-1950s, there were at least 39,000 still operating. Nebraska, the national leader in consolidating and closing school districts, also topped the list of states still having at least 3,000 or more one-room schools. An indeterminate number of these were built of sod, more reminiscent of the nineteenth-century frontier than the mid-twentieth century and the atomic age. Also maintaining over 3,000 one-room schools were Wisconsin and Iowa, followed by South Dakota, Missouri, and Minnesota with over 2,000.[11]

Despite what happened at the local level, or perhaps because of it, the federal government could not ignore the disparity among states and territories in tax-based school funding or the quality of instruction and classroom equipment. The inequities were underscored by the 1950 U.S. Census. Reporting on the median number of school years completed by persons twenty-five and over, the census found that the numbers ranged from 11.3 years of schooling for residents in the West; 9.6 years for the Northeast; 9.4 years for all other states outside the South; and 8.6 for southern states. Ranking at the top for the most educated populations were Utah (12 years of schooling) and California (11.6 years); at the bottom were Alabama and North Carolina, where the average was less than eight grades of completed schooling. The differences between states and regions could be explained in many ways, but the most obvious factors were locally depressed economies, attitudes toward education, and/or unwillingness on the part of communities and states to upgrade schools that served minority students.[12]

There were recurring demands from parents, educators, and policy-makers that the government take steps to equalize educational opportunities. And, one might expect that—if the nation's survival truly rested on education and if the postwar generation was to be the most academically successful—both the private and public sectors would work together in a common cause. The truth was far different. Regional, religious, and political factions were more likely to spar over school funding than come to any agreement.

In their arguments, opponents to federal aid failed to acknowledge, or chose to overlook, the government's long history of supporting some forms of education. Throughout the nineteenth century, federal monies were spent by the Bureau of Indian Affairs (BIA) to support Indian boarding schools, mission schools, and orphanages. In 1862 Congress passed the Morrill Act to establish state land-grant colleges that, along with classical studies, taught subjects related to agriculture, the mechanical arts, and military tactics. During the first half of the twentieth century, Congress also supported vocational education in agriculture, domestic sciences, and industrial arts when it passed the Smith-Hughes Act of 1917, several pieces of legislation in the 1930s, and the George-Barden Act of 1946. And, there was the massive postwar GI Bill, which gave thousands of returning servicemen an opportunity to attend college or receive advanced vocational training.

The government was also responsible for the National School Lunch Program (sometimes called the Hot Lunch Program). Established in 1946, it was administered through the U.S. Department of Agriculture (USDA) and championed by Richard Russell, a conservative Democrat from Georgia considered to be one of the most powerful men in the Senate. The program satisfied two needs. American agriculture got a boost because farmers received subsidies for their surplus goods, and America's children were guaranteed a nutritionally balanced hot meal. For thousands of youngsters the school lunch may have been their only complete meal of the day. During his presidential campaign in 1960, John F. Kennedy observed that in the Appalachians of West Virginia, "children took home part of their school lunch in order to feed their families."[13]

Although schoolchildren stood to benefit from the program, some conservatives opposed it. Senator Robert Taft of Ohio, for example, fought the measure because it was, in his view, another example of the federal government becoming too involved in people's everyday lives. Once quoted as saying that health, education, and welfare were "secondary functions" of the government, the very conservative Taft sometimes confounded his colleagues by actually supporting liberal programs such as aid to health care, housing, and education. In this instance, however, the man known as "Mr. Republican" stood firmly against the National School Lunch Program.[14]

Nevertheless, it was a popular idea because it seemed to be a natural progression in the history of private and public entities providing lunches to hungry, malnourished children. Since the early 1900s, women's groups, home extension clubs, home economics classes, and charitable organizations had sponsored programs in towns and rural communities, and during the 1930s, state welfare departments, working with the USDA and the WPA, began distributing farm surplus commodities directly to families and schools. After the war, a national program seemed an appropriate next step, providing nutritious meals to millions of children and assisting farmers and ranchers who received federal farm subsidies through the school lunch act.[15]

While children and farmers benefited, many argued that the program was also invaluable to national defense. After all, physical and mental disabilities brought on by childhood malnutrition followed youngsters into adulthood. From a purely economic standpoint, the malnourished child became a less productive adult. From a military position, the long-term effects of malnutrition led to the rejection, for medical reasons, of young men and women that otherwise would have served their country in the armed forces.

The National School Lunch Program provided grants-in-aid to states and territories, while the USDA supplied surplus commodities, such as cheese, raisins, and nuts, free of charge. The program was designed for all children, not just the needy. And, it was one of the few instances in which government funds made no distinctions between public and private schools. Parochial schools and private institutions for educating the deaf and blind took advantage of the program. Schools without cafeterias converted space in existing buildings or constructed free-standing structures on school grounds or moved in usable buildings such as military-surplus barracks.

No matter what sort of arrangements were made, thousands of youngsters stopped bringing their lunches to school. This is not to say that home-prepared meals were necessarily lacking, but school-cooked lunches ensured conformity of quantity and quality. Certainly, children were more likely to do well in school when they had a balanced, nutritious meal. Of course, youngsters could be picky eaters, especially when the food was not something served at home. One girl remembered: "I did not know for many years afterward that at least some of the cafeteria food came from commodities, but thanks to a teacher who told us to be grateful to Mr. Eisenhower, I equated the unfamiliar rice, which was glutinous and inedible, with the president." During the program's early years, "the school lunch menu most often resembled the 'blue plate special'" offerings found in diners, but societal changes found their way into school cafeterias. As McDonald's influence on America's food culture took hold, schools began to serve hamburgers and French fries, and when pizza lost its novelty for the average American family, it was added to lunchroom menus. Despite more choices, the program's original intent remained. It was "to safeguard the health and well-being of the Nation's children." Meanwhile, educators began to see school lunches as "an integral part of the total education program."[16]

By the mid-1950s, $83.2 million had been appropriated for the National School Lunch Program, and in 1954 the Special Milk Program was added under the Agricultural Act of that year. Federal funds for lunches were divided among states and territories through a formula based on need. The requirement that the program be administered through the state board of education was one reason for states that had yet to establish state boards to do so. Lunches were not free. There was a nominal fee, as there was for the extra half-pint cartons of milk purchased under the Special Milk Program. Youngsters unable to pay received free meals or paid a reduced price. Millions of students in elementary and secondary schools benefited. Many, however, did without. Those most likely to be excluded were minority and low-income students in rural and inner-city schools with no facilities for food preparation or with so few paying students that administrators could not carry the burden of providing free meals to the rest.[17]

Despite the government monies and grants that went to schools for various curriculums and programs, including the National School Lunch Program, opponents to federal aid either overlooked the government's existing programs or argued that serving some specific need did not require the government to take on more responsibilities. The Eisenhower administration was fiscally conservative, but in the area of education, it agreed with Truman's push to provide more construction funds.

Like Truman, Eisenhower was also concerned with the overall quality of the country's educational system. Overcrowded classrooms affected the quality of instruction, made it more difficult for teachers to maintain discipline, and often meant that youngsters with learning disabilities or behavior problems did not receive adequate attention from overworked teachers. To heighten public awareness and to budge Congress on construction funding, the administration supported a White House Conference on Education. In his 1955 State of the Union message, Eisenhower announced that America's "grave educational problems" were being studied and analyzed in anticipation of this national meeting. HEW was responsible for organizing the conference, and Eisenhower told HEW Secretary Oveta Culp Hobby, who came to her job after years of previous public service and as first commander of the Women's Army Corps during World War II, that he wanted "some guidelines for the solutions to [school] problems," not just a recitation of what was wrong.[18]

HEW had an appropriation of $200,000 for the meeting. Another $700,000 was allocated to the states and territories to defray a portion of the costs incurred while preparing for the conference. Eisenhower, who respected the organizational skills of men in big business, appointed Neil H. McElroy, president of Procter and Gamble (and later U.S. Secretary of Defense), to chair the conference's thirty-two-member national committee. This group, appointed by Ike, was an eclectic mix. Among its members were Mayme E. Williams (president of the National Congress of Colored Parents and Teachers), Ralph J. Bunche (undersecretary at the

United Nations), and William S. Paley (chairman of the board, CBS). The national committee developed agendas for state and local meetings, and it organized subcommittees that focused on specific topics. These ranged from assessing dropout rates to promoting vocational training to offering solutions to the teacher shortage.

The first phase of the White House Conference on Education consisted of meetings at the state and local levels. Representatives from public and private schools, parents, and educators were encouraged to attend. It was hoped that citizens would consider not only problems but find "some common answers . . . useful in every community where answers must be fully translated into action." People had to become involved or, as a Nebraska farmer explained, when people began talking and thinking, then "you've got something." Adding their voices were Republican congressmen Clifton Young of Nevada and Melvin R. Laird, from Wisconsin. Both taped television spots to be shown in their home states. HEW Secretary Hobby appeared with them to explain that the government already provided some aid to land-grant colleges, vocational education, and school construction. More, however, could be accomplished at both national and state levels.[19]

Groups met at community centers, local schools, and state offices. They addressed the issues of (1) the responsibilities of parents, the school district, the state, and the federal government; (2) improving efficiency and economy; (3) reversing the teacher shortage; (4) financing day-to-day operational costs; (5) building public interest in education; and (6) assessing the number of classrooms needed for the future and determining the safety of existing structures. Along with these primary issues, HEW also asked participants to discuss ideas for curbing juvenile delinquency and reducing school dropout rates. On the latter topic, historian Paula Fass has noted: "American educators were already beginning to measure the high school dropout rate and to worry about this as a sign of social failure, rather than celebrating the growing expansion [of high school education] as they had in the past." And, in light of the Cold War conflict that existed between the United States and the Soviet Union, HEW interjected the importance of reinforcing the ideals of democracy and improving technical/scientific training to heighten national security.[20]

While HEW planned for the national conference, two very different events turned the national spotlight on education. The first, which will be discussed later, was the Supreme Court ruling in *Brown v. Board of Education*. The second was the 1955 publication of Rudolf Flesch's *Why Johnny Can't Read: And What You Can Do about It*. The book alarmed parents and put educators on the defensive. Flesch argued that children in the United States were behind their counterparts in Western Europe where young readers were taught vocabulary and word recognition using the phonetic method. Phonetics was used in the United States, too, and had once been widely accepted. By the mid-twentieth century, however, education experts and textbook companies had steered schools and classroom teachers away from phonetics and toward the "word" method.

Flesch scathingly denounced educators who insisted that children exhibit "phonetic readiness" before they were exposed to this approach, and he accused leading authorities of knowingly promoting an inferior system. The "word" method, sometimes called "See and Say" or "Look and Say," required youngsters to recognize words through repetition. Millions of children were exposed to this method through the popular first readers *Dick and Jane* (Scott, Foresman) or *Jack and Janet* (Houghton Mifflin), but Flesch argued that the word method gave an advantage to youngsters who came from educated, book-reading homes, leaving those from less-educated households to struggle and possibly be labeled as "nonreaders" requiring remedial instruction. Essentially, said Flesch, "public schools are falling down on the job."[21]

Why Johnny Can't Read drew considerable public attention, but the book's subject had to jockey for position amid other concerns and issues discussed by two thousand participants at the 1955 White House Conference on Education. Attending were representatives from states and territories, members of Congress, and representatives from national organizations. Among these were the American Farm Bureau, the National Congress of Colored Parents and Teachers, and the National Education Association. Representatives from big business and organized labor came, too, because they had a vested interest in the education of future workers. They came by invitation. Thomas Lazzio, of AFL-CIO United Auto Workers, for instance, was nominated to represent labor by HEW Secretary Hobby and by two senators, but Lazzio received an invitation only after the FBI reported that he had never been investigated by the Bureau.[22]

Present on the first day of the White House Conference was Eleanor Roosevelt, who wrote in her "My Day" column, "I hope the delegates in attendance at the White House Conference on Education were encouraged by the speeches made by the President and Vice-President. I must confess I found very little that was new in these speeches." Nonetheless, she hoped that something positive would result. "We have discussed Federal aid too long and done too little, and our children are the ones who are suffering in too many areas of the country."[23]

Conference participants also wanted more than rhetoric. In its final report to the president, the national committee outlined goals for the nation's schools. The first, and most basic, was to ensure that students learned fundamental skills in reading, writing, and mathematics. Along with these, it was essential that youngsters receive lessons in citizenship. Traditionally, schools were the primary institution for teaching patriotism and national values. In addition, the report also called for more vocational programs, a national expansion of junior colleges, and a national increase in programs for the physically and mentally challenged and for "gifted" students.[24]

It may seem that conference delegates veered into uncharted territory by setting goals that singled out the special needs of some students. However, these topics had simmered on the back burner for years. The White House Conferences on Children and Youth in 1930 and 1940, for instance, discussed intelligence (IQ) testing, which since the introduction of the Stanford-Binet Intelligence Scale in 1916 was finding wide use and acceptance. These two conferences also considered the identification and treatment of behavior problems, as well as services provided to crippled children, the deaf, and the blind. It was little surprise then that these subjects should reappear at the 1950 White House Conference on Children and Youth, along with a new interest in the "gifted," who were often underserved because schools did not have the resources to encourage their abilities in academics, the sciences, music, dance, and art.[25]

The White House Conference on Education signaled a new direction in society's view of schooling. America's educational system had never been designed or intended to accommodate every student. Youngsters that did not fit into the "common school" education model either did without or found instruction outside the public classroom. The postwar era changed that. The United States was now an international power. It should have the wherewithal to give every child an education that best suited his or her needs, abilities, and talents.

American education was evolving. An eighth grade education was once considered an achievement; then a high school diploma. "To an increasing number of Americans," wrote historian Kriste Lindenmeyer, "earning a high school diploma looked like the minimum a young person needed to secure a better future. Leaving school early seemed like a poor choice." In fact, by the end of the 1950s, education beyond high school seemed increasingly necessary and desirable. Said one report: "We hold to the view that *all* [original emphasis] children be accorded the opportunity to go as far academically as they choose to do. This can include a 13th and 14th year or more. . . . Those who do not elect to go to college should have adequate opportunity to develop a skill of interest to them. However, all must be prepared for resuming or continuing education through life."[26]

The Great Depression cut short for many the dream of a high school or college education, but it did not dampen the fundamental belief that education was a stepping stone to a more productive, secure future. As America emerged on the other side of the depression and a world war, there was a sense of purpose in seeing that the postwar generation of children and teenagers had the opportunities others missed. Expectations rose. This generation was going to be the best-educated in history. Schools should be all things to all students. One of those trying to put this into perspective for the general public was Sloan Wilson. The author was just beginning to receive recognition for his 1955 novel *The Man in the Gray Flannel Suit*, but Wilson was also an outspoken advocate of public education and a participant at the White House Conference on Education. In *Harper's Magazine*, he offered his view:

As school enrollments increased, the demand . . . proved insatiable. At school-board meetings, wistful parents kept showing up to ask for something new. . . . shrewd managers of factories appeared to ask that vocational education be tailored to meet their immediate employment needs. People . . . asked why courses in driving automobiles couldn't be instituted. . . . Others requested courses in family life to help reduce the divorce rate, and instruction about alcoholic beverages to help reduce alcoholism. . . . And how about moral and spiritual values.[27]

The public wanted schools to teach more than the traditional class-room subjects while also producing "well-adjusted" and "well-rounded" individuals prepared for the world of work and the adult responsibilities of marriage and parenthood. Young people should emerge from their classroom experiences knowing how to cooperate with one another without sacrificing their creative self-expression. Schools and teachers were supposed to do more, but local districts were often reluctant to as-sume costs for teachers, equipment, special courses, or classrooms.

To offset what communities and states could not, or would not, do on their own, participants at the 1955 Conference on Education generally agreed that the federal government should become more involved. By a ratio of two to one, participants approved a proposal that federal funding be increased, especially for construction. Ten months before the confer-ence, the Eisenhower administration attempted to do just that. The pres-ident proposed a three-year $7 billion school construction project. Poorer school districts would have priority, although Ike refrained from making a point of saying that eligible school districts would include those that were overwhelmingly African American. Adam Clayton Pow-ell, Jr., the first African American congressman elected from New York and chairman of the House Committee on Education and Labor, wanted to attach an anti-segregation amendment to the spending bill, a move that Eisenhower tried and failed to dissuade. There was little chance of the bill passing with Powell's amendment. In fact, the administration already had a hard sell with fiscal conservatives, Catholic leaders whose schools would be excluded, and southern congressmen who feared that the price of construction funds would be integration. Despite the publicity gener-ated by the White House Conference on Education and the support it generated, Congress rebuffed the construction package in 1955.[28]

Congress also failed to pass a construction bill in 1956, although it was supported at first by both the House and Senate. The sticking point was distribution of funds. The formula was not a flat grant to states (favored by congressmen from large population areas), or equalization grants (supported by those from states with low tax revenues), nor the more complicated compromise of matching grants. Rather, the 1956 bill would have distributed monies on a per-pupil basis, giving the advantage to high population centers and less to school districts in sparsely populated states. Of the 1956 bill, columnist Drew Pearson wrote: "The school bill is stymied in the [House] Rules Committee and won't come out till near the end of the session. If it does Sam [Rayburn, Speaker of the House] knows it will cause a holocaust of a debate. . . . It will keep Congress in session for weeks. So the school bill simply won't pass." Another construction-aid bill failed in 1957.[29]

Despite the tension between members of Congress and what seemed futile attempts to fund school construction, Congress did enact other aid-to-education programs. These allocations went to improve services for the hearing and sight-impaired and the mentally challenged. In 1956, 1957, and 1958, Congress appropriated money for teacher training in special education. In 1956 and 1957, it passed bills to fund vocational rehabilitation facilities, to provide schools with modern diagnostic equipment for vision and hearing tests, and to provide money for the purchase of books in Braille. The aid went to specialized schools and training centers that were either privately run or state supported. It also went to public schools that were mainstreaming children with disabilities, either by placing them in regular classrooms or by providing special education classes within the whole-school environment. The practice was an innovation in education and not without its critics. Although it would not become widely utilized until the 1960s when additional federal assistance went to educating special needs children, federal funding during the 1950s laid the foundation. In 1950, for example, approximately 88 percent of the nation's students with visual impairments were enrolled in institutional-residential schools. By 1960 the percentage had dropped significantly; 53 percent of all visually impaired children, which included youngsters who had some sight but were diagnosed as legally blind, were enrolled in public schools. These aid programs were more in keeping with the conventional congressional approach that limited spending to a defined population group of students. This sort of funding was certainly more palatable than massive spending bills, but the federal-aid laws passed during the Eisenhower administration set a precedent for more extensive government action during the 1960s.[30]

The larger arguments over government's place in funding school construction and teacher salaries were certainly more divisive. Some asked if there would be a shift in power from state to federal, giving the latter control over the way schools were run and curriculum content. The federal role versus that of states' rights was a subtext to arguments and commentary. Yet, at the White House Conference on Education, those who denounced federal aid in any form were a small minority. Speaking for this group was an educator from Texas who warned that aid would lead to wholesale federal intervention. The majority did not agree with this doomsday prediction, but no one wanted the federal government in complete control. A conference statement declared "the federal government should never be permitted to become a deterrent to state and local initiative in education."[31]

Most attending the Conference on Education believed it possible for the states and federal government to work in limited partnership. Quoted by *Life* magazine during the conference, Columbia University professor John K. Norton took the position, often articulated by HEW Secretary Hobby and others in the Eisenhower administration, that funds already went to some programs. For *Life*'s reading audience, Norton drew attention to the country's sixty-nine land-grant colleges, seven of which were all-black. Land-grant colleges owed their existence and several of their programs to federal legislation and financial support. Yet, said Norton, government involvement had not translated into excessive control. This viewpoint was somewhat misleading, if not disingenuous. In 1953, the Eisenhower administration used the ties between the land-grant schools and federal money when it gave additional funds to all-black colleges for Reserve Officers' Training Corps (ROTC) and then used the National Defense Act of 1916, which established ROTC, to warn all-white land-grant schools that they would lose funds if their ROTC programs were not integrated.[32]

The administration took another tack to desegregate schools serving military dependents. Schools located on military bases and funded by the federal government were the most easily integrated. (This included schools on military installations in the South.) More difficult were base schools operated by local districts or situated on adjacent federal land; these received some federal funds, but primary support came from state and local taxes. When these districts received the order to integrate and balked, they were told that the government was prepared to consider "other arrangements." In less than three years these schools were integrated, and the federal government took control of forty-three out of sixty-three schools that refused to integrate. To those for whom states' rights meant the right to segregate schools, federal intervention in ROTC and military-base schools were perfect examples of where things could lead when the government was involved.[33]

The Executive Branch demonstrated that it would, and could, force desegregation in some areas, but it largely left the issue to state and federal courts where decisions were made on a case-by-case basis. In Kansas, for instance, the state supreme court heard eleven desegregation cases between 1946 and 1950; sometimes it found for the plaintiffs, sometimes not. When cases came before the U.S. Supreme Court, they were also confined to a defined set of circumstances. In 1950, the court overturned a University of Oklahoma policy that admitted a black student and then imposed segregation in every aspect of the student's campus life. In the same year, it also struck down a Texas statute that established a law school at a Negro college to keep African American students out of the University of Texas Law School. When the court agreed to hear the *Brown* case in 1952, it was not, however, considering just the child Linda Brown and her education. Similar cases questioning the doctrine of "separate but equal" were pending from Delaware, The District of Columbia, South Carolina, and Virginia. The court consolidated these cases into *Brown*.[34]

In its landmark *Brown* decision of 1954, the Supreme Court ruled that "separate educational facilities are inherently unequal," and in a follow-up opinion, it told segregated school districts to integrate with "all deliberate speed." Theoretically the separation of powers in the three branches of government removed the president from control over U.S. Supreme Court decisions, but a president could somewhat shape the court when a seat became vacant. Eisenhower had that opportunity and, along with Attorney General Herbert Brownell, made the conscious de-

The State Street School was the first elementary school in Topeka, Kansas, to desegregate after the Supreme Court's decision in *Brown v. Board of Education*. Pictured is the integrated first grade class. Kansas State Historical Society

cision to appoint civil rights advocate Earl Warren as chief justice. Although the court may have been inching closer to a decision like that made in *Brown*, it is debatable how long that ruling may have taken if not for the Warren appointment and Eisenhower's additional appointments of federal judges who would uphold *Brown*'s intent.[35]

Desegregation signaled a major social and cultural shift, and leaders of diverse backgrounds and outlooks felt that the American people needed time to adjust to changes in race relations. Moderation and patience were urged by Eisenhower and a number of politicians. In the South, some civic and political leaders took the moderate line. James P. Coleman, governor of Mississippi, called for "cool thinking." Both the governors of Alabama and Arkansas agreed that since desegregation was now the law of the land, the law would be obeyed. These voices were eclipsed by southern whites who intended to block integration. Among the more vocal was Senator Harry Byrd of Virginia, who called for "massive resistance." For many, including Byrd, the issue was not just school integration but integration's potential to break down social barriers that separated blacks and whites in all aspects of their daily lives. School integration was just a first step to lifting segregation restrictions in public transportation, restaurants, theaters, swimming pools, and other recreational areas.[36]

Following the *Brown* decision, the president received outraged letters asking the status of his grandchildren's school enrollment. Southern newspapers fanned the flames by accusing the Eisenhower administration of foisting integration on ordinary citizens while top officials put their children in private, segregated schools. In fact, the Eisenhower grandchildren, David and Anne, were in a private school, and younger sister Susan attended an integrated kindergarten. Vice President Nixon's daughters, Tricia and Julie, attended a public elementary school in Washington, D.C. The vice president felt it politically important that no one accuse him of "not believing in Washington's integrated institutions." Political expediencies aside, the school had its shortcomings, and in 1958, the girls were enrolled in the private, but recently integrated, Sidwell Friends.[37]

Bitterness, rather than acceptance, translated into vows to fight integration. Many school districts broadly interpreted the court's language of "all deliberate speed" as a license to do little toward that end. Resistance was fought out in the courts, but even reluctant compliance did not assure a peaceful transition. The Anderson County School Board in Tennessee, for instance, refused desegregation until a federal court order in 1956. There was a brief outburst of violence, but tensions seemed under control until the early morning of Sunday, October 5, 1958, when dynamite explosions destroyed the high school at Clinton. The school board took the position that the federal government was at least partly to blame. If not for *Brown* and court-ordered desegregation, the school would still be standing.

The school board wanted the government to help finance a new building, and to that end, it contacted the White House, along with Tennessee senators Albert Gore, Sr., and Estes Kefauver. The Eisenhower administration looked for a way to "quickly undo the effects of this terrible act." It found the answer in the federal program that gave school construction funds to districts impacted by federal military reservations and/or defense industries. The Oak Ridge Atomic Energy Commission reservation just happened to be about ten miles from Clinton.[38]

The administration's quick response suggested that it had learned a hard lesson from the previous year's violence in Little Rock, Arkansas. Like it or not, the government sometimes had to become more involved than cautioning moderation. Little Rock and the desegregation of Central High in 1957 became a symbol of white malice and black determination, as well as federal versus states' rights positions. The school board's initial plan for integration was one of gradual black admittance into the all-white high school. African American students had to apply and then meet the subjective criteria established by Superintendent of Schools Virgil Blossom. He made the final student selections. Those chosen became known to history as the "Little Rock Nine." Ernest Green, who turned seventeen during his senior year at Central, was the oldest; Carlotta Walls, at fourteen, was the youngest. The teenagers were not pushed into applying for admittance. In fact, the parents of fifteen-year-old Gloria Ray were "adamantly opposed." Ernest Green's mother was more resigned. "It was up to him," she said, "since he had to put up with whatever might happen there."[39]

What happened there during the opening days of the 1957 school year was an ugly mob scene. The crowd broke through police barricades. There were cries to lynch a student as an example to all. Black reporters were attacked. Americans saw the violence, relayed through television, and they heard radio broadcasts reporting the melee. One of those listening was a twelve-year-old boy, blind from birth, "There seems to be such a fuss about it because some of the children are different," he said. "And I can't understand at all what this great difference is. They say it's their color. . . . I guess that I am lucky that I cannot see differences in color because it seems to me that the kind of hate these people put in their minds must chase out of it all chance to grow in understanding." The sad truth was that color did make a difference. Eisenhower called in the 101st Airborne Division and federalized the Arkansas National Guard to bring order and protect the students. As Americans watched events unfold,

Students are escorted into Little Rock's Central High School. Library of Congress

they witnessed the willingness of one race of adults to do bodily harm to children of another race.[40]

Desegregation and racial tensions spilled over into questions about the schooling and treatment of other minority students. The Governor's Advisory Council on Children and Youth in Minnesota noted that, as growing numbers of Native American families left reservations for the state's urban areas, tribal children were no longer attending reservation schools. "[The child] now often attends the same school as his white age mates, where the instruction may be better but the reception is not always friendly." The prejudice and racism these students met was hardly different from that encountered by African Americans.[41]

Native American students were once largely segregated because they attended reservation or Indian boarding schools, but in the 1950s the government began to terminate its trustee relationship with tribal groups. This meant, among other things, transferring services from federal to state supervision and making education the responsibility of local school districts. The few exceptions were isolated areas such as the Navajo Reservation where the federally supported Navajo Emergency Education Program established additional schools for approximately 14,000 reservation children. As a rule, however, the federal government wanted out of Indian education, and by 1958 approximately 79,000 tribal children were attending public schools. States took responsibility for educating these children, but where large tracts of tax-exempt reservation land existed, states expected financial assistance from the federal government. In those cases, the school districts were compensated under the Johnson-O'Malley Act of 1934. This legislation, passed under the Indian New Deal, subsidized the cost of Native Americans using state-owned or state-funded schools, hospitals, and institutions such as schools for the deaf and blind.[42]

Tribal youngsters and other nonwhite children were not the object of the *Brown* decision. The pivotal argument in that case was whether the principle of "separate but equal" black and white schools was constitutional. The enforced integration of black students into white schools did not mean that other minority students would necessarily find the doors open. In North Carolina, for example, there were segregated public schools for Caucasian, African American, and Native American students. At a snail's pace, schools in that state began to desegregate along the white-black line, but in Dunn, North Carolina, Native American students remained segregated. Their parents sued the local school board, and seven teenagers staged a peaceful sit-in at the all-white high school. A United Press report told the story, alongside a picture of fourteen-year-old Dalton Grove, a "Victim of Segregation," dressed in suit and tie. For years, Indian students in the area, most of whom were members of the Croatan and Cherokee tribal groups, were bussed to the East Carolina Indian School. Parents felt that the school was inferior, and to reach the school, some students made a daily seventy-mile round trip. The Dunn school board did not relent to tribal pressure, however, and students continued to be bussed to the separate school until the early 1960s.[43]

Minority youngsters were not only categorized by race and ethnicity but by particular circumstances. One minority group was simply labeled the "children of migrant workers." In the 1920s and 30s this group was regularly studied by the U.S. Children's Bureau, which, in turn, used its findings to argue, without success, for child labor laws in agriculture. After World War II, these children attracted new attention. No one knew exactly how many there were. Estimates in the late 1950s placed the number at about 600,000. Who were they? President Truman's 1950 Commission on Migratory Labor defined them as "children of misfortune. . . . rejects of those sectors of agriculture and of other industries undergoing change."[44]

State statistics were more revealing. Colorado's migrant population was 85 percent Spanish speaking and most worked in the state's sugar beet fields. Much the same could be said of migrant workers in Nebraska, Kansas, Montana, and Wyoming. One or two generations earlier, U.S. Children's Bureau surveys demonstrated that sugar beet workers represented a variety of nationalities — German, Russian-German, Polish, Italian, Greek, Japanese, Mexican, and white, American-born workers. By 1950 things were dramatically different. Mexican workers, heavily recruited by sugar beet companies and railroads that shipped the product, were in the majority. Spanish-speakers were also dominant in the migrant population along the West Coast, although there were Anglos, too. Some of these were described as "remnants" of Dust Bowl families that left the Plains for California during the 1930s. Along the East Coast, from Florida to Maine, the population following the harvests was more diverse. There were Caucasians, African Americans, Puerto Ricans, Mexicans, Jamaicans, and Bahamians. A few thousand came to the States each year to work and then returned home. The majority of laborers, however, were full-time U.S. residents.[45]

After World War II, more agricultural workers were needed. Without them, farm production would not keep pace with the peacetime buying habits of consumers no longer restrained by wartime shortages and rationing. The nation's truck farms, orchards, and citrus groves required more laborers. To better understand the working and living conditions of migrants, as well as their impact on local health-care facilities and schools, President Truman established a migratory labor commission to study the workers and their families. One result was a plank in the Democratic party's 1952 platform that supported improving health, welfare, and education services to children of migratory workers.[46] Also showing greater interest in migrant children was the 1950 White House Conference on Children and Youth and the White House Conference on Education.

Schooling came under sharp scrutiny. Although no state or federal entity knew how many migrant children worked instead of attending school, there were attempts to get them into the classroom and to make the experience relevant. The Fresno County Project in California, for instance, was considered an exemplary example for its use of bilingual teachers and for teaching Spanish-speaking youngsters about their own culture. Meanwhile, day-care centers operated in several locales. Many were run by the National Council of Churches, helping families on two fronts. Mothers had a safe place to leave their children, rather than take them "into the heat and dust of the fields and orchards," and older children could go to school instead of being left in camp to babysit younger siblings while parents worked.[47]

In Arizona the chairman of the Governor's Committee on Migratory Labor railed against the church-run centers, calling them "communistic," but New York State welcomed the National Council of Churches. In the early 1950s, the organization's day-care centers began to receive state funds and soon became wholly state-financed, with additional contributions from the New York Federation of Growers and Processors. New York also cooperated with other states in schooling migrant children. At the 1954 East Coast Migrant Conference, for example, New York worked with other states along the migrant corridor to establish a standardized school transfer card. Youngsters carried the card from one school to the next, allowing administrators to know that "Jane had attended 21 days in Hamilton, New York, and 17 days in Exmore, Virginia, . . . [with] only five days missed in travel time."[48]

Teachers and school administrators gained a clearer idea of school attendance, grade level, and the number of youngsters that reappeared at schools year after year. As in other migrant work areas, counties or states ran their programs. Federal funds did not support these projects, although there were other government programs that aided migrants, including U.S. Public Health Service programs and Social Security benefits for widows and their children who were U.S. citizens.

Public education faced a number of daunting problems, but no one

Influenced by the U.S. Children's Bureau's Better Baby Movement, most states and territories by the 1950s required schools to record students' height and weight on report cards. Children of migrant workers are being weighed and measured at this New Jersey school. Library of Congress

was quite prepared for the ramifications of *Sputnik*. Launched by the Soviet Union on October 4, 1957, the orbiting satellite greatly influenced American education and redirected government resources. In retrospect, some educators felt that *Sputnik* was "a good thing." Without it there may not have been "a much-needed awakening to the fact that we [the United States] . . . were not doing all we might in the related fields of science and education."[49]

At the time, however, *Sputnik* brought alarm and recriminations. Speaking at a press conference on October 9, Eisenhower told reporters that there was "no reason to grow hysterical." This did little to silence the general uproar. The press and the public wanted to know who was to blame for letting the Russians get ahead of the United States. Some claimed that America had been overconfident and too focused on its highly publicized Vanguard Rocket Project, which was initially intended to map the earth's surface during the heightened cycles of solar activity in

1957 and 1958. Other critics pointed at rivalries between the armed services or set their sights on fiscally conservative Democrats and Republicans who supported cuts in the defense budget and missile program. On
Capitol Hill, the House Committee on Education and Labor heard a different answer from a spokesman for the National Education Association.
At least some blame lay at the schoolhouse door. "Any nation that pays
its teachers an annual average of $4,200 cannot expect to be the first in
putting an earth satellite into space," said the spokesman.[50]

It was hardly a secret that the Soviets put substantial resources into
science curriculums and technological education. Even before *Sputnik*,
the American media covered the subject. In March 1956, for example,
Life magazine ran an article on the "Golden Youth of Communism"
who spent "almost half their time on science and mathematics . . . [while]
in U.S. high schools half get no science at all." That had to change, as
sixth-grader David Obst was about to discover. Shortly after *Sputnik*'s
launch, David's teacher read a newspaper story to the class. "Russian
pupils go to school six hours a day, six days a week." They attended
school more days than American students, and they had more hours of
homework. David and his friends suspected that they, too, would have
more homework. They "hoped this would all go away but just then before Thanksgiving, the goddam Russians shot off *Sputnik II* and put a
little dog or monkey or something into the cosmos. Now we were really
in for it."[51]

In response to *Sputnik I* and *Sputnik II* (its payload included a dog
named Laika), the U.S. Department of Defense received funding for another satellite program, the Explorer Project, and the National Aeronautics and Space Administration (NASA) was created in 1958 after
Congress passed the National Aeronautics and Space Act. Meanwhile,
most Americans agreed that the "Space Race" demanded more from education and the country's next generation of scientists. Schools had to improve their curriculum and quality of teachers, and students had to work
harder. In the last months of 1957, Gallup polls showed that 70 percent
of those surveyed believed that it was up to students to compete with
their Soviet counterparts. Not only was this the new reality, but children
and teenagers became symbolic of another American challenge to the Soviet Union.[52]

Meanwhile, there was congressional reaction to *Sputnik*, with most lawmakers agreeing that it was in the national interest to promote science and math in the schools. How to translate the goal of producing more scientists, engineers, and mathematicians into practical fact was the point of debate. Staff on Senate Majority Leader Lyndon Johnson's Preparedness Subcommittee envisioned a "Johnson Plan," which emphasized a college scholarship program. Detlev Bronk, chairman of the National Science Board and charged with advising the president and Congress, offered a more expansive option. Speaking before the Senate Committee on Labor Relations and Public Welfare, he outlined a federal program that would support research and education, expand science and math studies in elementary and secondary schools, and place a new emphasis on teaching critical thinking. Among those on the senate committee supporting Bronk's plan were Senators John F. Kennedy and Barry Goldwater. The only committee member to oppose was Senator Strom Thurmond of South Carolina, whose rigid states' rights position precluded any support for federal involvement—even when that involvement was considered critical to national security and surpassing the Russians.[53]

In 1955, Neil McElroy told delegates at the White House Conference on Education that the country's schools were just as important to the nation's survival as the military. In 1957, *Sputnik* brought that message home. Education was tied to national defense and security, but before the country could reach the lofty goals of producing a greater number of highly skilled scientists and technicians, it had to confront the national illiteracy rate. From a military standpoint, this weakened America's potential fighting strength. Every wartime draft, beginning with World War I, rejected men because they were illiterate. Although illiteracy declined during the twentieth century, 19.2 percent of draftees for Korean War service were rejected for illiteracy and, according to the 1950 U.S. Census, there were about 8 million "functional illiterates" in the general population. This did not bode well for America's fighting forces or for a democratic form of government based on an informed electorate. Education was on the front lines in the Cold War struggle to maintain a democratic society.[54]

Reducing illiteracy and instilling patriotism were essential, but *Sput-*

nik forced Americans and their elected representatives to look to the federal government for action. Congressional support was assured when aid to education was presented as a necessary tool in national defense—much as the Eisenhower administration was able to fund construction of the national interstate highway system by tying it to defense and security. The result was the 1958 National Defense Education Act (NDEA), which Lyndon Johnson, who had himself once been a teacher, declared the "most important achievement" of Congress in that year. The act established a massive four-year spending bill. It funded student loans, at a cost of over $100 million, and spent $300 million for graduate fellowships and the purchase of scientific equipment for research facilities and college laboratories. Billions more went to public schools to expand science curriculums and teach modern languages. Teacher training at NDEA summer workshops began, and there was a rush to fund scholarships in college science programs.[55]

Although this was not the sort of construction or salary aid that school districts clamored for, they took what was offered. Money purchased modern equipment for science classrooms, slide and movie projectors, and the audio-visual aids that went with them. Yet, in many schools, especially those in economically depressed areas, NDEA's impact was hardly noticeable. Other classroom demands overtook promotion of the sciences and the addition of foreign language classes. And, in those districts where school administrators and teachers enthusiastically jumped at the chance to enhance science and math, the momentum was not sustained over the long term. Time itself was an enemy since most educators assumed that it would take time for the NDEA to show any results and for its influence to be fully evaluated.

In hindsight, it can be argued that the NDEA failed to deliver a sustained national superiority in the sciences and mathematics. Educators, U.S. presidents, business leaders, and members of Congress are still talking about ways to improve students' math and science skills. Yet, despite its shortcomings, at the time of its inception the NDEA produced some noticeable positive outcomes. The new emphasis on science and math encouraged students to pursue careers in those fields, as did the federally funded college scholarships. For some teenagers, like the "Rocket Boys" portrayed in Homer Hickam's memoir of high school boys building rockets in a West Virginia coal town, scholarships offered educational opportunities that otherwise would have been impossible.[56]

Of the education bill and the Cold War environment that influenced it, Democrat Jim Wright, elected to Congress in 1954 from Texas and later Speaker of the House, said:

> The Cold War dominated and in some ways distorted our whole national outlook. . . . The most often heard argument for its passage [National Defense Education Act] was not the need to improve learning opportunities for the sake of our kids but the fear that Soviet technology was getting ahead of us and the Russian schools were doing a better job than ours in preparing their youth for the space age.[57]

Sputnik, as well as school desegregation, had a major influence on America's educational system. They, however, did not present the only challenges faced by Presidents Truman and Eisenhower or the federal government. By the end of the 1950s, the burgeoning numbers of school-age children still outdistanced the number of available teachers and existing classrooms. In 1960, the country needed 195,000 teachers, and many school districts were so strapped for space that students either attended in double shifts or took their lessons in portable, mobile classrooms.

This state of affairs became a major topic during the 1960 presidential campaign, especially after Vice President Nixon refused to support the education bill of $1.1 billion put forth by Senators Patrick McNamara and Philip Hart, both Democrats from Michigan. The bill provided more money for school construction, something the Eisenhower administration tried to achieve on three earlier occasions and that both houses of Congress now seemed ready to support. The sticking point, however, was another provision in the bill—government funds to raise teachers' salaries. Supporters argued that salary increases would attract professionals who stayed away from teaching because the pay was less than what they could earn in other careers. (In 1960 the national average for teacher pay was just over $5,000.) Democrats, holding the majority in the Senate, believed that the bill had a good chance of passing, although some in the party, including education advocate J. Lister Hill, opposed the salary provision.

When the bill was defeated, the Republicans were blamed, and Nixon's very public position provided John F. Kennedy's presidential campaign with another point for criticism. During the first Nixon-Kennedy presidential debate of 1960, for instance, Kennedy pointedly stated his support for teacher compensation. In turn, Nixon responded that while he endorsed construction spending, he believed that "when the Federal Government gets the power to pay teachers . . . it will acquire the power to set standards and to tell teachers what to teach." Although Nixon's viewpoint was shared by people of all political stripes, it was muted when Kennedy's campaign speeches repeatedly returned to Nixon's position as an example of Republicans' desire to balance the budget at the expense of a quality education for America's children.[58]

Education was a multifaceted issue, and one that cut across all ethnic, racial, social, and economic boundaries. Of the many child-related topics discussed in the postwar era, education was the one most often addressed by lawmakers, presidents, and federal agencies. Alongside the basic necessities of building classrooms and finding teachers, there loomed demands that education do more for all youngsters, whether they be gifted, disabled, or marginalized. Most Americans considered many of the problems too large for local districts or state boards, and looked for federal intervention. Nevertheless, lawmakers were reluctant, if not outright opposed, to funding teachers' salaries and wholesale school construction. And, while a federal program helped feed a nutritious lunch to millions of schoolchildren, Congress only agreed to spend enormous amounts of money for specific forms of classroom instruction after the Soviets "beat" America into space. This was not funding for the love of learning or for the sake of a child's general education. It was a response to the threat of Soviet superiority.

As youngsters began to read with *Dick and Jane* and teenagers were introduced to algebra and physics, Congress and the presidents, along with state officials, hammered out the extent and the limits of federal involvement and intervention. As in other areas of child-related issues, the federal response was selective and often driven by Cold War rhetoric, arguments for shoring up national security, and perceived threats from the Soviet Union and Communist ideology. Nevertheless, federal policies became increasingly critical in determining what happened in America's classrooms. Overall, the Eisenhower administration of the 1950s fostered an unprecedented expansion of the federal government in education.

3

The Delinquent, the Dependent, and the Orphaned

"I am concerned about the opportunity that is put before every child from the day of his or her birth until he or she gets through high school."

—*President Dwight D. Eisenhower, December 6, 1958*

America was the land of opportunity. Children heard this from an early age. For proof, one had only to look at any number of inventors, industrialists, politicians, and presidents who came from modest beginnings. Eisenhower was no exception. In his experience, it was his parents and their home that prepared him for making the best of opportunities that came his way. That every child would have similar preparation and possibilities for self-advancement was Eisenhower's hope.

Millions of youngsters, however, were at a disadvantage. Child-care advocates in social welfare could point to any number of population groups—migrant children, African Americans, Latinos, Asians, and Native Americans—that were denied opportunities because of income, race, social barriers, and education. And, within these child populations were those that crossed racial and ethnic lines because they were the children and teenagers that society, welfare policies, and the courts designated as "dependent" or "delinquent."

Marriage, children, and family were national obsessions in the postwar period. A stereotype of the times was the child-centered, two-parent family. Yet, in 1949 an estimated 1.5 million minors did not live with their parents or with a surviving parent.[1] The number was expected to rise as the child population increased. Counted in the group of youngsters not living with parents were children and teenagers who were taken in by relatives because of family death, divorce, abandonment, or neglect. Also included in this group were the "dependent" residing in state or private orphanages, in foster homes, or in juvenile detention centers.

When mainstream society focused on marriage and the nuclear family, it was easy to look past the reality of youngsters living in circumstances that did not mirror the ideal of children being raised by biological parents in a stable home environment. In fact, most Americans had a rather sketchy notion of what happened to America's young when they entered the social welfare or justice systems. In a general way, people knew that there were orphanages, and perhaps they were familiar with foster care. Thanks to the media and congressional hearings, the public also heard and read a great deal about juvenile offenders and the courts.

Often what people thought they knew came from popular magazines that sometimes touched on the serious topics of delinquency or foster families. It was just as likely, however, that perceptions were shaped by movies and television. This was true of delinquency. The topic had been used by Hollywood filmmakers for years. *Public Enemy* (1931), for instance, followed characters whose juvenile offenses led to more serious crimes when they became adults. Other films, including *Angels with Dirty Faces* and *Boys Town* (both from 1938), took another avenue. Delinquents might be flawed, but they were not beyond redemption. From depression-era entertainment to the popular culture of the postwar era, delinquency continued to appear as a movie theme. Then, in 1957, it found a place on Broadway. *West Side Story* (later made into a movie) combined *Romeo and Juliet*, ethnic tensions, juvenile crime, and two competing gangs—the Puerto Rican Sharks and the Caucasian Jets.

While audiences may have left the theater humming "When you're a Jet, you're a Jet all the way," juvenile delinquency was a glaring social problem that drew the attention of both Presidents Truman and Eisenhower. Delinquency was on the rise, but its incidence was not confined to the United States. After World War II, Japan, West Germany, Austria, Sweden, France, New Zealand, and Australia grappled with widespread gang activity, rising juvenile crime, and an upswing in middle-class involvement. Even the harsh tactics employed by authorities in the Soviet

JUVENILE CRIME

FAMILIARITY WITH VICE
SOON LEADS TO CRIME

THREE STORIES OF THE STREET

Jakey supplements his meager breakfast with apples stolen from the grocer's barrel

Leo and Willie just returned from Reform School, delinquents as a result of street work. Their other brothers are going the same way

Seven year old newsie who sells until midnight. He has learned to gamble

SUCH BEGINNINGS LEAD TO

"THE MAJORITY OF BOYS WHO COME BEFORE THE JUVENILE COURT HAVE BEEN STREET WORKERS"

As this 1913 exhibit on factors leading to juvenile delinquency demonstrates, delinquency was a long-term national problem. Library of Congress

Union could not entirely curb "tough gangs that often terrorize people on the streets [of Moscow and provincial towns]." It was little wonder that Eisenhower, speaking before the 1960 White House Conference on Children and Youth, called delinquency a "world wide problem."[2]

Eisenhower knew that juvenile delinquency was not a new social issue in the United States. Even in his relatively sheltered life growing up in small-town America, there were a few delinquents. Writing to a cousin in 1905, fifteen-year-old Ike mentioned that three local boys were on their way to the state reform school "for chicken stealing."[3] Incarceration was the time-honored response to delinquency, and both boys and girls were committed to institutions for behavior that state laws defined as delinquent. The laws were often exhaustive since they included both criminal acts and those that might lead to delinquency. Included in the latter were frequenting pool halls or railway yards, smoking cigarettes, or spending more time on street corners than in school.

In the nineteenth century, a few private charities initiated intervention programs meant to redirect the paths of potential delinquents, but it was not until the end of the 1800s and the early 1900s that preventive measures such as organized sports and other supervised activities became widely accepted as the means to "save" youngsters from going "bad." Adult-directed recreation taught moral and social values. Organized play was a defense against juvenile delinquency, filling youngsters' time with something constructive. Delinquency was an ongoing topic among welfare workers, police officers, judges, and officials in state and local governments. The subject was discussed at the 1909 White House Conference on Children and Youth, and it returned at each successive ten-year meeting as a social problem that simply would not go away.

Although delinquency occurred in rural America and in towns of all sizes, the public generally regarded delinquency as behavior confined to the lower socio-economic classes. Urban tenements of the nineteenth century were notorious for neighborhood gangs that followed no laws but their own and periodically fought one another to protect their territory. Irish gangs in New York, for instance, fought each other when they were not defending their turf against the anti-Irish, anti-Catholic Bowery Boys gang. The scenario of urban gangs had not changed by the mid-twentieth century. In fact, the number in metropolitan areas was increasing nationally as more Latinos, Puerto Ricans, and African Americans from the rural South migrated to cities and took up residence in poor, economically depressed neighborhoods.

Solving all the social and economic problems found in urban slums and tenements was an impossibility, but one step toward eradicating delinquency, suggested many activists and reformers, was to eliminate the worst urban neighborhoods and rebuild them. New housing would lift morale and instill pride. In turn, neighborhoods would become safer, and delinquency rates would fall dramatically. Slum clearance and urban renewal were advocated by a number of sociologists, welfare workers, and congressmen. Among the latter was Senator Paul Douglas, a Democrat from Illinois, who said in *Collier's* magazine "living conditions, and not race or religion or color, largely determine delinquency rates."[4]

The numbing poverty and desperation of life in the slums certainly contributed to juvenile crime, but for most Americans, delinquency seemed far removed from their lives. That is until it became a middle-class problem in the postwar years. In the late 1940s and throughout the 1950s, juvenile delinquency found middle America. Among adults, there was a growing fear that delinquency and bad influences lurked around every neighborhood corner and in the nicer sections of town. The press, Hollywood, and popular magazines fueled the imagination. "Juvenile Crime: Is Your Boy Safe?" asked a *Newsweek* article. There was more to think about in such articles as "Child Criminals Are My Job," "Delinquency: Big and Bad," and *Time* magazine's seven-part series on "The Shook-Up Generation."[5]

Meanwhile, a spate of "delinquent" movies made their appearance. Many were low-budget B films, but that could not be said of two well-known films of the period. *The Blackboard Jungle* (1955), with its riveting rock 'n' roll soundtrack, brought a frightening realism to the subject of urban delinquency while *Rebel without a Cause* (1955) took delinquents out of the inner city and put them in the financially comfortable, white middle class.

The characters in *Rebel* were the new reality, said the U.S. Children's Bureau. By 1954, juvenile delinquency was on the rise "in more fortunate neighborhoods and homes." The sharpest increases over the national average were being seen in small cities and towns. A *Newsweek* survey agreed. Delinquency was spreading "to the suburbs and rural sections, taking root at white-collar and well-to-do levels." As one example, the magazine told the story of twenty-five teenage girls, from "good" families in Washington State, involved in an organized shoplifting ring. In a rather prescient forecast, one commentator predicted the social upheaval that occurred in the 1960s—but his statement was made within the context of juvenile delinquency in the 1950s. "It may be that we are soon to witness the birth of political awareness among American gangs," he wrote. "And it may be that middle-class youth will revolt more pronouncedly against social pressures and gather together in defiant groups in order to render their protests more effective."[6]

While a chorus of opinions, commentary, and conjecture surrounded the topic of delinquency in the 1940s and 50s, the most accurate information came from the federal government. Both the U.S. Children's Bureau and the Department of Justice kept track of trends and collected national statistics. During the war years, juvenile crime spiked when children, the "latchkey kids," and teenagers were left to their own devices. Unsupervised, they contributed to higher delinquency figures. Arrests for minor infractions such as school truancy went up, as did those for robbery, assault, and underage prostitution. Increase in the latter, said local officials and a number of private surveys, was directly tied to the expansion of existing military bases and the creation of new ones.[7]

As early as 1942, the Social Services Division of the Children's Bureau warned at a meeting of the newly created Commission on Children in Wartime that "increased delinquency was a natural function of war." Within recent memory was the "abnormal increase" that occurred during World War I; further back in time, the social and economic upheaval created by the Civil War fed delinquent crime. Given what they knew about the past, the U.S. Children's Bureau and Department of Justice anticipated rates to increase, and by 1945, U.S. Attorney General Tom C. Clark informed President Truman that the overall numbers for juvenile arrests and incarcerations were "alarming." The increase in some categories of crime-related activities during the war years was in excess of 350 percent.[8]

Immediate action was called for, and with Truman's support Attorney General Clark convened the National Conference for the Prevention and

Control of Juvenile Delinquency in 1946. One result was a new policy, instituted by Clark, for federal judicial districts. Judges could defer criminal charges against juvenile offenders if the youngsters seemed to be candidates for rehabilitation. The policy was later codified in the Federal Youth Corrections Act of 1950, giving courts more latitude and a greater number of options for sentencing. The act also required rehabilitation treatment in special facilities for offenders under the age of twenty-two convicted in federal courts.[9]

Most youthful offenders, however, did not break federal laws or end up in federal courts. They passed through the local juvenile court system—a system devised by early twentieth-century reformers to separate youthful offenders from adults charged with crimes. If juveniles were sentenced by the court, they were incarcerated in reformatories operated by a state or territory's correctional department or they were remanded to training schools run by departments of public welfare and corrections or by private charities. When the Federal Youth Corrections Act became law, there were approximately 29,000 teenage boys and girls in these institutions. Another 15,000, noted the U.S Census of 1950, lived in "detention homes" where temporary care was provided to those who, "by reason of delinquency, dissolution of the home, or other crises," awaited welfare workers and the courts to decide the next step. Although some commentators believed that the incidence of juvenile crimes would fall as the country returned to normalcy after the war, there was no drop. In fact, the number of adolescents and older teenagers brought before judges more than doubled between 1948 and 1956. The year 1954 showed "an all-time high."[10]

Tougher juvenile codes and tighter enforcement was partly responsible for the rise, as was a justice system that became increasingly watchful and inclined to act. Youngsters that made a nuisance of themselves by congregating on the street or running through neighbors' yards were less likely to be simply reprimanded by a neighbor or the stereotypical kindly cop on the beat. Instead, there were formal complaints and hearings before a judge.

Despite the collection of statistics and studies of juvenile crime, no one could pinpoint one single, overriding factor responsible for the national increase. Was this a sign of the country's moral decay predicted by the Communists? Were young people acting out because they felt there was nothing to lose when faced with the prospect of nuclear annihilation? More importantly, who or what was responsible for this state of affairs? Social commentators, community leaders, law enforcement experts, and welfare workers felt that there was plenty of blame to go around. Slums and poverty were factors, but many agreed with Senator Robert C. Hendrickson, a Republican from New Jersey, who pointed a finger at apathetic or too-permissive parents, saying that "not even the Communist conspiracy could devise a more effective way to demoralize, confuse, and destroy [the United States]."[11] Parenting, or more specifically the absence of it, may have been a factor, but certainly it was not the only culprit. Television, movies, bad neighborhoods, gangs, inadequate schools, lack of community leadership, comic books, and rock 'n' roll all came in for their share of condemnation.

Rock 'n' roll was an easy target. The music itself suggested rebellion against the social order. The same was said about popular music in the 1930s and 40s when the conductor for the New York Philharmonic called the jitterbug "the greatest single contributing factor of juvenile delinquency among American youth today." Although young people and the older generation are often at odds over music, rock 'n' roll seemed to represent a particular threat to both morality and the status quo of race segregation. The music crossed racial and class lines, challenging traditional boundaries and attitudes. Whites, African Americans, and Latinos shared the music, and what was worse, said anti-rock protesters, teenagers of racially different backgrounds sometimes attended the same performances and mixed on the same dance floors. The lines blurred between "race" music and the popular mainstream. Teenagers did not question a performer's race or did not, if they knew, seem to care. Teenage singer Leslie Uggams thought Buddy Holly was African American, "just another brother out there doing his number"—until she saw him onstage at the Apollo Theater. "But he was terrific," she said, and that was what mattered. Then, there was the music's sexual edge, enhanced by performers like Jerry Lee Lewis, Little Richard, and Elvis Presley. Presley was a phenomenon. Even President Eisenhower was aware of him, if for no other reason than the hundreds of letters received from teenage girls begging the president to keep Elvis out of the army.[12]

Rock music was just one piece of America's popular culture during the postwar years. Big bands, crooners, ballads, and romantic tunes also claimed huge followings. When, however, the lyrics and rhythms of rock 'n' roll were compared against such top-selling songs as Eddie Fisher's "Oh, My Pa-Pa" or Patti Page's "Doggy in the Window," rock seemed more rebellious and shocking than it really was. Many adults were not persuaded that rock 'n' roll was simply another form of music. Instead, they saw it as a force that could lead young people astray. Jack Lait and Lee Mortimer made just this argument in their successful book *U.S.A. Confidential*. Rock 'n' roll, they said, encouraged delinquency with its "hot jive and ritualistic orgies of erotic dancing, . . . with African jungle background." "We know," wrote the journalists, "that many platter-spinners are hopheads. Many others are Reds, left-wingers, or hecklers of social convention."[13]

If rock 'n' roll contributed to delinquency, it was certainly not alone. To ferret out the causes behind the indisputable rise in juvenile crime and to assure Americans that it was just as concerned as the general public, a Senate committee convened congressional hearings. Senator Robert C. Hendrickson pushed for the hearings, as did Estes Kefauver, who became a household name during the Senate's investigation into organized crime. "Youth, indeed, is the greatest wealth of the nation," said Kefauver. "We must not waste our resources by allowing vast numbers of our young to enter a destructive rather than a constructive way of life." In November 1953 the Senate Subcommittee to Investigate Juvenile Delinquency convened under the chairmanship of Hendrickson. Also on the committee were Kefauver, William Langer (R-North Dakota), and Thomas C. Henning, Jr. (D-Missouri). In a letter to Hendrickson, President Eisenhower wrote that he considered delinquency "a problem filled with heartbreak. . . . [and] one of the most complex social problems facing the nation today." Eisenhower promised Hendrickson that the committee's "suggestions for action" would receive the "wholehearted assistance of those Executive Departments which are concerned with the problem."[14]

The committee held hearings in Washington, D.C., New York, California, Colorado, and North Dakota (testimony there dealt solely with delinquency among Native Americans and the contributing factors of

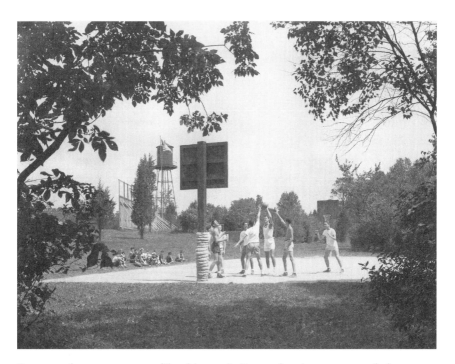

Sports and summer camps, like this one in Pennsylvania, were regarded as significant solutions in stemming delinquency. Library of Congress

poverty, unemployment, and alcohol use). During its multicity tour, the committee heard testimony about drug use, the ethnic and racial makeup of gangs, school dropout rates, gang wars, and "rumbles." They listened to descriptions of California's "Displaced Children's Specials," which transported runaways and parolees from California Youth Authority institutions back to their home states. Dramatically described by the *Saturday Evening Post* as "Heartbreak" trains, these "Specials" sometimes returned the same runaways time and again. Lastly, the committee was confronted with statistics for juvenile crime. In 1953, juveniles (anyone under the age of eighteen) committed over 50 percent of all auto thefts in the nation; they were responsible for 48 percent of all burglaries; 15 percent of the rapes; and 4 percent of all homicides.[15]

The committee, chaired by Kefauver after Hendrickson did not run for reelection and was appointed ambassador to New Zealand, met in other locales in 1954 and 1955. It heard about successful programs in the fight to combat delinquency. Some were state-run. Others were privately operated by charities, religious organizations, or civic groups. A large number of programs involved summer camps that removed youngsters from big-city temptations. In-city groups focused on getting young people off the streets and into structured sports and recreational activities; the majority of these, such as basketball and boxing, were clearly aimed at boys, who statistically outnumbered girls in the delinquent population. The committee also considered topics not addressed during its initial inquiries. One was the influence of the mass media, including comic books.

The committee's concern was not with romance comics, the teenage antics of characters such as "Archie" and his friends, or even with war comics and their depictions of violence in battle because, said Kefauver, "authorities agree that the majority of comic books are as harmless as soda pop." The committee was primarily interested in the "horror and crime comic books [that] are peddled to our young people of an impressionable age." A reported 20 million copies of the ten-cent horror comics were sold each month in the United States, to both youngsters and adults. No one knew how many minors bought the comics, but the senators expressed alarm as they pored through piles of exhibits that included such titles as *Voodoo* and *Uncanny Tales*.[16]

Called to testify were publishers, cartoonists, and anti–comic book crusaders. The latter was led by psychologist Fredric Wertham, whose book *Seduction of the Innocent* claimed that his studies demonstrated a direct correlation between delinquency and comic books. This assertion was challenged by a number of criminologists, as well as psychologists opposed to Wertham's view. Ultimately, the committee announced in its final report that it would not condone censorship. Nor was the committee convinced that comic books were a major factor. Reading a comic book did not turn someone into a delinquent—any more than television shows or motion pictures did. The committee agreed that the comic book industry could do more to regulate itself, but parents and communities had the power, if not the responsibility, to control access and to redirect youngsters' reading habits.[17]

A number of communities and states responded to the potential comic book menace with legislation. By 1955, fourteen states regulated the sale and production of comics, with three states banning some titles outright. Nine other states had either considered legislation and then failed to act or were in the process of writing regulatory laws. Although the Senate committee's final report spoke against government censorship, the comic book industry decided to act on the assumption that federal control might come at a later date. It established the Comic Magazine Association of America and had its own stamp of approval for printed material. As the first of new industry-approved comics were about to hit the stands, the *New York Times* noted that the heroines would be wearing more clothes and the violence would be "toned down."[18]

Delinquency destroyed potentially productive lives, tore apart families, and presented a challenge to law enforcement and the courts. Rising crime rates required more money for additional law enforcement personnel, court facilities, detention centers, and probation services. Delinquency presented two separate but intertwined issues. The first was finding ways to regulate and control behavior; the second was funding both preventive programs and those that began at the time of arrest and court appearance.

As Senate hearings continued, the Children's Bureau and the Department of Health, Education, and Welfare (HEW) organized a special conference in June 1954 entitled "Moving Ahead to Curb Juvenile Delinquency." Participants asked what more could be done. There were already over 90,000 organizations nationwide involved in special projects to combat the problem. Scouting, boys' and girls' clubs, organized sports, and summer camps were among the most active preventive programs. Nevertheless, said HEW Secretary Hobby, these were "sprawling and uncoordinated." Programs and projects often overlapped, and in most cases there was no real coordination between state and city governments, local communities, or private organizations running these programs. Also problematic was finding the right approach to treatment and prevention when delinquents exhibited such a "great variety of personality and behavior problems." As the conference ended, it was decided that HEW and the Children's Bureau could play a leading role in coordinating projects from the top, using federal money to support their efforts.[19]

President Eisenhower raised the issue of juvenile delinquency in his 1955 State of the Union message, proposing federal legislation that would provide states and U.S. territories with financial resources to fight the problem. As he spoke on the subject, he also became the first U.S. president to address a national audience on the dangers of the international trade in narcotics, as well as its connection to delinquency. The government, said the president, had a responsibility to all of the country's citizens to protect them from illegal drugs and to "combat narcotic addiction in our own country."[20]

There had been a subculture of drug use and trafficking in the United States for decades. Several states had laws, dating back to the 1800s, that addressed opium smoking or allowed only licensed physicians to prescribe cocaine. In 1914, the first national drug law, the Harrison Narcotic Act, was enacted; it required manufacturers, physicians, and pharmacists handling "hard" drugs to be licensed and then taxed. And, in 1930 the Federal Bureau of Narcotics was established. Its chief concern was opium and heroin being smuggled into the country. Marijuana use also came under closer scrutiny. In the late 1930s, the film *Tell Your Children* (later retitled *Reefer Madness*) was released as a warning to teens, and cities and states began to seriously study drug use and distribution. In New York City, a committee of doctors and psychiatrists appointed by Mayor Fiorello LaGuardia determined that marijuana use was on the rise in the city, and lest anyone think that this was strictly confined to large metropolitan centers, in America's heartland, the Kansas Bureau of Investigation's first marijuana case occurred in 1939. Although drug use and addiction remained at the edge of America's mainstream culture, it gained more attention after World War II. The Boggs Act of 1951 and the Narcotic Control Act of 1956 increased penalties for drug possession and distribution, and Eisenhower brought the subject of illegal drugs before the American public when he connected them to juvenile crime.[21]

There were degrees of delinquency. Incorrigible gang members who trafficked in drugs or carried illegal firearms were in no way the same sort of delinquents whose major offenses were school truancy, hot-rodding, or sneaking an underage drink. All minors brought before the courts were, however, a national problem. The Eisenhower administration asked Congress for financial aid to curb delinquency. When it refused, Representative Victor L. Anfuso, a Democrat from Brooklyn, New York, proposed that Ike establish a presidential commission on crime and juvenile delinquency as a springboard to get the legislation he wanted. The commission would study the various ways states dealt with delinquency and incarceration, would revisit the question of comic books, would recommend legislation to control the sale of firearms to minors, and would determine the extent of narcotic use.

Representative Anfuso was particularly concerned with illegal drugs. By the mid-1950s, unsubstantiated press reports claimed that New York City had more juvenile drug users than in all of Western Europe. Following Anfuso's suggestion, the presidential commission was considered but not appointed. Its creation was redundant when a three-year congressional investigation and a national conference on delinquency had already compiled reams of testimony, reports, and statistical data. Despite the work put into studying the problem, Congress was not prepared to spend federal monies to assist state and local agencies. Eisenhower's requests for funds were blocked in 1956 and 1960. Supporters of federal aid—and there were many, including former president Herbert Hoover, who included the subject in his speech at the 1960 Republican National Convention—refused to give up. Then, with the momentum generated by the 1960 White House Conference on Children and Youth and a change in presidential administrations, Congress acted in 1961. The program, begun under the Kennedy administration as the Juvenile Delinquency and Youth Control Act, provided $10 million a year in federal grants for pilot projects, training programs, and studies conducted by state, local, and nonprofit agencies.[22]

The problems of delinquency and its prevention were recurring issues with each generation. So, too, were the questions of what constituted the best treatment for orphaned and dependent children. The first White House Conference on Children and Youth, held in 1909, focused on dependent children, standardizing policies for their care and safeguarding their welfare. Each successive conference addressed the dependent child population. Children and teenagers grouped into the category of dependent were a varied lot. They were youngsters whose parents, for any number of reasons, could not or would not care for them; they were children whose mental or physical conditions required institutional care; and they were the orphaned.

In 1949, the Social Security Administration, which provided survivor's benefits through Social Security funds, estimated the number of orphans (youngsters under the age of sixteen with no living parent) at 100,000. On the face of it, the number was astounding, but during the twentieth century the number of orphans actually dropped as adult mortality rates declined. In 1920, for example, orphans made up 16.3 percent of the total child population; by 1954, the number was at 5 percent. Statistics also showed that in 1949 only three out of every one hundred orphans lived in an orphanage.[23]

Orphanages had been part of the American landscape since the early 1800s. The numbers increased throughout the nineteenth century and into the early twentieth. Many, such as those for African Americans, Jewish children, or Native Americans, were very specific about the race, ethnicity, or religion of the children taken in. Other orphanages, however, cared for youngsters from varied backgrounds. While the physical layouts of some orphanages comprised central buildings with dormitory settings, others housed child residents in cottages to provide a semblance of family living.

Orphanages were certainly not all the same, but their diversity was usually lost on the public. What most Americans thought they knew about orphan homes and orphans came from literature or Hollywood. More than one generation grew up reading Horatio Alger's tales of boys who got themselves off the streets or out of institutions by their own grit and gumption. Readers knew the story *Anne of Green Gables*, first published in 1908, or they followed the adventures of "Little Orphan Annie," either through the comic strip or radio program. And, thousands of fans flocked to see Shirley Temple's orphan-girl *Curly Top* (1935), happily adopted into an affluent home.

Too often, however, "orphan" and "orphanage" brought to mind those nineteenth-century institutions described by Charles Dickens, no matter how much orphanages had changed, modernized, or applied progressive methodologies over the decades. Undoubtedly some institutions were badly run or mistreated their charges, but most did their best with what they had. A former resident said of his life in a North Carolina children's home during the 1950s: "Throughout my life, I've heard the orphanage experience condemned by any number of people who knew it only from the way orphanages are portrayed in novels and movies. . . . I

With assistance from a care provider, two girls at the Nebraska Children's Home Society decorate a birthday cake. Like other child welfare organizations of the time, the society encouraged foster care placement and adoption of its charges. Nebraska Children's Home Society

knew my home did not fit the grim Dickensian mold. . . . I grew up in a home with 150 or so other girls and boys—and I'm damn proud of it, and thankful."[24]

Orphanages housed parentless children, and they provided refuge for youngsters whose parents sought out the institutions when the family experienced personal or financial crises, such as the death of a spouse or loss of a job. The orphanage provided a safety net when few social welfare or reform programs dealt with the family unit. Parents saw orphanages as a stopgap. When a family's situation improved, parents reclaimed their children, but for many youngsters the ups and downs of family life meant spending time in and out of orphanages.

Although orphanages had long been accepted as a form of child welfare, their numbers began to decline for several reasons. During the 1930s, many privately supported orphanages were forced to close their doors for lack of funds, and many more orphanages were affected by the New Deal's Aid to Dependent Mothers, which allowed youngsters to stay with their families rather than seek aid and shelter from an orphanage. Many institutions also redirected their resources. Rather than provide long-term, in-house care, they began to concentrate on home placement through adoption or foster care. Although orphanages had a long history in American social welfare, they lost favor among trained professionals, experts in child development, and a growing cross-section of the American public. Youngsters, it was argued, should grow up in a home environment—if not with their own families, then in foster care.

Foster care and adoption were considered to be the best alternatives to institutional care. And, of the two, foster care was more likely to affect a larger population of children since it was employed to house both orphans and those children who could not, for any number of reasons, live with parents or relatives. Recognizing that fact of life, foster care was specifically mentioned in the eighteen-point "Pledge to Children" drafted by the 1950 White House Conference on Children and Youth. The pledge promised to "work to conserve and improve family life and, as needed, to provide foster care according to your [child's] inherent rights." This strongly echoed the 1930 White House Conference on Children and Youth's "Children's Charter," which called foster care "the nearest substitute" to a loving, protective home.[25]

Clearly, foster care was recognized as an important adjunct to child welfare, but there were obstacles to finding homes. A problem, often heard echoed today, was the "dire shortage" of available homes. Many states found it impossible to increase the "board rate" paid to foster parents. New Mexico's Department of Public Welfare noted that good homes were difficult to find because the state was asking families "to give love and care to children unrelated to them for less than it actually costs."[26]

Even the best of foster parents were seriously reconsidering their commitment. Concerns were reported throughout the nation. Illinois officials bemoaned the low number of foster homes in Chicago and the nonexistent supply in several downstate counties. Delaware, in 1950, noted that four agencies in the state arranged foster care for children of all racial and religious backgrounds, but each faced similar difficulties. Welfare workers believed these stemmed from more women working outside the home, families "preoccupied" with their own lives, and the postwar housing shortage. The Michigan Youth Commission concurred. Couples would not take in another child when homes were already over-crowded. The housing shortage, said the commission, especially affected finding homes for minority children.[27]

Federal agencies, including the Children's Bureau, were aware of the problem, but they were not in a position to act beyond conducting studies that supported state reports. Indirectly, however, the federal response to the housing shortage—funding public housing projects and providing veteran benefits that included home loans—gradually alleviated the housing crisis. In turn, it became less of a factor in the search for couples willing to act as foster parents. There were never enough, however, and the numbers of children requiring foster care only increased with the growing child population of the 1950s. By that time, most of the children placed in foster homes were not orphans, but youngsters with at least one living parent. The "most common reason for foster home place-ment" said the research study *Children in Need of Parents* in 1959 was "neglect and abandonment . . . followed by death, illness, economic hardship, and marital conflict."[28]

Adoption also drew the attention of the general public and federal agencies. What adoption meant seemed self-explanatory, but the concept of legal adoption, as a relationship that differed from the English Com-mon Law of guardianship, only dated back to the mid-nineteenth cen-tury in America. States varied in their adoption statutes. Some established adoption laws in the 1850s and 1860s; others, not until the 1920s. Generally, these laws provided children legal status within their adoptive families, set guidelines for agencies handling adoptions, and mandated standards for protecting the child's "best interest." There was, however, no uniformity in state statutes.

The U.S. Children's Bureau and organizations such as the Child Wel-fare League of America, which traced its beginnings to the 1909 White House Conference on Children and Youth, spent the first decades of their existence in trying to establish national adoption standards and to eradicate "black market" placements. Although they were influential in seeing states tighten their laws and force "baby sellers" out of business, there were still questions about the process of adoption.

When the White House Conference on Children and Youth convened in 1950, professionals' concerns were substantiated by state reports. Wisconsin and Texas noted that "too many" home placements occurred "without supervision of an authorized welfare agency." Texas hoped to correct its problems with new legislation that gave the state department of welfare greater investigative power to ferret out illegal "black market" adoptions. From Missouri came the complaint that about half of the adoptions in that state were handled by "untrained juvenile court staff." (This would not have pleased President Truman, who proudly told delegates at the 1950 White House Conference on Children and Youth that as a judge in Jackson County, Missouri, he ignored critics and hired trained welfare workers.) A constant in every state and territory were the number of adoptions secured through private intermediaries. These were often doctors or lawyers. In fact, the acrimony was palpable between professional social workers and private citizens who arranged adoptions. A report from Kansas, for example, complained that efforts to strengthen the state's adoption laws (the first was enacted in 1864) were "met with cold indifference and often opposition from the medical doctors who by some strange logic" believed that they were better equipped than trained workers to place children.[29]

Doctors, along with lawyers, believed that they filled a need for couples who shied away from what they considered the intrusive bureaucracy of licensed adoption agencies and their drawn-out waiting periods. Many couples did not want to wait for a child that an agency decided was a "perfect" match. Nor did they want to endure months of extensive interviews, psychological testing, or trying to meet every demand—some of them unreasonable—placed on them by social workers. Adoption through a private party meant less red tape, a shorter waiting period, and greater confidentiality. Although states, urged on by professional social workers, attempted to exert more control over private adoptions, the number of both private and agency adoptions increased near the close of World War II and continued to grow. Adoption was becoming a widely used practice to expand the family unit. Telling his own story, one adoptive father wrote that he and his wife were against adoption until their friends adopted. "We suddenly began to realize that we were missing something in life."[30]

For many, desire for a child was heightened by the postwar era's idealization of parenthood. Women, said popular culture, could only find ultimate fulfillment as mothers. Fatherhood was a desirable role for men. The print media said so, as did the television fathers in *The Adventures of Ozzie and Harriet, Father Knows Best, Make Room for Daddy*, and *Leave It to Beaver*. Although sometimes bemused by their offspring, these fathers were emotionally involved with their families. They represented society's changing view of fatherhood. Father was still the family patriarch, but he was also a pal who spent time with his children offering fatherly advice and sympathetic direction.

Personal identity and marital happiness were tied to children. The message was conveyed through articles in popular magazines, television, and Hollywood's new emphasis on stars as parents. Celebrities were photographed and filmed with their children at birthday parties, on outings, and during casual days at home. Magazines and entertainment executives drew the line, however, at showing women who were obviously pregnant. All that changed when Lucille Ball's pregnancy became part of the story line in *I Love Lucy*. The 1953 episode "Lucy Goes to the Hospital" was watched by over 70 percent of television households. Adding to the list of celebrity parents were a number of well-known personalities who adopted children. Among them were Roy Rogers and Dale Evans, George Burns and Gracie Allen, Joan Crawford, and Bette Davis.

Between 1944 and 1953, the number of adoption petitions filed in U.S. courts rose from 50,000 to 90,000, and for the remainder of the 1950s, the yearly average ranged between 90,000 and 95,000. Children adopted by a stepparent or relative made up almost half of all adoptions; the remaining were adopted by nonrelatives. Despite the general assumption that nonrelative adoptions were of children born to unwed mothers, almost half were the children of married women. Studies in California, for instance, found that 45 to 47 percent of all adoptions in that state involved children of married couples. Parents explained their reasons for giving up a child in a number of ways. Financial problems made it difficult, if not impossible, to provide for a child. Some couples thought that they were too young to take on the job of parenthood. And a mobile society made child rearing all the more difficult when young parents were far away from the support of an extended family that might offer advice, financial help, and help with child care. Other couples believed that already shaky marriages would only get worse if there was a child. The California findings reflected circumstances and attitudes in other areas of the country.[31]

Parents who gave up their children supplied the "adoption market." So did unwed mothers. Pregnancy out of wedlock was seldom admitted to in public, and if a woman did not quickly marry, she was discouraged from keeping her child. Any woman who kept her child was considered flawed. She was rejecting society's willingness to rehabilitate her by allowing her to send the child away and then start over as if nothing had happened. In the 1950s sociologists began to survey and analyze women living in homes for unwed mothers. After administering a battery of tests in one group study, a sociologist used what he called his "interpretative impressions" to conclude that women who refused to give up their children were emotionally immature. Although they scored well on a test that calculated their "femininity," the sociologist believed that women who refused to relinquish their children really had no "traditional feminine interests, warmth or concern for others." American culture preached the desirability and fulfillment of motherhood, but it also chose to stigmatize the unmarried mother. The reality was that social pressures, combined with limited economic prospects, primed women to opt for adoption.[32]

Other than the U.S. Children's Bureau's promotion of foster care as a way to give children a "normal home life," the federal government did not involve itself directly with foster care or adoption legislation during this period. Legislation did not begin to appear until the late 1970s, and then it specifically addressed issues such as the transracial adoption of Native American children into white homes. In the postwar era of the 1940s and 50s, the government's role was played out through federal agencies. The Children's Bureau conducted studies on adoption trends and acted as the voice for professional standards. And, the U.S. Bureau of Indian Affairs (BIA) promoted its own adoption program. For years a number of private agencies and orphanages had placed Native American children into adoptive homes. One of those adopted out of Oklahoma's

Murrow Indian Orphanage in the 1950s recalled: "We rejoiced always at an adoption at Murrow; we truly did. Riding far above the undercurrents of jealousy and loss was a wave of excitement and hope. Every adoption promised redemption for all the lonely little orphans."[33]

In 1958, the BIA decided to do what private and state-funded agencies were already doing. It would directly involve itself, as a federal agency, in the adoption of Native American children. With the help of the Child Welfare League of America, it established the Indian Adoption Project (IAP). While the Child Welfare League was careful to note that it did not view the program as a "solution for the mass of Indian children suffering from long-standing national neglect and abuse," it considered adoption an attractive alternative for some. As it turned out, the project never reached the scope once envisioned. After a decade of activities in seventeen states with native populations, the IAP placed only 395 children into adoptive homes. There were several explanations for the low number. IAP was reluctant to allow Indian families to adopt Indian children, favoring Caucasian families. And, without the cooperation of tribal governments, the project faced outright disapproval. In addition, some states initiated policies that gave them a larger role in the social welfare of tribal people. The State of South Dakota, for instance, with a large Native American population, began to pay the hospital and medical expenses of unwed mothers so they would not be "forced to release [their children] to whomever would pay the bills." Nevertheless, the BIA called its project a success because it "stimulated adoption of Indians in the care of state agencies."[34]

The number of children adopted by American families also increased as people responded to the wrenching circumstances of children affected by war. An emotional outpouring led to an unprecedented wave of international adoptions. Following World War II, orphans came to the United States from Europe. Some were flown to America, but the first groups were transported by troopships, along with others leaving war-ravaged countries. A crew member of one ship wrote: "We watched them come aboard at Bremerhaven [Germany]. . . . First came the orphans, then the aged and finally the families." One of the child passengers recalled, "Although at 6 years of age I was too young to form strong opinions about the cuisine I distinctly remember eating the first orange of my life aboard the USAT *General R. L. Howze*."[35]

The child was one of the thousands of "displaced persons" left up-rooted and homeless by the war. "Displaced" is too mild and benign a word to describe who these people were and their circumstances. They were from France, Belgium, the Netherlands, the Baltic States, Poland, and Yugoslavia. During the war, most had been transferred by the Nazis into Germany and German-occupied regions where they were forced to work in German industries or were sent to concentration camps. After the war, the number of displaced persons only increased as thousands of East Europeans fled Soviet-occupied areas for the Allied Zones in Germany and Austria. Between the end of war hostilities on May 8, 1945, and July 1947, approximately 7 million of the displaced were repatriated back to their home countries, particularly to France, Belgium, and Holland, but an estimated 1 million remained in and around camps set up to provide shelter, medical attention, and food.[36]

Those who could not, or refused to, return to their country of origin could not remain in the camps indefinitely, and it was feared that their continuing presence would produce severe economic and social reper-cussions in Germany and Austria. One alternative was resettlement. Several countries were willing to accept the displaced. To facilitate migration, the Intergovernmental Committee for European Migration (ICEM), consisting of twenty-six countries, was organized. Belgium, England, France, Norway, and Latin American countries took in thou-sands. So did South Africa, Israel, New Zealand, and Australia. The dis-placed also came to America, but it was apparent that the United States was reluctant to take what many considered its fair share of refugees. Testifying before the House Subcommittee on Immigration and Natural-ization in July 1947, Secretary of State George C. Marshall cautioned that the United States should "practice what we preach. . . . In doing so, we will also confirm our moral leadership and demonstrate that we are not retreating behind the Atlantic Ocean."[37]

Just four months before Marshall appeared before the subcommittee, Illinois Republican William G. Stratton introduced a bill in the House of Representatives to admit up to 400,000 displaced persons over a four-year period. There was considerable public support. The National Feder-ation of Women's Clubs, for example, voted overwhelmingly to support the bill. In the *New York Times*, Earl G. Harrison, former commissioner of Immigration and Naturalization, argued that these new immigrants would strengthen America, and RKO-Pathe produced a documentary to generate public sympathy. The film, *Passport to Nowhere*, made a plea for compassion as it prominently featured the faces of babies, children, and teenagers living in camps for displaced persons.[38]

Although some private citizens expressed concern that helping "the abandoned and unwanted children of Europe" would take attention away from America's own dependent children, public opinion sided with the Stratton Bill. The Truman administration favored it, but the bill, said *Time* magazine, "was dying on the vine." Many in Congress considered the immigration of so many "a politically explosive issue." Some feared that immigrants would glut the labor market at a time when the unemployment rate was less than 4 percent. Others argued that these "foreigners" would transport anti-democratic ideas. Worse, some might be die-hard Communists slipping into America under the guise of being refugees.[39]

Congress finally passed a bill in June 1948. Compromises and revisions that suited both the House and Senate had produced legislation that Truman was loath to sign. Nevertheless, he did "in the hope that its injustices will be rectified by Congress at its first opportunity." The injustice that offended many was blatant discrimination against Jewish and Catholic immigrants. Truman felt, however, that it was this bill or nothing while thousands languished. Under the bill, a Displaced Persons Commission was established to oversee refugee immigration, and Truman took the opportunity to appoint men who shared his desire to aid as many as possible. Commissioners Harry S. Rosenfield, Edward O'Connor, and Ugo Carusi were chosen because they would broadly interpret the Displaced Persons Act.[40]

Senator Pat McCarran, a Democrat from Nevada who later lent his name to the 1952 McCarran-Walter Act and its rigid entry quotas, was outraged. He accused the Displaced Persons Commission of not only being lax in its oversight but of turning a blind eye to forged documents, perjured statements, and fraud among refugees who hoped to come to America. The senator was certain that the commission was allowing Communists into the country. McCarran, said Senator Paul Douglas, exercised his power on the Senate Judiciary Committee and the Appropria-

Children wait for a meal at a camp for war refugees. The Displaced Persons Act of 1948 allowed 3,000 war orphans into the United States as adoptees; the number was later increased. U.N. Relief and Rehabilitation Administration, Courtesy Harry S. Truman Library

tions Subcommittee "like a despot." His constant harangues and charges against the commission caused some to leave the job, and those who stayed often found their work criticized or stymied. Nevertheless, the commission had some impact on restructuring the quota system to allow more Jews into the country and to eliminate a preference for agricultural workers, a group favored because the country at the time needed them.[41]

The Displaced Persons Act of 1948 allowed 200,000 displaced persons into the United States (the number was later amended to over 400,000). It also admitted 2,000 refugees who fled Czechoslovakia after the Soviets took control there, and it allowed for 3,000 orphans. A child was designated a "displaced orphan" and eligible for adoption if the child was orphaned because both parents were dead or had disappeared without any hope that they would someday be located. An adolescent boy in a displaced persons camp in Germany, for instance, was deemed ineligible because both parents were still alive in Czechoslovakia, but a nine-year-old residing in a Greek orphanage qualified because both parents died during the war, the father in a concentration camp and the mother when Germans set fire to a church.[42]

Government employees working for the U.S. Displaced Persons Commission and aid workers at the camps in Germany and Austria sought to verify as thoroughly as possible that a child was not being abandoned by a living parent. Eligibility was also defined by age. When the commission began its work, potential adoptees could be as old as sixteen, but the later amended Displaced Persons Act dropped the age to ten and under. These displaced orphans were eligible for adoption by American families that sometimes, but not always, were somehow related. Once a youngster was deemed eligible, the U.S. Committee for the Care of European Children reviewed adoption applications and made arrangements for visas, legal formalities of adoption, and transportation. A number of private charities worked with the committee, including the Church World Service and the American Hellenic Education Progressive Association. The latter dealt solely with Greek orphans, assuming the cost to transport the children to their adoptive American families.[43]

Being a war orphan did not, however, mean that the child was available for international adoption. England, France, and the Scandinavian countries, for instance, took a dim view of their native-born children being removed from local orphanages for overseas placements, and American families of Greek or Italian origin wishing to adopt children from those countries often found it difficult because a child had to be first of all a "displaced person." Simply being an orphan did not qualify. Although some children from Greece and Italy met the criteria and were admitted into the United States as adoptees, many others were not. After being told that his eight-year-old orphaned relative did not qualify as displaced—she was still in her home village—a man bitterly wrote his senator, John Foster Dulles: "Communists are coming into our country [U.S.] everyday, and I can't see why this little one who does not know what it is all about cannot arrive quota or no quota." Those most likely

Youngsters at a displaced persons camp pose with Edwin W. Pauley, who was serving as President Truman's personal representative on the Allied Commission on Reparations with the rank of ambassador. Courtesy Harry S. Truman Library

to qualify were displaced children in Germany and Austria at the end of the war. Among them was a Latvian boy who wrote President Truman from his new, adoptive home in Michigan: "Thank you so much for the nice things you have done. . . . My life has changed like magic. . . . I am beginning to forget the bad things that happened to me in the war."[44]

Admission of orphans into the United States was expanded by the Refugee Act of 1953 during the Eisenhower administration. The president considered the act to be a piece of emergency legislation that allowed the United States to deal with not only persons displaced by World War II but with new refugees escaping Soviet-controlled countries behind the Iron Curtain. There were 3.5 million refugees in Germany, Austria, Italy, Greece, and the Netherlands. So many homeless in need of basic help, employment, and shelter could easily upset the delicate balance of post-war recovery in Western Europe. The Refugee Act allowed 214,000 victims of war's aftermath, oppression, and persecution to receive visas, but they had to have a job and housing waiting for them in the United States. These were assured through sponsorships provided by local committees in thirty-seven states and by organizations, including the Lutheran Refugee Service and the National Catholic Welfare Service. The act also gave 4,000 visas to orphans under the age of ten "who are being brought to the United States to be, or who have already been, adopted by an American citizen and spouse who will assure proper care of such a child."[45]

About half of the available 4,000 visas were issued by June 1955, but a report to the president cautioned: "There is a constantly increasing interest on the part of Americans desirous of adopting orphans and although the total quota of 4,000 may not be reached, there is now a definite possibility that a larger number of visas will be issued to orphans than was heretofore anticipated." In fact, President Eisenhower found it necessary in 1956 to issue a public statement regarding the difficulties American citizens faced when they adopted and then learned that the child could not come to the States because quotas were filled. The president was sympathetic and promised immediate action to amend the law for adoptable children. Part of the reason for an exhausted quota system was the scope of the 1953 Refugee Act. It not only included Europe but the Far East. This opened the door for adoption of Korean, Chinese, and Japanese children.[46]

Although there were tens of thousands of war orphans in Hong Kong, China, and Japan, the most publicized in the United States were the children uprooted and orphaned by the Korean conflict. Through newspaper stories and magazine articles, the general public learned that Col. Wallace I. Wolverton and Lt. Col. Russell L. Blaisdell, both chaplains with the Fifth Air Force, moved almost 1,000 Korean children out of Seoul, fearing that they would die when the Communists overtook the city. In what was called "Operation Christmas Kidlift," the children were airlifted to safety at Cheju-do Island on Korea's southern coast. The American public also saw President Eisenhower appear for the American-Korean Foundation's appeal to aid "distressed" Korean children, and Americans were told about church missions and the efforts of

U.S. servicemen. In one instance, the *New York Times* featured the crew of the USS *Missouri* and the nine-year-old boy that became their "foster" son through the International Foster Parents Plan. There was also the eleven-year-old boy who received prosthetic limbs and was flown to a new home at Boys Town in Nebraska because several U.S. soldiers "interceded" on his behalf.[47]

Humanitarian efforts were undertaken by soldiers, private citizens in the United States, relief organizations, and international groups. The media focus on children brought adoption into the picture. Pearl S. Buck, Pulitzer and Nobel Prize winner, and her husband served as examples when they adopted several Korean children and facilitated adoption for others after establishing the adoption agency Welcome House. The agency concentrated on placing American Asian children who were abandoned outcasts in their own country and a "very difficult problem" for the U.S. government. Officials believed that North Korea might use "GI Babies" in propaganda to denounce the presence of American and United Nations forces fighting in the conflict, but more pressing were the immediate needs of the children. By 1954, Armed Forces Aid to Korea had built fifty orphanages. Characterized as an "anti-communist goodwill project," some of these orphanages began as nothing more than a tent with soldiers gathering food and clothing. Meanwhile, the United Nations Korea Civil Assistance Command, largely staffed by U.S. military personnel, had the task of providing economic, medical, and agricultural help to South Koreans, as well as giving aid to orphans.[48]

Media coverage of Korean assistance projects and stories of Korean orphans prompted American families to consider adoption. Harry and Bertha Holt of Oregon provided a case in point. After seeing a church-sponsored film on the plight of Korean children, the Holts adopted eight. Their story was told to the American public through articles appearing in *Reader's Digest*, the *American Mercury*, *Look*, and *Life* magazines. Of course, this couple, which already had six children of their own, was not alone in Korean adoptions. They, however, became central to thousands of Korean adoptions after they founded an international adoption agency and began to fly orphans to the United States for waiting adoptive couples.[49]

The Far East became a focal point for international adoption, although

This image of a Korean boy and the U.S. serviceman adopting him was titled "He knows where home is!" and appeared in a U.S. Department of Defense publication for military couples. Taken from *Manual on Intercountry Adoption*, Dwight D. Eisenhower Library

couples once again turned their attention to Europe in October 1956 when thousands of Hungarians fled Soviet tanks and troops sent to crush the country's revolt against Kremlin control. Believing that this newest crisis was similar to the postwar aftermath of displaced orphans, American couples began to contact government agencies to apply for Hungarian children. Some couples were responding to an NBC program on the refugees, who would eventually number 200,000. Other would-be adoptive parents were spurred on by an Associated Press story of a nine-year-old boy who arrived at a Red Cross shelter in Austria after he "lost his parents [in Hungary] during the early fighting and crossed the border unescorted." Although the President's Committee for Hungarian Refugee Relief tried to explain that there were very few true orphans since the majority of children left Hungary with parents or relatives, it received hundreds of applications. In one instance, a couple hoped to get President Eisenhower's personal help by including a letter of recommendation from their senator, Frank Carlson of Kansas. Undaunted by the probability that adoptions would not be possible, almost 400 hopeful couples contacted the Committee for Hungarian Relief.[50]

For the first time in American history, the concept of international adoption found a place in mainstream society. The idea was suggested, but not pressed, after World War I when Herbert Hoover, head of relief efforts in Europe and himself an orphan, dismissed suggestions made by American Relief Administration social workers that orphaned youngsters be relocated to the United States. As dire as the situation was, Hoover believed that children should not be uprooted from their country of birth, its cultural and religious foundations.[51]

At the end of the Second World War transporting children out of the chaos and destruction of postwar Europe was viewed differently. People saw international adoption as a humanitarian act, and couples accepted it as a means to expand their nuclear family, although would-be parents often found themselves grappling with federally mandated quotas and lawmakers' entrenched suspicions of more lenient policies.

Whatever impulses motivated adoptive couples, they were influenced to some extent by the postwar culture of a child-centered family. At the same time, however, these couples were quietly redefining the family context. White middle-class couples, the most likely to adopt, brought racially and ethnically diverse children into their homes, their neighborhoods, and schools. And, they did this at a time when white schools were still largely closed to children of some racial backgrounds, when communities often segregated housing by race and/or religion, and when racial equality and civil rights were heatedly contested and debated.

With this new interest in international adoptions, it went without saying that youngsters were being rescued from dire, even life-threatening conditions. Yet, even in the humanitarian language of child rescue and a new chance at a better life away from political chaos and war, there was a Cold War subtext. Hungarian refugees were fleeing communism; Korean orphans were the victims of a war brought on by Communists; and in another part of the world, much closer to the United States, children and teenagers were airlifted out of Cuba after Fidel Castro's Communist forces overthrew Batista's U.S.-friendly government.

Beginning in late 1960, when Eisenhower was still president, and continuing through 1962 during the Kennedy administration, over 14,000 children and teenagers were flown out of Cuba. These refugees were youngsters whose parents feared for their children's safety in the immediate upheaval of Communist control. Parents worried that closure of parochial schools signaled Communist indoctrination, that older teenagers would be pressed into military service for Castro, and that rumors that their children would be relocated to Eastern Europe for their education might prove true. Carlos Eire, airlifted to the United States with his older brother, recalled that one of his mother's worst fears was that her sons would be "packed off to Russia or East Germany or Czechoslovakia, of us disappearing in some foreign land and never returning."[52]

As it turned out, the foreign country from which they never returned was America. The airlift, known as Operation Pedro Pan, was intended to only temporarily separate families. They would be reunited when parents were able to join their children in the United States or when the youngsters could return to a Castro-free Cuba. Organized by the Catholic Welfare Bureau, with some support from the federal government, the plan was for children to live with relatives, in foster homes, or in Catholic-run "camps" located in Florida until families were reunited. Some families, however, remained forever separated. It became clear, particularly after the Cuban Missile Crisis, that it would be even more difficult for parents to leave Cuba, or for children to return. In 1963 the U.S. Information Agency produced a twenty-five-minute film, *The Lost Apple*, because thousands of children, still living in the Florida camps, needed foster homes. Without them, the youngsters would join other Pedro Pan refugees already housed in orphanages. Some have suggested that the Central Intelligence Agency (CIA) was behind the film, intending to use it for anti-Communist propaganda, and it has been said that the CIA fueled the fears of Cuban parents and then ran the temporary camps using Catholic nuns and priests as "fronts." The conjectures remain just that, but the youngsters of Pedro Pan were, and remain, symbols of the struggle between the Free and Communist worlds.[53]

Adoption and foster care were cornerstones to child welfare programs in the United States. Their effectiveness was compromised, however, by a shortage of social workers. The public and politicians, caught up in the much more visible shortages in housing and teachers, were largely unaware that social workers were in short supply. Federal agencies, however, noted the decline at a time when they were increasingly needed. Arthur Flemming, who succeeded Oveta Culp Hobby as head of HEW, called the demand for trained professionals of "national significance." At least 10,000 were needed immediately, but the prospects were not encouraging. Only about 4,000 students were enrolled in graduate schools of social work during the 1956–1957 school year. States and major cities trying to upgrade and expand their social services were stymied. Federal programs suffered, too. HEW, the largest employer of social workers in the federal government, saw the shortages affect the U.S. Public Health Service, as well as federal help for crippled children, the deaf, the blind, and "children who are without the care and support of one or both parents." Fourteen other agencies, including the BIA and Veterans Administration, also needed more social workers.[54]

Flemming's concerns coincided with the Eisenhower administration's request that Congress authorize money for training social workers. Congress had supported similar appropriations in the past for the U.S. Public Health Service, vocational rehabilitation, and child welfare services. Additional personnel were critical if the government was to meet the requirements of the 1956 Social Security Act, which emphasized strengthening families and substantially increased the federal share of public assistance funds. The congressional response to Eisenhower's budget request was the Government Training Act of 1958. This gave federal agencies authority to oversee employee training, allowing them to use resources not available within the government. Agencies could retrain existing staff, many with backgrounds in something other than social work. The result was a slight, but noticeable, increase in federally employed social workers.

The BIA, for example, had five social workers assigned to South Dakota's Native American populations in 1950; after passage of the 1958 act, there were thirteen—six the products of retraining.[55]

Government involvement with social services, adoption practices, and curbing delinquency was not an entirely new responsibility brought on by the postwar era. To some extent, federal agencies had been involved with child-protection issues since the early 1900s, and the Children's Bureau had been the chief federal advocate for the dependent and marginalized. However, there were new challenges. Whereas people in the nineteenth century "did not *automatically* [original emphasis] think in terms of government as being an obvious or appropriate source of a solution," state and local agencies of the mid-twentieth century often looked to federal aid and laws for direction and tangible support.[56]

The federal government, through HEW and the Children's Bureau, supported foster care over orphanages and advocated strong state guidelines for adoption. Through legislation, the government made more international adoptions possible by increasing the number of orphans allowed into the country, and it continued to fund programs intended to strengthen the family unit. Federal programs and public policies could not, however, eradicate every social and economic problem that created dependent or delinquent children. There would never be enough resources or a firm consensus on what worked best and for the largest number of people. This was particularly true of juvenile delinquency. Urban renewal did not eradicate delinquency, as predicted. Programs intended to divert youngsters from going down the wrong path found it difficult, if not sometimes impossible, to break through the sense of belonging and prestige youngsters associated with gang membership or to redirect youth who felt alienated from their families and social surroundings. And, rehabilitation techniques used to modify the behavior of the incarcerated were increasingly judged to be ineffective.

Whether the issue was delinquency or child-welfare programs for dependent children, the best that presidential administrations and federal agencies could sometimes do was to keep a spotlight turned on an issue. The concerns expressed by Presidents Truman and Eisenhower were real. So were those emitting from Congress and federal agencies that periodically sounded new alarms. In place of concrete action, backed by federal funds, the government oftentimes took the position of standing vigilant, trying to keep problems from worsening while at the same time providing more youngsters with stability and the chance to have the kind of growing-up years America expected for its youth.

A Healthier Generation

"The national health has become, quite properly, a matter of government concern."

— *President Harry Truman, October 29, 1949*

During his time in office, Truman pushed for new hospital construction, increased funding for medical research, modernization of mental health facilities, and a national health insurance program. When he spoke in 1949 of government's role in national health, he was thinking of his own health-care agenda, but some aspects of the nation's health had long been of concern to the government, eliciting the involvement of federal agencies. In the early 1900s the U.S. Public Health Service was charged with controlling the spread of contagious diseases, and during the Progressive Era, the newly created U.S. Children's Bureau established programs to protect maternal and child health. During the administration of Franklin Roosevelt, both agencies took on new responsibilities when the Public Health Service Act of 1944 initiated grants-in-aid programs that expanded existing mandates to include research and treatments for tuberculosis and cancer.

Truman, however, wanted more. He believed that government should extend its role in issues related to health care and its availability to all citizens. The president emphasized health care in his 1947 and 1948 State of the Union messages, and he directed Oscar R. Ewing, head of the Federal Security Agency, to organize a 1948 national health-care conference to analyze the efficiency and availability of existing medical care and services. It was also charged with identifying the most critical health problems facing Americans. A centerpiece in the administration's Fair Deal programs became national health insurance. Truman was determined to enact a program that President Roosevelt had considered but never advanced.

A national health insurance program took precedence over other proposals that may have increased health-care coverage to some but not all in the population. This included a piece of legislation proposed by the Children's Bureau. Simply labeled the Children's Act of 1949, it would provide "outside the Social Security Act, a new and broader charter for the Children's Bureau." Through the bureau, an administrator would be authorized to make grants that, if enough funds were appropriated, would provide free medical care to all mothers during pregnancy and for all children under the age of eighteen. It seemed that the words of the 1930 White House Conference of Children and Youth Charter declaring health care a child "right" would finally be accomplished. In reviewing the proposal, the Bureau of the Budget advised the White House that, while this sort of specialized program had a better chance of "early enactment" than Truman's more ambitious health insurance program, the Children's Act could weaken the chances for health insurance. Congress might support one, but not both pieces of legislation. The report went on to add, "This is primarily a political determination."[1]

There was a good possibility that the Children's Act could have passed, providing every child and teenager in America with health care. There was already a precedent for aid to mothers and children through the 1935 Social Security Act's Title V. Officially known as the Maternal and Child Health Act, Title V provided states with federal grants "to promote, improve and deliver" maternal and child care, as well as provide aid to crippled children. At the time it was established, Title V was considered the "most significant piece of legislation charting federal responsibility for services for maternal and child health."[2]

So, in a sense, the proposed Children's Act of 1949 was not something radically new and unknown. Arguably, it simply provided aid to more children than were already covered by Title V. In addition, aid to some women and children was already available through the Children's Bureau, which had involved itself for years in health care. From its very beginning, the Children's Bureau conducted field studies of maternal and child health, and it routinely published and distributed information on infant and child care. In fact, by the end of the 1950s, the bureau was celebrating the tenth edition of its publication *Infant Care*. To mark the occasion an Illinois couple and their two young children were invited to the White House where they were presented with the 40 millionth copy of the booklet. First published in 1914, the publication was "not only the standard guide for millions of new parents" in the United States, but it had been translated into several foreign languages and distributed abroad. Aside from its many publications, the bureau was also the driving force behind the Better Baby Movement, which began after World War I and received tremendous grassroots support for seeing that thousands of infants, toddlers, and young children received free medical examinations while mothers were counseled in basic first aid, home nursing, and nutrition. Then, during World War II, the bureau ran the Emergency Maternity and Infant Care program for the wives and children of servicemen.[3]

Truman, however, chose to set aside the Children's Act of 1949 for his chief objective, a national health insurance program. The Children's Act, while a good idea in principle, could distract lawmakers and the country from the primary focus of a program that encompassed every American. This included children whose health, he told Congress, "should be recognized as a definite public responsibility." The Republican-controlled Congress and congressional conservatives did not respond with action. Instead, Republicans saw an opportunity to fight the big-government philosophies of Roosevelt's New Deal and of Truman's administration while the president was besieged by labor unrest, a housing crisis, domestic inflation, and international tensions. In turn, Truman used Congress's inactivity to stir up the party faithful at the 1948 Democratic convention. When he accepted his party's nomination as presidential candidate, Truman announced that he was calling Congress back into session to act on a number of things, including the insurance program.[4]

More than any other health-related topic, health insurance sparked a firestorm of controversy over government's place in medical assistance. Under Truman's plan, national health insurance would be funded through payroll deductions, and every citizen would receive medical and hospital attention, regardless of ability to pay. Supporters of other Truman programs would not side with the president on health insurance. It smacked of "socialized medicine." This deadly label in a period of rising tensions with "socialistic" countries actually echoed the charges of "European Socialist and Bolshevist" made almost twenty-five years earlier when Congress passed and later repealed the Sheppard-Towner Act for maternal and child health care. Nothing could be more deadly in American politics than a socialist label.[5]

In the 1940s, this point of view continued. Some in Congress, such as Harry Byrd of Virginia, called Truman's program "socialized medicine," as did various commentators around the country. Pharmaceutical companies backed away from the plan, afraid of severe government caps on drug prices. To the din of contentious debate, the American Medical Association (AMA) added its powerful presence to lobby against the idea. Said Oscar R. Ewing of the organization's involvement: "[AMA] didn't want the Government to have a thing to do with medicine. They opposed every bill that was introduced in Congress that even remotely would involve Government in medicine."[6]

To counteract those against a national health insurance plan, the Committee for National Health was organized by private citizens to educate the public and to promote "prompt passage of the needed legislation." On the committee were doctors, writers, businessmen, clergy, and a number of notable public names. The latter included Eleanor Roosevelt and Abe Fortas, who served in the Roosevelt administration. Also notable were the 200 individuals that added their signatures to the committee's newspaper ads endorsing Truman's plan; the well known included Fiorello LaGuardia, mayor of New York; Hollywood producer George Zukor; actor Frederic March; and writers Thomas Mann and Rex Stout. The force of personality and celebrity did not, however, influence the public. And, just the suggestion that this was socialized medicine sent congressional support in the opposite direction.[7]

Also unpopular was Truman's plan to reorganize the Federal Security Agency into a federal department to be called the Department of Health, Education, and Security. "Through the new Department," said one report, "it will be possible for the country to give its young people the consideration which is theirs by right." No longer would there be a patchwork approach that served some and not others. The basic idea was to consolidate federal health programs under one administrator, rather than leave them under various departments. Agencies affected included the Bureau of Indian Affairs, the U.S. Public Health Service, the Chil-

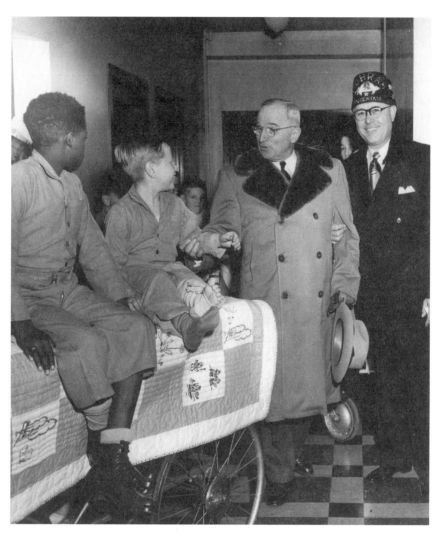

Truman, shown here visiting the Twin City Shrine Hospital in Minneapolis, was unable to establish a national health insurance program, but with the Hill-Burton Act of 1946, he achieved federal grant funding for the construction of community hospitals, rehabilitation centers, and nonprofit hospitals. Courtesy Harry S. Truman Library dren's Bureau, the Social Security Administration, and the Department of Agriculture. These either indirectly contributed to better health care with funds and public education programs, or they provided direct medical treatment through clinics and mobile field health services. The Bureau of Indian Affairs, for instance, ran infirmaries in Indian schools, operated over one hundred health clinics on reservations, and had almost fifty hospitals before its health-care programs were transferred to the Public Health Service in 1955 and renamed the Indian Health Service.[8]

Arguably, Truman's plan to place various programs under one department would reduce overlap and costs. The only exception to reorganization was health care provided to military personnel and their dependents; they remained the concern of their particular branch of service. The Senate produced a bill to establish this new department, and two bills were introduced in the House, where there was generous support. The department, however, never materialized. Some in Congress thought another federal department unnecessary, and others linked reorganization with Truman's hopes for national health insurance. Opposition melted away, however, when the Eisenhower administration proposed and got the new cabinet-level Department of Health, Education, and Welfare.

Although Truman was stymied in his overall attempts to reconfigure the country's system of health care, he enjoyed some measure of success. The Hill-Burton Act of 1946, named for Democratic Senator J. Lister Hill of Alabama and Republican Senator Harold Burton of Ohio, initiated a grant program for hospital construction at $75 million a year. The act was extended and then expanded during the 1950s, providing funds during a decade when the increasing child population alone demanded more treatment facilities. The Hill-Burton Act provided federal grant money to build community hospitals, nonprofit hospitals for the chronically ill, nursing homes, convalescent homes and rehabilitation centers, and nonprofit outpatient diagnostic and treatment centers. In 1946, Congress also approved the National Mental Health Act. Through its grants-in-aid program to states, there was additional funding for training mental health workers, promoting research, and encouraging both state-run and private facilities to adopt new treatment methods. In 1947 the U.S. Public Health Service awarded its first mental health research grant to a non-governmental facility, laying the foundation for legislation in the 1950s that gave federal aid to clinical research in the treatment of mental illness and basic aspects of psychopharmacology.[9]

New hospitals and treatment facilities, as well as other federal health-care programs, touched thousands of lives. The vast majority of Americans, however, were unaware of the government's level of involvement in funding and program support. For the average citizen, medical care was a personal relationship between the patient and a private physician. Parents were strongly encouraged to have their infants and toddlers periodically checked by a doctor to determine their progress in gaining weight and reaching milestones such as talking, crawling, and walking. As youngsters grew older, however, parents were generally more inclined to seek out a doctor or hospital only when they were needed, not as preventive measures to ensure good health. For much of their information, young parents turned to child-rearing books, government publications, and articles found in popular magazines. *Parents Magazine*, *Family Circle*, *Good Housekeeping*, and many others offered practical advice on a wide range of subjects. Considerable space was devoted to health-related topics, whether the subject was proper nutrition, recognizing tonsillitis, or how to react effectively when a child got into potentially dangerous household products.

Printed materials, including government pamphlets printed in both English and Spanish, were accessible to most Americans, as were physicians, hospitals, or health clinics. Nonetheless, some population groups remained underserved because of their race, inability to pay, or location. Urban hospitals and clinics serving the poor were overburdened, and in many remote rural areas, medical facilities were either scarce or nonexistent. In an attempt to bridge the gaps, many states used Maternal and Child Health grant money from the U.S. Children's Bureau to extend and improve basic services in rural areas—and to some degree, to the children of migrant workers. And, the Children's Bureau tested a pilot project of mobile clinics in Colorado, Idaho, and Oregon. Despite these efforts, collected data demonstrated that sparse and inconsistent medical services resulted in a high incidence of rickets, scurvy, and pellagra among low-income children in city slums, in the rural South, and in migrant families. In fact, the migrants were 55 percent more likely than the other two groups to suffer "disabling illnesses."[10]

Some afflictions were obviously tied to low income, poor diet, and/or lack of medical attention. Some illnesses, however, touched all social classes, all races, and all economic levels. Infectious diseases could be treated with new types of antibiotics including sulfadiazine, introduced in the early 1940s, and penicillin, which became available to the civilian population in 1944. For most "childhood diseases," however, there were no defenses. Until 1963 there was no vaccination against measles, which infected 3 to 4 million children and adults every year, and each year left at least 1,000 with chronic disabilities such as blindness. Until 1967 there was no vaccine for the mumps, contracted by at least 200,000 each year. A vaccine for chickenpox was not used in the United States until 1995.

To combat contagious diseases in the immediate postwar era, physicians had a very small arsenal. There was the smallpox vaccine, first developed in the early nineteenth century; a diphtheria antitoxin, first available in 1894; a diphtheria toxoid produced in 1923; sulfonamide drugs developed during the 1930s to combat infections and infectious diseases; and by the mid-1940s, the combination DTP vaccine was used against diphtheria, tetanus, and whooping cough. New developments "have come thick and fast," wrote one doctor in 1955. Yet, many contagious diseases were not preventable and were regarded as a part of growing up. Although any of the childhood diseases could be fatal or result in long-term health problems or disabilities, most children recovered with nothing more than a memory of itchy rashes or hacking coughs and time spent in bed instead of at play or in school.[11]

Contagious diseases were dreaded, but few brought more fear than infantile paralysis—polio. Although adults contracted the disease, children and young people under the age of twenty were the most likely victims, and every summer swimming pools, playgrounds, and youth camps quickly closed after a reported case. About 20,000 cases occurred each year, but there were almost 58,000 in 1952 during the worst epidemic on record. Ironically, in that same year, Dr. Jonas Salk and his colleagues, including Dr. Julius Younger, developed a vaccine that they believed held great potential for eradicating polio. Pilot trials were held in the Pittsburgh area, followed by field trials designed by Dr. Thomas Francis. The trials involved 1.8 million children in the United States, Canada, and Finland. The study was financially supported by the National Foundation

Discovery of the polio vaccine was celebrated at a Rose Garden ceremony where President Eisenhower honored the work of the National Foundation for Infantile Paralysis (represented by Basil O'Connor, left) and Dr. Jonas Salk (next to the president). Also pictured is Oveta Culp Hobby, secretary of the U.S. Department of Health, Education, and Welfare. Dwight D. Eisenhower Library

for Infantile Paralysis (NFIP); more commonly known as the March of Dimes, the NFIP was created by President Roosevelt in 1938.[12]

On April 12, 1955, Doctors Francis and Salk announced that the trials showed the vaccine to be safe and effective. The vaccine was hailed as a life-saver and one that would one day eliminate the need for iron lungs, painful operations, and years of therapy and rehabilitation. Just ten days after the announcement, President Eisenhower honored Salk and the NFIP at a Rose Garden ceremony where he offered a "presidential thank-you" on behalf of himself, "all 164 million Americans . . . [and] all the people of the world." He presented Salk with a special citation for his "historic contribution to human welfare." Another citation was given to the NFIP for its support of all scientists who contributed to this historic breakthrough.[13]

The vaccine was such an important discovery and its potential so great that Americans clamored to have their children vaccinated as soon as inoculations began. That was a problem. Not enough vaccine was readily available. Youngsters who had participated in the field trials needed their follow-up "booster" shot, and millions of children were waiting for their initial vaccination. To head off the possibility of the vaccine ending up on the black market and sending costs soaring, HEW Secretary Hobby, under Eisenhower's directive, organized a conference of doctors and pharmaceutical representatives to lay the groundwork for production and distribution. It was agreed that the NFIP would act as distributing agent and that the government would control distribution by deciding the order of vaccinations. The initial group would include children who needed the booster and all five-to-nine-year-olds since they were, according to medical evidence, at the greatest risk for contracting the virus. After this group received vaccinations, children aged one to five would be next in line. By the end of May 1955, Eisenhower announced that more than 5.5 million children had received their vaccinations, "including one of my grandchildren, a first grader." The grandchild was David Eisenhower, who faced his shot surrounded by reporters and news photographers.[14]

President Eisenhower wanted to ensure that everyone was vaccinated. No child should have to suffer through the effects of polio or die. And, no parent should have to stand by and helplessly watch that happen. From a personal standpoint, Eisenhower knew the devastation of losing a child to disease. In 1921 the Eisenhowers lost their three-year-old son to scarlet fever. Ike later wrote that he and Mamie were "completely crushed," and over forty years later, when he thought of that time, "the keenness of our loss comes back to me as fresh and terrible as it was in that long dark day."[15] No doubt the death of his own child played on the president's mind as he considered government's role in protecting children from another dreaded disease.

The White House and HEW began to work with Congress for a comprehensive bill that would give federal grants to states and U.S. territories for free vaccinations. Hobby, however, tried to dissuade the president or

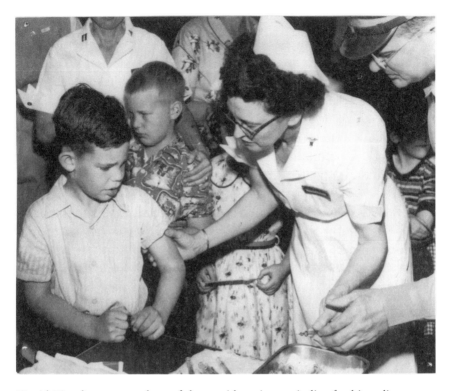

David Eisenhower, grandson of the president, is next in line for his polio vaccination. Dwight D. Eisenhower Library

at least forestall such a program. She suggested that they wait until they knew how many states would take it upon themselves to provide free vaccinations. Philosophically, Hobby was opposed to any government role in health-care and was once quoted as saying that she had come to Washington to "bury the dream of socialized medicine." Eisenhower, who declared his opposition to socialized medicine before the AMA and promised not to make the government the "big poobah" of medical affairs, saw things differently when the matter was protecting children from polio. Adamantly, he insisted that the government take a leadership role. According to Surgeon General Leonard Scheele, Ike gave Hobby her "marching orders" to see that legislation happened.[16]

There were numerous consultations with members of the congressional leadership, as well as testimony before the Senate Labor and Public Welfare Committee, chaired by J. Lister Hill. Surgeon General Scheele later said that little actual testimony was given. Hill, a moderate and known for the 1946 Hill-Burton Act funding hospital construction, told Scheele to make his statement short. The committee would approve Eisenhower's program. "You can say we're for children," Hill told the doctor.[17]

The Senate passed the Poliomyelitis Vaccination Assistance Act in July 1955. The final bill, somewhat reworked by House versions and compromises, was signed into law on August 12, 1955. Those opposed to government intervention in health issues and the most likely to cry "socialized medicine" kept a low profile. As for Eisenhower's role, he could consider this one of his administration's most important pieces of legislation for America's children. The act authorized federal grants to states for the free vaccination of pregnant women and everyone under the age of twenty. States were required to make the vaccine available to all eligible persons, regardless of ability to pay, and the vaccine was distributed to the territories of Alaska, Guam, Hawaii, Puerto Rico, the U.S. Virgin Islands, American Samoa, as well as the District of Columbia and the U.S. Canal Zone.[18]

Despite the large number of children receiving the vaccine soon after it became available, the national immunization program had a rocky beginning. Although HEW personnel spent innumerable man hours working with drug companies on manufacture, distribution, and quality control, there were problems. First, there was the initial shortage. Then, 200 cases of polio resulted from contaminated lots produced by one California drug company. Seventy-nine children and over one hundred family members and other "community contacts" were affected. Most were badly paralyzed; eleven died. Democrats lambasted the White House and in particular Hobby. "I found," recalled Dr. Scheele, "that more often than not, somebody—a Democrat—would say, 'It wasn't the surgeon-general. It was that woman over there in the Department of Health, Education, and Welfare, Mrs. Hobby. She should be fired.'" Partisanship fueled some of the complaints against Hobby, but she made herself vulnerable to attack with statements that made her sound uninterested and uninformed. When, for example, she defended the shortage by saying that "no one could have foreseen the public demand for the vaccine," she was roundly ridiculed by the press and her congressional detractors.[19]

In the rush to make the vaccine available, mistakes were made. This did not, however, halt the need, or demand, for inoculations. "One great question remains," said the *New York Times*, "When can millions of children get it?" A projected 100 to 150 million doses were expected for 1956, and when the vaccine became available, children and their parents lined up at thousands of hospitals and clinics throughout the country. Sometimes the lines snaked down the street and around the block. At Eisenhower's urging, Congress extended the $28 million grants program to June 30, 1957. By that time, there was enough vaccine to inoculate adults, and the NFIP chose Protection, Kansas, because of its name, to kick off a national vaccination campaign. The small town of about 500 residents became the first community in the nation to be "100% protected."[20]

While the Salk vaccine was celebrated as a medical miracle, there were thousands of children and teenagers for whom the discovery came too late. A woman who contracted polio at the age of three in 1954 later wrote:

What do I remember of my initial experience of polio? A memory so vague as to be less than dreamlike. Eerie gowned figures. A glass wall. After that a single clear memory of the hospital in Syracuse [New York], where I spent the acute phase of my illness. I was no longer in a solitary room but a ward that I shared with three or four other children. One of them, an older girl—four, or maybe even five, she seemed almost an adult to me.[21]

Eisenhower cautioned the public and government officials that the country could not forget those still in iron lungs, confined to wheelchairs, or learning to walk with leg braces. The president was personally reminded of them when he received letters from families and friends of polio patients. Among them was a letter asking him to write a note of encouragement to a thirteen-year-old girl who "as many other Polio patients in the past years has fought endless battles to be normal again." For this girl and others like her, the president insisted, "Help must continue. . . . There is need for further research, for expanded professional knowledge, for continued care and rehabilitation."[22]

Most Americans knew that the March of Dimes raised money for research and rehabilitation and that a number of service clubs and private organizations provided hospital care, therapy, and financial support. Among them was the Capper Foundation for Crippled Children in Eisenhower's home state of Kansas. Less recognized by the public was the amount of government funding that went toward rehabilitation. Of the $15 million annually given to the states through the Children's Bureau, a portion aided polio patients. Another portion helped finance special projects for children crippled by cerebral palsy. Federal funding dated back to the Social Security Act of 1935 and the creation of Crippled Children's Services under the U.S. Public Health Service. Through this program, grants-in-aid to states contained several components. Money was used to locate children and teenagers who needed help, to provide diagnosis, hospitalization, and surgery, and to offset costs of rehabilitation services.

Each state defined "crippled" and "crippling condition" by its own standards. During the 1950s, states began to stretch definitions to qualify more youngsters for the grants provided through Crippled Children's Services. Young people who had handicaps of an "orthopedic nature" or who required plastic surgery because of a birth defect, accident, or burns were included by most states. A few states added children with rheumatic fever, those with hearing problems or eye conditions that could be treated with surgery, and those with epilepsy. The lists grew longer, and the number of federal dollars increased, although the states continued to bear the larger financial responsibility in the grants arrangement.[23]

Federal-state programs also helped fund vocational rehabilitation for young people with physical or mental disabilities. The amount of federal dollars rose from $23 million in 1953 to almost $40 million in 1957. By 1956, one of every six persons aided by this government program was a teenager, fifteen through nineteen years of age. And, an amendment to the Internal Revenue Code, passed by the 83rd Congress, entitled parents of mentally handicapped children to a higher tax deduction for the expenses of child day care. When Senator Gordon Allott, a Colorado Republican, asked how federal programs benefited his constituents, he was told that they were being served through the tax benefits and several federal-state programs for rehabilitation of youngsters with physical or mental disabilities. "As you know," came the assurance, "the total fitness of all American children is a matter that is much on the President's heart."[24]

One example of the president's concern was his creation of a national conference on physical fitness. At the time that parents and educators were digesting the contents of the bestselling book, *Why Johnny Can't Read*, another warning went up. Not only did "Johnny" have problems in reading, he was failing at push-ups. President Eisenhower was presented with the news at a White House luncheon largely attended by well-known amateur and professional athletes. Among the invited were golfers Jack Fleck, Robert Trent Jones, and Barbara Romack; baseball's Willie Mays and Hank Greenberg; tennis champion Tony Trabert; boxers Archie Moore and Gene Tunney; track star Wes Santee; and basketball's Bob Cousy and Bill Russell. Also attending the July 1955 luncheon were Hans Kraus and Bonnie Prudden, co-authors of a number of articles related to physical fitness. Their most recent report, published in the *New York State Journal of Medicine*, formed the basis for a luncheon presentation regarding the physical fitness of young people.[25]

Using the Kraus-Weber Tests for Muscular Fitness, 4,400 American youngsters, ages six to sixteen, were compared to 3,000 students of the same ages from Switzerland, Italy, and Australia. The tests evaluated youngsters' abilities to do a set number of such things as leg lifts, sit ups, and toe touches. The results were hardly encouraging. Fifty-six percent of the American children failed at least one test component, and usually more. Meanwhile, only about 8 percent of the overseas group failed even one test component. The conclusions seemed clear. American youth were out of shape, and likely to remain that way unless pushed into physical activity.[26]

Eisenhower, who played football and baseball as a young man and remained active as a golfer and fisherman, believed that sports not only added pleasure to one's life but fostered moral values. After the luncheon, he sent a note to Vice President Nixon asking him to take up the matter with HEW Secretary Hobby and Surgeon General Scheele: "After what we heard at luncheon today, I really think that we should try to

Whether they engaged in a recreational activity or a competitive sport, the President's Council on Youth and Fitness wanted children up and moving. Pictured is an archery class at a Topeka, Kansas, park. Kansas State Historical Society

take the lead in doing something along the lines suggested by Mr. Kelly." (This was either John B. Kelly, Sr., or John B. Kelly, Jr.: both were at the luncheon and both were Olympic scull rowing medalists.) Although Mr. Kelly's suggestion is not extant, the end result was the President's Conference on Fitness of American Youth.[27]

The vice president took the lead in organizing the conference. Among those invited to attend were representatives from health and education associations, directors of local and national fitness programs, industrial leaders such as Harry Bullis, chairman of General Mills, and leaders of the Boy and Girl Scouts, the YMCA, 4-H, and Boys' Clubs of America. Also included were a number of "outstanding, serious-minded sports figures," some of whom were present at the White House luncheon. Slated to meet in September 1955, the conference was delayed when, in an ironic twist of fate, President Eisenhower's own health was in jeopardy. He suffered a heart attack.[28]

Ten months later, in June 1956, the meeting convened at the U.S. Naval Academy in Annapolis, Maryland. Conference participants were asked to discuss the effectiveness of existing programs; the quality and availability of sports facilities; community support for youth sports and playgrounds; ways to encourage youngsters to take part in all kinds of sports; and the establishment of guidelines to measure short-term goals such as doubling participation in high school and college athletics. A national focus on physical fitness would first and foremost improve the physical well-being of children and teenagers, but there were arguably side benefits. One hoped-for outcome was getting kids off the streets and reducing juvenile delinquency.

At Annapolis, Eisenhower announced, via a message read by Vice President Nixon, his intention to create the President's Council on Youth Fitness. (President Kennedy changed the name to the President's Council on Physical Fitness in 1963.) Eisenhower followed up his statement by issuing an Executive Order that established a council composed of Vice President Nixon (who later turned over his chairmanship to Interior Secretary Fred Seaton), five cabinet members, and a President's Citizens Advisory Committee. The 120-member Advisory Committee included teachers and administrators from elementary schools, high schools, and colleges. There were also representatives from the medical community and from youth organizations. To coordinate meeting times and agendas, Shane MacCarthy, who held a variety of government posts, was named executive director. The advisory committee was required to meet at least once a year with other members of the President's Council on Youth Fitness, while subcommittees met more often.[29]

The President's Council was not designed to take control of existing fitness programs in schools and communities or to provide federal or private funds for projects. And, it did not introduce fitness testing into physical education classes, as did the later Kennedy program. From the outset, Eisenhower made it clear that he did not envision "an over-riding Federal program." Rather, it was the "task of the Federal Government . . . to assist the educators and the many fine organizations, now dealing with the problem, that they may improve and advance projects which are already underway." It was the job of the council to raise public awareness and to stimulate community action. The intent was to "help improve the physical and mental health of the Nation's young people" and "to alert America on what can and should be done to reach the much-desired goal of a happier, healthier, and more totally fit youth in America."[30]

Despite this high purpose, members of the President's Council had their own particular interests and agendas, which they felt obligated to protect. The most obvious division was between those who advocated competitive sports and those who disdained competition because they saw it as discriminatory, keeping the nonathletic child on the sidelines. There should have been room for both those who supported competition and those who preferred to frame physical activity as recreational, but lines were drawn. Helen Rowe, an associate director of the Camp Fire Girls, worried that she might not have the chance to argue the "dangers of competition" because, in her opinion, the conference was tilted toward "competitive sports for all children and youth." Coaches and professional athletes did not agree. Earl H. Blaik, director of athletics for the U.S. Military Academy at West Point, for instance, complained to Nixon's staff that only about 4 percent of the President's Council on Youth Fitness represented high school and college competitive sports. Blaik and his colleagues wanted a stronger presence. Trying to smooth over the discord was MacCarthy, who sought to remind the council that "the aim and hope are activity for all."[31]

Despite their differences, council members agreed that they should find ways to engage the public and encourage greater local and state support for the many groups, educators, and civic projects that tried to involve youngsters in physical activities. They could educate parents on the importance of exercise to their children's physical and mental health. The President's Council felt that it served a real need as "subtle physical erosion" seemed to be taking place among young people. Physical education classes in schools were often slighted by budget limitations on equipment and staff. People sat in front of televisions instead of being physically active. The car replaced walking or bicycling, especially as suburbia continued to sprawl. "Here in America," MacCarthy told *Sports Illustrated*, "our pattern of living has become so mechanized and education so crowded that it has pushed physical training into a secondary position." People lived more comfortably because of new technology, but there was a danger of becoming too sedentary. For youngsters this could

easily lead to poor health and a physical "softness" that was both dangerous to them and to their country.[32]

Just as Cold War rhetoric found its way into discussions on education
and youngsters' psychological well-being, it found a place in physical fitness. Should a Third World War happen—and many believed it would
come with a nuclear attack—the United States would not have the time it
had with World War II and Korea to turn "pampered, soft and flabby"
recruits into physically ready combatants. The inactivity of "modern
youth" posed serious problems for a quick military response.[33]

Hypothetically, this was a valid argument, although projections prepared for President Eisenhower by the Net Evaluation Subcommittee of
the National Security Council presented an entirely different picture of
the aftereffects of strategic air strikes. In the event of a nuclear attack,
said the committee's report, 65 percent of the country's population
would be killed or need medical treatment; the economy would collapse;
and the army would more likely be assigned to keeping law and order,
rather than be engaged in conventional combat against the Soviets. "It
would be a long time," said Ike, "before a country so struck would be
shipping out any troops to fight any other kind of war." There was, nevertheless, the possibility that America might become involved in "con-
tained" warfare somewhere in the world—although the president did not
believe that any armed conflict was guaranteed to remain limited or con-
tained. Still, in instances of limited fighting, troops would be needed, and
Americans should understand the dangers to themselves and their country if young people were not physically ready. President Truman had already sounded a warning in 1945 when he told Congress that during the
war the military had rejected about 30 percent of all men, and about the
same percentage of women, as physically unfit. Although any number of
health problems and disabilities could keep some young people out of
the military, lack of exercise should not be one of them. The President's
Council on Youth Fitness took its mandate seriously, and despite dis-
agreements among its members, it put great effort into public information campaigns and encouraging local and state programs aimed at
producing healthier, more active children and teenagers.[34]

In the sometimes hysterical Cold War environment and predictions
that Communists were plotting to overthrow the United States, another

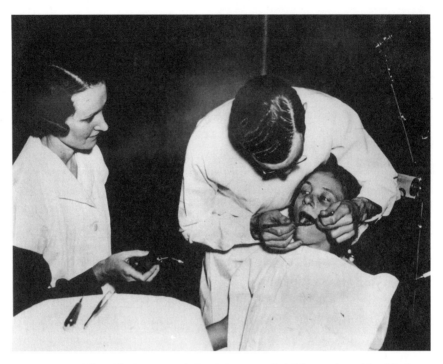

Supporters of fluoridation argued that it improved children's dental health, but it was a controversial issue. Kansas State Historical Society

health measure, fluoridation, became a divisive issue. The principle behind adding fluoride to municipal water supplies was simple. It was shown to reduce dental cavities in children. The first studies took place during the 1930s where fluoride occurred naturally in drinking water. In the 1940s, studies moved to evaluating the effectiveness of fluoride as an additive. Test trials were conducted in Michigan. In New York State, two cities in the lower Hudson Valley were selected by the state department of health for a multiyear study. In Wisconsin, a group of very vocal and determined dentists argued that all public water supplies be fluoridated. They, as well as other fluoridation supporters, were brought up short, however, by the American Dental Association (ADA) and the U.S. Public Health Service. Both refused to endorse fluoridation until 1950 when the final results of the Michigan trials showed a significant drop in tooth decay among children.[35]

By the mid-1950s, fluoridated water supplies existed in cities and municipalities in some southern cities, in much of the eastern United States, and sections of the Midwest. Early in the fluoridation movement, local water districts or city governments simply made the decision to introduce fluoride. By 1955, however, an increasing number of towns and cities put the question to the public, and when local residents had the opportunity to express themselves, they often rejected fluoridation.

It was not unusual for opponents to equate fluoridation with socialized medicine—only in this case, it was socialized dentistry. Many conservatives claimed that the government was taking away individual liberty and free will by forcing people "to ingest a medication regardless of whether the individual wanted or needed it." Others regarded fluoridation as a Communist plot to take over Americans' minds and actions. If fluoride could be introduced into the water supply, who was to say that something more sinister could not be added? Americans had heard reports and read stories about American soldiers taken prisoner in Korea and then "brainwashed" by the Chinese Communists, and Richard Condon's 1959 *The Manchurian Candidate* gave readers a frightening story of what brainwashing could do. Considering the tenor of the times, vocal opponents to fluoridation argued that it was not beyond the realm of possibility for foreign enemies to use drinking water as a brainwashing weapon.[36]

The depth of animosity and fear surprised pro-fluoridationists. For them, it was an issue extremely important to children's health. Fluoridation reduced tooth decay and in turn lowered dental-related illnesses. Rather simplistically, supporters assumed that once public education campaigns explained that this was an inexpensive measure with great benefits, the idea would be accepted. They were wrong. Citizens spoke out at town meetings and at the ballot box. Although there was no federal plan to make fluoridation a national project, people wrote their congressmen and contacted the White House. The gist of these messages was captured in one letter to President Eisenhower. Fluoride, said the letter, was simply "deadly and toxic," and the government should put a stop to all "propaganda" claiming otherwise. The outcry influenced public attitudes and some professional organizations. In Texas, for example, a few municipalities fluoridated their water supplies in the early 1950s, without protest, but in 1955, the Texas State Medical Association announced that it would not endorse fluoridation or reconsider its position on the matter for at least another five years.[37]

The public expressed growing concern over what was entering water and food supplies. At every turn, it seemed that a new, potential danger was headline news. Not only did people worry about what came out of their water taps, but what fell out of the skies. Early in the 1950s when the Nevada Proving Ground became operational, the Atomic Energy Commission (AEC) played down the potential hazards of radioactive fallout from aboveground testing. In 1951, for instance, the AEC acknowledged that high levels of radioactivity had been reported as far away as upper New York State, but it quickly added that there was no "possibility of harm to humans or animals."[38]

This, of course, was not a one-time event. The hydrogen bomb was first tested in the fall of 1952, staggering the imagination in its destructive capabilities. Testing at the Nevada test site continued, particularly in 1955 and 1957, and high-yield weapons that could not be tested in Nevada were detonated on Bikini and Eniwetok atolls in the Pacific in 1956. During the mid-1950s, Great Britain also tested nuclear devices in the Pacific, and the Soviet Union continued with its own testing and development of nuclear weapons. Clouds of radioactive fallout would dissipate over time, but they also traveled great distances. The Americans most likely to be repeatedly and immediately affected by fallout were those living closest to the Nevada test site. Residents of Nevada and Utah were told that their potential exposure was low, especially if they stayed indoors for a few hours after an aboveground test.

People had become accustomed to the fact that they might be exposed to radiation in limited, controlled situations. Procedures using radium were used to treat middle-ear deafness, skin diseases or abnormalities, and some forms of cancers. Medical X-rays were standard for examining lungs and broken bones. Dentists used X-rays to check for cavities. Nor were X-ray machines limited to hospitals and doctors' offices. They were used in several industries, in laboratories, and in research centers. They could even be found in shoe stores throughout the country. Looking more like a carnival attraction that told your fortune, these X-ray machines gave youngsters a view of their tarsal bones when they stood with their feet under a slot in the machine. Americans were exposed to radiation in numerous ways, but they were repeatedly assured that limited exposure to X-rays and radium-based medical treatments was not life-threatening.

Nuclear bombs and radioactivity were another matter, but Americans deflected their fears with ridiculous, sometimes humorous distractions. Toy makers capitalized on the lighter side of the atomic age, offering youngsters their very own Lone Ranger Atomic Bomb Ring, an Atomic Board Game (the object was to "bomb" Nagasaki and Hiroshima), Junior A. Bomb Darts, and the "Educational, Fun and Realistic!" Geiger counter. "There were no bad effects from radiation exposure," wrote Richard Miller in his study of atomic testing and its influence on popular culture. Filmmakers and cartoonists found new opportunities for story lines. Monsters like "Godzilla" and "The Beast from 20,000 Fathoms" were unleashed by the hydrogen bomb. Ants, mutated by radioactivity, became giant killers in *Them!* (1954). On a much lighter note, radiation gave a poor prospector (played by Mickey Rooney in *The Atomic Kid*, 1954) the ability to beat the slots in Las Vegas, and exposure to radiation turned an ordinary guy into *The Atomic Man* (1955) with the ability to anticipate events before they happened. Even cartoons incorporated "the bomb" and featured such characters as "Atomic Rabbit."[39]

Audiences may have been more amused than terrified by cartoon characters and creatures seen on the big screen, but as allegories for the effects of the atomic age, the stories and what they represented left an uneasy feeling. Civil Defense messages on radio and television, as well as films such as *Duck and Cover*, told people what they should do in the event of a nuclear attack. Far less was said about protection against radioactivity, which could not be seen, felt, or tasted. The public was told that levels of radioactivity were found in rain water and snow, and just to be on the safe side, public officials warned against making snow ice cream. Fallout fell with precipitation. It could be anywhere.

Then, Americans were told that milk supplies might be contaminated with radioactive fallout. How much a child's body could tolerate or how long it stayed in the system was difficult to estimate. There was little hard data regarding radioactivity's long-term effects on the human body, although many scientists had already extrapolated the lessons of Hiroshima and Nagasaki to conclude that slow exposure to aboveground radioactivity had its dangers, including childhood leukemia. The amount of contaminated foodstuffs ingested and the length of their effects on a child's physical development and future good health were, however, unknowns.

Neither the Atomic Energy Commission nor the U.S. Public Health Service was able to reassure the public that there was no danger. Once tests conducted by the Public Health Service showed radioactivity in milk, the agencies repeatedly emphasized that the amount was "well within the limits as established by the National Committee on Radiation Protection and Measurement." They had to concede, however, that it was "likely that a sizeable proportion of the strontium-90 that stays in the body comes from milk and its products."[40]

During the presidential campaign of 1956, the issue of radioactive contamination was raised, however briefly, by Democratic presidential hopeful Adlai Stevenson and his running mate Estes Kefauver. First, Kefauver accused the Eisenhower administration of misleading the public when it made assurances that no one was adversely affected by a series of nuclear aboveground tests that took place in 1955. Stevenson then pledged that as president he would make a nuclear test ban his first priority. Just days before the election, Stevenson created a small stir when he mentioned strontium-90 contaminated milk. Since youngsters were the primary consumers of milk, said Stevenson, they were the most likely to suffer the consequences of radioactive fallout. Lewis Strauss, chairman of the Atomic Energy Commission, vehemently countered that Americans were not being poisoned by clouds of radioactivity that slowly dissipated after a test. And, Eisenhower made a brief statement on the country's need to develop weapons for defense and as a deterrent against war. Although there were scientists who opposed the "bomb" and who predicted dire long-term health effects for the living and "the yet unborn," neither the media nor public opinion presented a united front, demanding more information or the end of testing. Certainly, voters were not swayed. If anything, the recent Suez Crisis in Egypt and the Soviets' violent response to the uprising in Hungary were arguments for a hefty nuclear arsenal and continued testing. Eisenhower and his running mate Richard Nixon won with almost 60 percent of the popular vote.[41]

Federal agencies responsible for areas that affected the nation's health were standing on the threshold of new medical concerns and science. Finding ways to monitor and control the levels of radioactivity in the food supply was just one of several food-contamination issues facing federal agencies. Speaking to the American people after the Public Health Service issued an extensive study and review of milk contamination in 1959, HEW director Arthur Flemming acknowledged that radiation presented a health danger. His emphasis, however, was on federal agencies and their work to mitigate the threat.

> Radiation is not new in our environment. . . . There are many sources and kinds of radiation, such as cosmic rays and medical x-rays, . . . but the problems of radiation in the nuclear age are obviously growing ones and will be with us from now on. . . . Many scientists are seriously concerned with the cumulative effects on human beings of repeated small exposures of radiation, and research is being done by the Public Health Service, The Atomic Energy Commission, and others to ascertain these effects. We are developing plans to enable the Food and Drug Administration to engage in research in this area.[42]

While Americans were beginning to ponder what radioactivity meant to them and their families, they were told that something else was getting into milk. Penicillin, used to treat mastitis in dairy cows, was appearing in small quantities. There were two approaches to the problem. The first was to prohibit any practice that endangered the food supply and the public, even if that meant economic hardship for dairy producers. The second approach was to allow use of antibiotics under government-regulated restrictions. "I think it is fair to say that the public policy in the United States . . . is best reflected by the acts of Congress," said John L. Harvey of the Food and Drug Administration. "As a nation [we] have decided that there are many aspects of modern civilization which offer a hazard to health and welfare, but which can be adequately controlled so that the benefits can be enjoyed."[43]

Just two months after Harvey's pronouncements, his superior, HEW Secretary Flemming, seemed to somewhat contradict the assumption that controls would still allow some level of impurities in milk. Speaking at a press conference in December 1959, Flemming noted another impurity finding its way into milk—pesticides. In studies conducted in 1958, the Food and Drug Administration found minuscule levels of pesticides, and Flemming wanted to assure the public that the government had a policy of no-tolerance "for any amount—no matter how small—of any pesticide residue in milk." Companies involved in the interstate shipment of pesticide-contaminated milk would be prosecuted under the Federal Food, Drug, and Cosmetic Act. However, there was a loophole. Shipments within a state did not fall under the government's mandate to prosecute offenders, and states were under no obligation to align their laws with federal guidelines. Depending on the product's point of origin, it was still possible for youngsters to consume contaminated milk.[44]

Since passage of the 1906 Meat Inspection Act and Pure Food and Drug Act, government agencies have inspected meat, regulated drug and alcohol content in over-the-counter medicines, and set standards for the purity of foods sold to consumers. By the late 1950s, the Food and Drug Administration (which was under HEW), the USDA, and the Public Health Service faced the challenge of herbicides and pesticides entering the food chain at an alarming and accelerated rate. Chemicals that controlled noxious weeds and insects infesting crops were not new to agricultural production. A number of chemical compounds were used during the 1930s and 40s, but in the postwar years, large-scale farming and the application of hundreds of new chemicals sharply escalated. In 1933 farmers spent $29 million on pesticides; in 1958, the amount was $260 million, an increase of 800 percent in twenty-five years. The amount of pesticide residue released into the environment was "becoming more frequent and acute." Its effect, said one government report, was a challenge requiring immediate research.[45]

The 1962 publication of Rachel Carson's *Silent Spring* alerted the public to the environmental dangers and health hazards of pesticides, but federal agencies were well aware of particular problems long before Carson completed her book. In 1945, for example, a Kansas farm newspaper used information provided by the USDA to warn that DDT (dichloro-diphenyl-trichloroethane) was not necessarily a "wonder drug" for pest eradication. It had little, if any, effect on some insects; repeated use over long periods of time could turn the ground toxic and unfit for agriculture; and there was little information at the time regarding its effect on humans, although "jitters and nervousness" had been reported by people who came in close contact with the chemical.[46]

Government officials and scientists faced a quandary. Without knowing with any certainty how various herbicides and pesticides might affect the human body or what long-term risks they might pose to the development of a child's brain, nervous system, or internal organs, officials were not sure what to tell consumers. If Americans were frightened away from certain food products because of supposition, the country's farmers and ranchers would suffer economically. And, despite concerns over DDT, it was considered a "miracle drug." Its numerous uses made it a staple for application on farms and ranches. Thousands of communities also relied on it for eradicating mosquitoes and the gypsy moth. In fact, aerial spraying aimed at the gypsy moth and other pests was just as likely to shower people, and trucks spraying DDT sometimes attracted youngsters who ran behind playing in the pesticide-laden fog meant for mosquitoes. How to control the use of chemicals while protecting the public and keeping agriculture productive left many in government scratching their heads. In 1959, Don Paarlberg, special assistant to President Eisenhower, wrote:

> There is a troublesome and growing problem with respect to pesticide residue in milk, meat and other food products. These residues (chiefly from chlorinated hydrocarbons such as DDT) are in some cases exceeding present tolerance levels set by the Food and Drug Administration. Human health is concerned. . . . Both Agriculture and HEW . . . have said relatively little about it hitherto because of some perplexity as to how to proceed, and much concern for the attitude of the American people if scare stories should be written.[47]

Federal agencies were, in fact, facing a number of "scare stories" that panicked and confused the public. There were the announcements of milk contaminated by pesticides, by an antibiotic, and by radioactive fallout. Radioactivity was also found in some grains, including wheat, and another report suggested that a portion of the chickens processed for public consumption were infected with a pesticide. Then, just before the

1959 Thanksgiving holiday, HEW announced that trace amounts of the herbicide ATZ (atrazine), a possible carcinogenic, was found in a substantial portion of the cranberry crop. Although ATZ had a relatively low toxicity, its long-term effects could result in malignant thyroid tumors.

ATZ was approved for use in 1958 by the USDA to control weeds in cranberry bogs, but it was only supposed to be used during the post-crop season. Some cranberry growers evidently misused the herbicide, and when the Food and Drug Administration tested several shipments of berries in the fall of 1959, it found contaminated lots. HEW Secretary Flemming told the public on November 9 that neither the government nor the consumer had any way of knowing if fresh berries or canned produce and juices were safe. The public had to use its own discretion when purchasing these products. However, Flemming assured them that the National Cranberry Association, better known as Ocean Spray Cranberries, Inc., was cooperating with the government to identify contaminated batches and to ensure that nothing of this kind happened again.[48]

Supermarkets pulled cranberry products from store shelves. Sales dropped to near zero. Representatives from the cranberry industry were furious. The governors and congressmen of Massachusetts, New Jersey, Wisconsin, and Oregon, where most cranberry bogs existed, were up in arms. Representative Frank Thompson, Jr., a Democrat from New Jersey, demanded that the federal government compensate growers. Congressman Hastings Keith, a Republican representing Massachusetts, proposed an independent investigative panel, without any representatives from the federal government. USDA Secretary Ezra Taft Benson publicly criticized Flemming because American farmers were hurt. To show his confidence Benson, said *Time* magazine, "performed a kind of ritual sacrifice by gulping down a bowl of cranberries in public." In Wisconsin, presidential candidates John F. Kennedy and Richard Nixon both "cheerfully" consumed cranberry products while on the campaign trail. Soon after these "feats of leadership," reported *Time*, additional tainted batches of cranberries were seized in Wisconsin.[49]

Flemming was skewered by politicians and the public. In hundreds of letters and telegrams to the White House, he was criticized and some-

times colorfully defamed. The general tone of this outpouring was captured in a letter from two grocers in Houston, Texas:

> Let's sack poor Mr. Fleming [*sic*] fast. . . . The merchants are fighting
> mad. Here right at Thanksgiving and Christmas! You know how
> people are about cancer. Even the thought of cranberry sauce makes
> them faint. Women calling us up on the telephone crying that they fed
> a can of it to their family, and they all are going to die, and what are
> we going to do about it? What are WE going to do about it? Hell,
> lady, call Mr. Eisenhower and ask him what he's going to do about
> it.[50]

The "great cranberry scare" was a lesson in how little ordinary citizens in an increasingly urbanized society knew about where their food
came from or how it was produced and processed. For his part, Flemming was doing his job by following federal legislation. In 1958 an
amendment to the Food, Drug, and Cosmetic Act strengthened the authority of the Food and Drug Administration. The amendment, known
as the Delaney Amendment, was added by Representative James Delaney, a New York Democrat who came to Congress during the Roosevelt administration as a liberal but became increasingly conservative
during his three decades in Congress. The Delaney Amendment inaugu-
rated the federal government's role in protecting the public from cancer-
causing agents. It "categorically forbade the presence in foodstuffs of any
additives shown by experiment to cause cancer in test animals." Although the Food and Drug Administration was uncertain of ATZ's toxicity, it fell within the parameters of a carcinogen. Flemming believed that
he was bound to follow the law and that it was in the public's best interest for him to do so. From his point of view, the Food and Drug Administration was, at the time, the "only consumer-oriented agency in the
government."[51]

By the end of the 1950s and the close of the Eisenhower administration, the line between private health care and government actions was
less distinct. Although Truman's plan for national health-care insurance
was long abandoned, federal agencies continued, sometimes at an accelerated rate, to act on issues related to public health care. The Children's

Bureau, BIA, and Public Health Service provided medical assistance to the poor and to minority populations. They administered grants-in-aid to states for specific programs, while HEW offered expertise in science and technology to identify and counteract threats to the country's food and water supplies. Americans thought of medical care in personal terms—hospitalization or visits to the family doctor—but they also expected the government to protect their health. Whether or not the public agreed on government programs and policies, ensuring a healthy population was a matter of national concern. A sick nation depleted the country's economic viability, jeopardized national security, hampered military preparedness, and robbed youngsters of their promised bright futures.

How the government should be involved was often a point for debate. Certainly, political ideologies and viewpoints shaded the discussion, creating issue-driven legislation. The legislation and presidential initiatives were, however, rather prolific and wide ranging. They dealt with such diverse issues as building hospitals, funding rehabilitation and mental health services, providing clinics to underserved ethnic and racial groups, highlighting physical fitness, providing the polio vaccine free of charge, and taking steps to control hazardous chemicals and additives in the food supply. The physical well-being of children and teenagers translated into a national asset. "The national policies," said Eisenhower in 1956, "will be no more than words if our people are not healthy of body, as well as of mind. . . . Our young people must be physically as well as mentally and spiritually prepared for American citizenship."[52]

Conclusion

"Deeply embedded in my dedication and devotion to America is a great faith in and affection for America's youth. They are our nation's hope."

—*Dwight D. Eisenhower, July 29, 1960*

Children and teenagers of the postwar era were told that they lived in a country where anything was possible, but while they were encouraged to find self-fulfillment and expression, they were also told that they were responsible for preserving the democratic society in which they lived. They were the country's next generation of military and citizen soldiers. On their shoulders rested preservation of the country's ideals and way of life.

While Eisenhower attempted to engage the Soviet Union in arms control negotiations, beginning with the president's 1953 "Atoms for Peace" speech, he (like Truman before him) and the American people believed that the United States was fighting for its very survival in a Cold War. The Soviet threat, warned Eisenhower, was not something imagined and blown out of proportion. "Soviet spokesmen, from the beginning, have publicly and frequently declared their aim to expand their power, one way or another throughout the world."[1]

This was the world being passed to the next generation. At the same time that children and teenagers were encouraged to advance their educations, become physically fit, and develop their individual talents, they were seen as the country's "most cherished hopes" for the future. One day, they would be the adults contributing to the country's economy and carrying on its inherent values while also defending it against the non-democratic, totalitarian forces of the world.[2]

A lot was expected of the postwar generation. Conversely, if young-sters were to fulfill their prescribed roles, society had a responsibility to help them along the way. It could do that in innumerable ways, but a ba-sic step was accepting that childhood was the right of every child. The concept was first articulated in the late nineteenth century. By the early twentieth century, the idea was firmly established in social thought. Few questioned that childhood should combine playtime, schooling, home nurturing, religious instruction, and character-building home chores. This was the cultural ideal and goal, although the realities for individual youngsters were quite different.[3]

During the Progressive Era and the years immediately following World War I, a number of leaders in the areas of child health and welfare began to discuss and enumerate the rights of children beyond the basic standard that children had a right to experience the childhood society en-visioned for them. The 1930 White House Conference on Children and Youth enumerated children's rights in an eighteen-point charter. Twenty years later, the 1950 conference reiterated its recognition of rights in a "Pledge to Children." By the midcentury mark, American culture ac-cepted the idea of child rights. These rights were articulated by adults, who said less about rights in terms of those guaranteed to all American citizens by the U.S. Constitution and more about specific rights associ-ated with childhood and the growing-up years. In this regard, the United States was in step with other industrialized countries that had, in their own ways, embraced the concept to the point that the United Nations first referred to children in two articles of the 1948 Universal Declaration of Human Rights and then enacted a Declaration of the Rights of the Child in 1959.[4]

America's support for the U.N. declarations was both an affirmation of societal thought regarding childhood and a reflection of the U.S. gov-ernment's interest in children beyond the country's borders. Two years after the 1948 Universal Declaration of Human Rights, the Truman ad-ministration invited forty-four German educators and child-care experts to the White House Conference on Children and Youth. It was not un-usual for foreign visitors to attend conferences. They had been doing so since the second meeting in 1919, but Truman did not expect the German guests to be mere observers. It was hoped that the conference model would be transported back to Germany, much as U.S.-assisted technology and funds were being used to rebuild that country's economy and infrastructure through the European Recovery Program (the Marshall Plan).

The German visitors expressed admiration for what they saw, but resisted transplanting the American model. When later interviewed, a number said that they found some "American theories about children" confusing because, unlike Germany where children's attributes were considered largely a product of heredity, Americans gave considerable weight to environmental influences and "social heredity." As disconcerting to the German visitors, accustomed to a rigid hierarchy based on education, expertise, and social station, was the casual, democratic mix of participants. A renowned educator exchanged ideas with a high school teacher; a settlement house worker was as free to express an opinion as the director of a nationally known charity; and a youth delegate engaged in a "friendly disagreement" with a respected child-care expert. The American model did not seem a good fit for export.[5]

Rejection on this front did not dissuade the federal government from pursuing other international projects. The U.S. Children's Bureau, for instance, placed "qualified specialists in the fields of child welfare and maternal and child health" in foreign countries through its Division of International Cooperation. Meanwhile, the U.S. Department of State "continued to support in ways that are appropriate the efforts of American voluntary agencies operating abroad, many of whose programs directly aid children and youth of those countries." The U.S. government also provided strong support to the work of UNICEF and the World Health Organization.[6]

American society pictured itself as caring about children and regarded its families as child-centered. The self-image was fixed, but it was also rife with contradictions. While the middle class began to sentimentalize childhood in the latter half of the nineteenth century, influencing perceptions forward into the twentieth century, society could also be ambivalent about children and childhood or express outright fear of what one reformer labeled the poverty-stricken, uneducated "dangerous classes."[7] Nonetheless, by the mid-twentieth century, Americans preferred to think of themselves and the country in which they lived as committed to children. Yes, there was a fear factor attached to delinquency, and there was no doubt that jarring social and economic inequities turned the cultural ideal of childhood into nothing more than a stereotypical cartoon. Still, Americans acted on the belief that they valued their young and had their best interests at heart.

Childhood had achieved a new importance, both culturally and politically. The question Americans asked was how they and their government leaders could best meet their obligations to the next generation. Poverty and attitudes about ethnicity and race continued to result in a multitude of children and teenagers being treated as less than first-class citizens. Rapid social, economic, and political changes during the 1940s and 50s introduced elements of fears and uncertainties, and the burgeoning child population presented challenges for the institutions responsible for their health, education, and welfare.

In the face of issues that sometimes seemed too large for parents, communities, or states to take on alone, they looked to the federal government to play a larger role in giving children and teenagers the full measure of what society promised to them as citizens with rights. To negotiate the uncertainties of the postwar world, people increasingly turned to experts for advice, whether it was in child rearing or to better understand rapidly changing technology and medical science. It was not so great a leap, then, for the public to turn to their elected officials and federal agencies for greater response and direction. This is not to say that government involvement was welcomed with open arms or that Americans wanted federal programs and laws to be all things to all people.

While the public accepted, even expected, that their local and state governments would intercede and regulate such things as child welfare laws, compulsory school attendance, and child labor, people were less sure of federal intercession. Many opposed federal involvement if that meant increasing the national debt to pay for programs, and there was the nagging question of state autonomy. Policies dictated from above and federal grants-in-aid could potentially diminish a state's right to decide what best served its population and specific needs. It was not so far-fetched to predict a future in which states turned over more control in exchange for federal dollars. Voicing this opinion, a man wrote President Truman that any government aid to education set a dangerous precedent for all sorts of other legislation. The result would eventually make the government a "nurse maid to the States as well as the people."[8]

Certainly, most Americans realized that a number of government agencies offered various forms of assistance to some segments of the population. Although they may not have been able to name every program or the agency responsible, responses to a White House questionnaire demonstrated some level of knowledge. The questionnaire, sent to newspaper editors in 1954, asked how people in their respective towns perceived existing social and domestic policies. Fairly typical was the report from an editor in Knoxville, Tennessee: "Regarding public health, housing, social security, unemployment insurance, etc., I think there is general satisfaction with the progress being made." An editor in Albuquerque agreed that most people approved the current policies, but he added a caveat. "Some business people believe the social welfare program too deeply imbedded for Ike to do anything about it except to continue more of the same."[9]

It was true that some projects had become so entrenched that people took them for granted and relied upon them, and even when people said that they disliked increased government spending and the larger government bureaucracy that came with additional programs, they accepted, even sometimes demanded, childhood policies that required more spending and bigger government. The cultural and political environment offered contradictions. More was expected from government, but lawmakers did not intend to rubber-stamp every proposal just because it was supposed to help children.

Perhaps Congress could not, or would not, undo what was already in place, but many representatives and senators reasoned that they could limit the extent of any new mandate or program. Some lawmakers argued that it was fiscally irresponsible to increase existing programs or add new ones. Many lawmakers were uncomfortable with what appeared to be a slow expansion of the federal role in directing child-related policies, interfering with states' rights, or policing parental prerogatives. Too much involvement in the latter could conceivably mirror the Soviet Union where the state exhibited no qualms when it took decisions about child rearing and education out of the hands of parents and acted as a parental surrogate.

At the same time, it was apparent that neither local communities nor states had the resources to solve many of their largest problems alone. It was not unreasonable to say that many felt overwhelmed by complex issues that grew exponentially with the increase in a youthful population, or felt that significant change would happen only when the federal government became involved. Overcrowded classrooms, too few teachers, overburdened juvenile courts and detention centers were just a few of the concerns.

Lawmakers and the political parties they stood for were not immune to the needs. They did not agree, however, on the extent of federal response or, in some cases, the desirability of federal involvement. Ideology and partisanship formed viewpoints and arguments, as did a deeply ingrained reluctance to intrude on state or parental rights. In family matters, Congress was likely to act only when legislation was meant to strengthen the American family, which was often portrayed as a fragile entity buffeted from all sides by events that would destroy it. If families weakened, it was argued, the country's democratic way of life would suffer. Youngsters were the beneficiaries of family-help programs, such as Aid to Dependent Children, and they were assisted indirectly by legislation that encouraged housing construction, controlled rents, or provided unemployment insurance to out-of-work adults.

New initiatives related to youngsters also appeared in relation to Americans' anxieties over Soviet intentions and the general Cold War environment of the 1940s and 50s. Certainly, the National Defense Education Act was a direct response to fears that the Soviets had jumped ahead of the United States in science and technology, but support for other programs and policies were also couched in terms of national defense. The National School Lunch Program, efforts to curb juvenile delinquency, and promoting physical fitness were tinged with Cold War references. There was an inescapable link between international events and domestic policies affecting facets of American childhood.

Policies that impacted children and teenagers were both a product of the times and of America's political system. Partisan politics, fiscal concerns, cultural and social values each contributed to debates over government's role. The discussions were littered with denunciations of communism, socialized medicine, juvenile delinquency, divorce, and

working women. These were counterbalanced by the realities of everyday life and the needs of children and their families. It was difficult, if not
impossible, to ignore issues affecting children or to pretend that no inequities existed between states and regions, or between racial, social, and
economic groups. Some communities and states demonstrated little interest in helping minority groups, and even those that might have done
so often did not have the resources to provide the same level of services
found in other sections of the country. Like it or not, people inside and
outside the federal government felt that the country had an obligation to
act, especially when one considered the country's future and what it held
for children.

Harry Truman, the Democrat with a domestic agenda that echoed the
New Deal, and Dwight Eisenhower, the fiscally conservative Republican
determined to balance the national budget, were poles apart in how they
viewed the role of government and social policies. Nevertheless, they
agreed that America's young were the country's great hope for maintaining a democratic, economically sound, and secure America. On a few occasions the presidents' words had the sound of pure rhetoric, but more
often than not, they were heartfelt statements. And, more importantly,
they were acted upon, as both men conceded that there were times when
only they and Congress could step in as advocates for children and
teenagers.

It has been argued that government policies affecting children usually
occur as an incremental change. In other words, lawmakers react to public pressure or lobby groups and mandate some form of service or type of
reform that usually affects only a segment of the population. Over time,
the resulting programs then evolve, are readjusted, or are sometimes
eliminated. There are, however, occasional seismic events, such as the
discovery of the Salk vaccine or the appearance of *Sputnik.* When these
occur, the reaction is a comprehensive program that affects youngsters
from all backgrounds and circumstances.[10]

Incremental changes impacting a defined group were true for most
government programs during the postwar era. Federal funds for new
school construction, for example, only benefited youngsters living in
military/defense boom towns. And, federal spending that went toward
Native American education or mobile health services for migrant work-

ers were obviously intended for those groups alone. Comprehensive legislation that affected children and teenagers from every economic and social level came about through broad social and/or political changes. Court-mandated desegregation, for example, not only altered the racial mix in classrooms but laid the groundwork for desegregation of all public places. And, dramatic legislation occurred when the White House and Congress quickly approved bills to provide every child with the polio vaccine and later to significantly bolster math and science education in the schools.

In the years immediately after World War II, it was almost impossible to ignore society's preoccupation with teenagers and baby boomers. What they read, and watched on television, where they played, and popular culture's impact on their behavior were all fodder for social commentary, parenting literature, and advice columns. And, as no other generation before them, children and teenagers were scrutinized and discussed at the highest levels of government. Besides the myriad of child-related issues examined and debated at the 1950 and 1960 White House Conferences on Children and Youth, youngsters were researched and dissected by the U.S. Children's Bureau as it conducted studies and issued reports. America's youth were the subjects of federally sponsored conferences on education and juvenile delinquency. Meanwhile, a congressional committee spent approximately three years probing delinquency, and a presidential commission preached the values of physical fitness.

White House Conferences on Children and Youth intended to do several things. They drew the country's attention to the subject of children and brought together people of very different backgrounds and interests. The expected outcome was, first of all, people going back to their communities with new ideas and a renewed sense of purpose. Secondly, the meetings would point out areas where federal action was needed or garner support for existing programs. The 1950 conference, for example, not only applauded the Truman administration for its urban renewal and public housing programs but demanded more. In other instances, however, no amount of activism or lobbying could nudge lawmakers into action. Other types of conferences came to the same result. One goal of the White House Conference on Education was to push Congress into authorizing funds for school construction, but the plan failed. To jumpstart federal funding for anti–juvenile delinquency programs, Eisenhower supported congressional investigation and HEW's conference on delinquency. These efforts did not produce the desired results. White House conferences and presidential commissions sometimes failed, but before concentrating on what was not accomplished, it might be well to consider that they occurred at all.

Out of conferences, investigations, and reports emerged recommendations, as well as proposals for legislation. Occasionally conference or congressional reports also asked the government to reconsider programs that, once implemented, produced unforeseen problems. Follow-up meetings to the 1960 White House Conference on Children and Youth, for instance, expressed concern that federally funded vocational programs were inadequate and outmoded. They were not keeping pace with changing technology, leaving teenagers unprepared to enter the modern job market and earn a livelihood.[11]

There was also a growing concern that Aid to Dependent Children was out of control. By 1958 annual expenditures totaled more than $8 million. While there were calls to raise government funding in relation to increased costs of living, many inside and outside the government worried that federal policy made it easier for men to abandon their families and for unwed mothers to have more babies. Rather than keeping families intact, said critics, the program rewarded broken, fractured relationships. The program seemed to have lost its original purpose of helping dependent children who had lost either one or both parents to death. And, when the number enrolled in the program doubled between 1957 and 1967, legislation was amended to slow what was by then known as Aid to Families with Dependent Children. Participants were required to take part in work training while "undeserving" enrollees were weeded out by a new emphasis on assistance to children of unemployed fathers.[12]

In follow-up meetings to the 1960 White House Conference on Children and Youth, a considerable amount of criticism was directed at urban renewal. State and federal entities too often rushed forward with projects without giving much thought to the families affected. The program was, said one follow-up group, a "national disgrace." On paper, slum clearance and urban renewal looked like positive solutions to reducing juvenile delinquency, creating safer environments for children, and shoring

For critics of urban renewal, the Barry Farms Housing Development in Washington, D.C., pictured here in the mid-1940s, became but one example of poor foresight and planning when urban planners reconfigured neighborhoods during the 1950s. Library of Congress

up family stability. The reality, however, was often grim. Neighborhoods were wiped out, often replaced by highways and office buildings, not homes. Families were forced to move, but newer public housing often became just as blighted as those poverty-stricken neighborhoods it was meant to replace. Problems of poverty, joblessness, and illiteracy did not magically disappear.[13]

Urban renewal may have been well intentioned, but was not thought-out in many instances. This did not dissuade voices from the private sector and from within some government agencies from pushing for more programs, funding, and federal involvement in many aspects of everyday life. When the 1950s came to an end, reformers and child-care advocates argued that there was still much to be done. The country continued to suffer from a shortage of classrooms, teachers, school counselors, and day-care centers. Malnutrition remained a problem in some population groups, as did lack of access to prenatal and developmental medical care. The country's juvenile courts were still overwhelmed, and educators were blamed for not finding the magical formula that made learning a stimulating adventure for those teenagers most likely to drop out.

Across a broad spectrum of professions and child advocacy groups, it was agreed that advancements had been made in education, health, welfare, and strengthening family life. Nevertheless, there was no time for self-congratulation or complacency. More had to be done to sustain programs and to advance new ones. The United States was an international power that should expend more of its resources on children. The government, it was argued, should reexamine its priorities. After all, said one report from the early 1960s regarding Social Security expenditures: "26 billion dollars are spent for the aged and 8 billion dollars spent for children, although there are three times more children."[14]

Of course, not every recommendation or proposal for legislation was acted upon. Lack of action spoke volumes about the importance lawmakers or the public attached to an issue, as well as a political climate responsive to change. Policymakers, for instance, generally refused to back government-funded day care, believing that this would only encourage women to work outside the home rather than perpetuate the stereotypical model of the family unit. And, arguing fiscal responsibility, the Eisenhower administration did not seek funding for physical fitness programs but put its faith in a presidential commission to raise public awareness and community support. Nevertheless, discussions and conversations that surrounded policy strategies informed public policy. Certainly, at times the debate surrounding an issue projected the political climate and political ideologies at work. Federal policies were often reactions to a set of circumstances, broad social issues, and the ability of a political party to push through its domestic agenda.

For their part, children born in the immediate postwar era and those who were teenagers were largely unaware of the part government and lawmakers played in their lives. If their childhood memories or reminiscences recall school-cafeteria hot lunches, a polio shot, or more science and math homework, it is unlikely that there is an immediate connection to people in the halls of Congress or in the Oval Office. Yet, there were numerous ways in which government programs and dialogue influenced their experiences, whether it was something as simple as getting an extra pint of milk at school or the more dramatic experience of sitting in a mixed-race classroom. Life changed for children, but not at the same pace for all. Some youngsters gained more from federal policies than others, depending on where they lived, their race or ethnicity, and family circumstances. American culture had decided, however, that children of every background sometimes required more support than their families or communities were able to provide.

Teenagers and children of the 1940s and 50s were a driving force in the social fabric of the country. Conversely, they absorbed society's notion of them. If they seemed too sedentary, too materialistic, or too self-involved, they were scolded for not living up to their potential. On the other hand, they were called national resources, expected to be happy, and encouraged to seek more personal accomplishment and success than any earlier generation. They lived in a culture that preached the rights of children and encouraged the dichotomous ideas of personal fulfillment and group cooperation.

The issues and concerns surrounding the next generation were many and complex, but through the discourse, what was said about the next generation was fundamental to forming society's view of childhood and the role government should play in its protection and elemental experiences. Often reluctant to become more involved, the federal government, nevertheless, assumed an unprecedented degree of responsibility for children and teenagers.

The years between 1945 and 1960 were not staid or stagnant as some have suggested. They were a transitional period between the few legislative mandates enacted before World War II and the storm of changes that arrived in the 1960s and 70s when federal programs brought about new and often sweeping initiatives, such as the 1965 Head Start program. Head Start and other programs from President Johnson's War on Poverty and Great Society emerged from a specific intellectual and political context of the civil rights movement, national economic growth, and a heightened awareness of poverty levels in the country. However, it is short-sighted to postulate, as some have, that the origins of Johnson's

At Tekakwitha Orphanage, which primarily served the Sioux in South Dakota, children gather around Sister Kathryn DeMarrais in this 1955 photograph. Three years later, the Bureau of Indian Affairs initiated the Indian Adoption Project, generating tribal opposition and the eventual passage of the 1978 Indian Adoption Welfare Act. SDS-W Archives, Milwaukee

legislation date back only to President Kennedy's New Frontier bills on poverty, medical care, and education.[15] Johnson's social philosophies were rooted in the Great Depression and Roosevelt's New Deal, but many of his administration's programs had connections to mandates enacted during the immediate postwar era. The 1946 National School Lunch Program, for instance, was the basis for the 1968 Child Care Food Program, which provided meals to day-care centers, and then expanded to add school breakfasts to the Hot Lunch program.

Federal aid-to-education funding that supported teacher training in special education and improved services to the hearing- and sight-impaired during the 1950s opened the door to more aid for physically and mentally challenged children in the 1966 amended version of the Elementary and Secondary Education Act of 1965 and through the 1975 Education of All Handicapped Children Act (later codified as the Individuals with Disabilities Education Act). The decided difference between legislation of the 1950s and later statutes was, however, the latter's punitive components. Under the 1966 legislation, public schools that discriminated against disabled students by turning them away received no federal aid, and the 1975 law went further by requiring that special needs children attend regular classrooms whenever possible. For youngsters whose first language was not English, the Bilingual Education Act of 1968 was hailed as the first of its kind. It was unique in that there was no federal precedent, but since Truman's commission on migratory labor in the late 1940s and bilingual education initiatives in several states during the 1950s, federal agencies had hovered at the edges of equalizing access and opportunity for non-English speakers.[16]

In other aspects of federal legislation, there is no doubt that groundwork for the Kennedy-endorsed 1962 Educational Television Facilities Act, which provided construction grants for educational television, was laid in the 1950s by critics of television programming and by U.S. Children's Bureau studies. And, the BIA, another federal agency, made an unintended legislative contribution. Its conflict with tribal groups over its Indian Adoption Project influenced the Indian Child Welfare Act of 1978, which established federal requirements for home placement of tribal children in the custody of state welfare systems.

In the 1960s and 70s, the intellectual construct of children's rights also took a turn, evolving from the established tenets of the right to a childhood to arguments of legal rights like those afforded adults. Advocates for child rights put forward the argument that minors, particularly older ones, were capable of making decisions on such issues as parental/guardian custody, emancipation from parental control, educational choices, and medical care (including the right to birth control information—something approved by the 1960 White House Conference on Children and Youth—and the right to obtain contraceptives or seek an abortion without parental/guardian consent). The legal right to make personal choices also extended to the voting booth. If young men were old enough to be drafted for military service, they were old enough to vote. In 1965, the Voting Rights Act lowered the voting age to eighteen. In 1971, the Twenty-Sixth Amendment to the Constitution, giving voting rights to eighteen- to twenty-year-olds, was ratified.[17]

In 1970, the last officially named White House Conference on Children and Youth occurred during the Nixon administration. The meeting's overall discussions centered on how to preserve the family unit amid what sometimes seemed the absolute chaos of social and cultural upheaval, whether it be over Vietnam, integration, widespread use of recreational drugs, emergence of a new women's movement, or the sexual revolution. Those attending the conference did not foresee that they were participating in the last of what had become an expected event.

Although Jimmy Carter sponsored a White House conference in 1979 devoted to strengthening American families, the meeting was narrow in focus and did not follow the organizational process of earlier White House Conferences on Children and Youth. Carter's approach signaled an end to a tradition begun in 1909. Ronald Reagan shut the door on it. There was no funding for a national event, but states could ask for federal aid if they wished to hold their own individual meetings. This was in keeping with the conservative policy of making big government smaller, but critics saw Reagan's refusal to sponsor a White House Conference as another example of his administration's assault on federal assistance to children. During Reagan's years in office, Aid to Families with Dependent Children was cut by 13 percent; job training for young people by 53 percent; and child nutrition programs by 28 percent.[18]

In the years that followed, presidential administrations sponsored conferences, but they adopted the Carter model, selecting specific topics with a smaller number of participants. White House–sponsored meetings have included a 1997 conference on early childhood development, the 2000 conference on teenagers, a 2002 meeting regarding missing, exploited, and runaway children, and the 2005 Helping America's Youth Conference.[19]

In the postwar era, the force of presidential agendas and personalities, along with a willing Congress, intersected with political ideologies and shifting social climates. From the years of Truman's Fair Deal through Johnson's Great Society, federal participation in child-related issues expanded. Chronology cannot be assumed to demonstrate a tidy link from

This poster from the 1960 White House Conference on Children and Youth underscored the Cold War rhetoric of U.S. freedom versus Soviet totalitarianism. Dwight D. Eisenhower Library

one piece of domestic legislation to another. Nevertheless, legislation of the Great Society, while reflecting the nation's mood at a specific place in time, did not spring out of a void. There was a foundation for federal action that grew incrementally stronger through the early part of the twentieth century and noticeably expanded in the immediate postwar years. From the end of World War II to the close of the Eisenhower presidency in 1960, Americans and their leaders gave considerable attention, not just lip service, to issues that directly affected the country's children and teenagers. Often the federal response was nuanced by Cold War fears and rhetoric, but inherent in the politics of childhood was society's concept of its responsibility to the young. Acting on their behalf was an investment in what Eisenhower referred to as "our nation's hope." Parents, communities, and states each had a part to play. So did Washington. During the postwar years, there was an increased expectation, and acceptance, that the federal government would have a broader role in promoting the health, education, and welfare of the national child community.

Appendix: White House and Federal Agency–Sponsored Conferences and Commissions, 1946–1960

1946   National Conference for the Prevention and Control of Juvenile
       Delinquency; National Chair, Tom C. Clark, U.S. Attorney
       General
1950   White House Conference on Children and Youth; Executive
       Committee Chair, Melvin A. Glasser, former administrator,
       American Red Cross; National Committee Chair, Oscar R.
       Ewing, director, Federal Security Agency
1952   White House Conference on Children and Youth, Follow-Up;
       National Committee Chair, Leonard W. Mayo, director,
       Association for the Aid for Crippled Children and past-
       president, Child Welfare League of America
1954   Moving Ahead to Curb Juvenile Delinquency Conference; U.S.
       Children's Bureau and U.S. Department of Health, Education,
       and Welfare, organizing agencies
1955   White House Conference on Education; National Chair, Neil
       H. McElroy, president, Procter and Gamble; U.S. Department
       of Health, Education and Welfare, organizing agency
1956   President's Conference on Fitness of American Youth; National
       Chair, Vice President Richard M. Nixon
1956   President's Council on Youth Fitness; National Chair, Vice
       President Richard M. Nixon; Executive Director, Shane
       MacCarthy, educator and public servant
1960   White House Conference on Children and Youth; Executive
       Committee Chair, Arthur S. Flemming, secretary, U.S.
       Department of Health, Education, and Welfare; National

Committee Chair, Ethel Brown, past president, National
Congress of Parents and Teachers

1960   National Conference on Day Care of Children; U.S. Children's
Bureau and U.S. Women's Bureau, organizing agencies

NOTES

INTRODUCTION

1 Walter I. Trattner, *From Poor Law to Welfare State: A History of Social Welfare in America*, 4th ed. (New York: Free Press, 1974), 196; Kriste Lindenmeyer, *"A Right to Childhood": The U.S. Children's Bureau and Child Welfare* (Urbana: University of Illinois Press, 1997), 253.

2 Paula S. Fass and Michael Grossberg, eds., *Reinventing Childhood after World War II* (Philadelphia: University of Pennsylvania Press, 2012); Edward F. Zigler, Sharon Lynn Kagan, and Edward Klugman, eds., *Children, Families, and Government: Perspectives on American Social Policy* (Cambridge, UK: Cambridge University Press, 1983); Judith Sealander, *The Failed Century of the Child: Governing America's Young in the Twentieth Century* (New York: Cambridge University Press, 2003); Lindenmeyer, *"A Right to Childhood"*; Steven Mintz, *Huck's Raft: A History of American Childhood* (Cambridge, MA: Belknap Press, Harvard University Press, 2004); Julia L. Mickenberg, *Learning from the Left: Children's Literature, the Cold War, and Radical Politics in the United States* (New York: Oxford University Press, 2006); Juel Janis, "Health Policy for Children," in Zigler, Kagan, and Klugman, eds., *Children, Families, and Government*, 356.

3 Steve Gillon, *Boomer Nation: The Largest and Richest Generation Ever and How It Changed America* (New York: Free Press, 2004), 6, 41.

4 William M. Tuttle, Jr., *"Daddy's Gone to War": The Second World War in the Lives of Children* (New York: Oxford University Press, 1993), 241.

5 Ibid., 44; James Gilbert, *A Cycle of Outrage: America's Reaction to the Juvenile Delinquent in the 1950s* (New York: Oxford University Press, 1986), 19.

6 "Speaking of Pictures: Teen-age Ballet," *Life* 19 (May 28, 1945): 12; "Teen-age Boys Are Just the Same as They've Always Been," *Life* 19 (June 11, 1945): 91–97.

7 "Law Change Urged to Admit Refugees," *New York Times*, April 2, 1947, p. 11. The article, arguing for U.S. admittance of refugees, expounded on the country's current population figures.

8 Lindenmeyer, *"A Right to Childhood,"* 1; "Minutes of Executive Committee Meeting, October 22, 1949," Midcentury White House Conference on Children and Youth 1950 file (1), box 6, White House Conference on Children and Youth Records, 1930–1970, Eisenhower Presidential Library, Abilene, KS (hereinafter cited as WHC, EL).

9 David G. McCullough, *Truman* (New York: Simon & Schuster, 1992); Stephen E. Ambrose, *Eisenhower: The President*, vol. 2 (New York: Simon & Schuster, 1984); Jim Newton, *Eisenhower: The White House Years* (New York: Doubleday, 2011); David A. Nichols, *A Matter of Justice: Eisenhower and the Beginning of the Civil Rights Revolution* (New York: Simon & Schuster, 2007).

10 Elaine Tyler May, *Homeward Bound: American Families in the Cold War Era*, rev. ed. (New York: Basic Books, 1999); Joanne Meyerowitz, ed., *Not June Cleaver: Women and Gender in Postwar America, 1945–1960* (Philadelphia: Tem-

ple University Press, 1994); Lary May, ed., *Recasting America: Culture and Politics in the Age of the Cold War* (Chicago: University of Chicago Press, 1989); Lizabeth Cohen, *A Consumers' Republic: The Politics of Mass Consumption in Postwar America* (New York: Vintage Books, 2003); John Bradley, ed., *Learning to Glow: A Nuclear Reader* (Tucson: University of Arizona Press, 2000).

11 Tom Brokaw, *Boom!* (New York: Random House, 2007); Victor D. Brooks, *Boomers: The Cold War Generation Grows Up* (Chicago: Ivan R. Dee, 2009); Gillon, *Boomer Nation*; Landon Y. Jones, *Great Expectations: America and the Baby Boom Generation* (New York: Coward, McCann & Geoghegan, 1980).

CHAPTER 1. WHITE HOUSE CONFERENCES ON CHILDREN AND YOUTH: THE PUBLIC DISCUSSION

Epigraph: "President's Proclamation," *Midcentury White House Conference on Children and Youth Bulletin* 5 (June 20, 1951): 1.

1 Oscar R. Ewing, "The Task of the National Citizens Committee: Speech before the National Committee, September 8, 1949," p. 2, box 7, Background Material file, WHC, EL.

2 "National Midcentury Committee for Children and Youth, Inc.," memo, December 1952, box 14, Two-Year Anniversary Conference file, WHC, EL; "Proposal for Organizing Statistical Material for White House Conference Background Reports, February 17, 1950," box 6, Advisory Council for Federal Government Participation file, and "Federal Agencies" Follow-Up 1952 file, WHC, EL; "Annual Report of the Interdepartmental Committee on Children and Youth, July 1, 1954–June 30, 1955," box 25, Interdepartmental file, Oveta Culp Hobby Papers, Eisenhower Presidential Library (hereinafter cited as Hobby Papers, EL). In 1965 the War Orphans' Educational Assistance Act was expanded to cover dependents of servicemen killed or permanently disabled as a result of service after the end of the Korean conflict.

3 "Minutes of the Executive Committee Meeting, Oct. 22, 1949," box 6, Midcentury White House Conference on Children and Youth, 1950, file (1), WHC, EL; Memo, Robert E. Hampton to David W. Kendall, December 17, 1958, box 846, OF-15560A-7 file, Central Files, EL. For letters endorsing conference participants, see box 1669, White House Conference on Children 1502 file, Official Files, White House Central Files, Harry S. Truman Presidential Library, Independence, MO (hereinafter cited as Central Files, TL.)

4 Hubert H. Humphrey, *The Education of a Public Man: My Life and Politics* (New York: Doubleday, 1976; reprint, Minneapolis: University of Minnesota Press, 1991), 98.

5 U.S. Department of Commerce, "1950 Census of Population: Advance Reports," *Publication No. 16* (July 1953): 2.

6 F. A. Steel, "The Cult of the Child," *Littel's Living Age* 237 (April-June 1903): 761; Catherine J. Ross, "Advocacy Movements in the Century of the Child," in Zigler, Kagan, and Klugman, eds., *Children, Families, and Government*, 171. Key's work, first published in 1900 in Swedish, was translated into English and published in 1909.

7 Lindenmeyer, *"A Right to Childhood,"* 253.

8 Dominique Marshall, "Children's Rights and Children's Action in International Relief and Domestic Welfare: The Work of Herbert Hoover between 1914 and 1950," *Journal of the History of Childhood and Youth* 3 (Fall 2008): 353–354, 378–380; Katherine B. Oettinger, "The Growth and Meaning of the White House Conference on Children and Youth," *Children* 7 (January-February 1960): 5; "Platform Recommendations and Pledge to Children," p. iii, box 9, Follow-Up Meeting file, WHC, EL.

9 Nicholas Sammond, *Babes in Tomorrowland: Walt Disney and the Making of the American Child, 1930–1960* (Durham, NC: Duke University Press, 2005), 362–363, 375; Julia Grant, *Raising Baby by the Book: The Education of American Mothers* (New Haven, CT: Yale University Press, 1998), 204; Peter N. Stearns, "Defining Happy Childhoods: Assessing a Recent Change," *Journal of the History of Children and Youth* 3 (Spring 2010): 176–177.

10 *White House Conference on Children in a Democracy, Washington, D.C., January 18–20, 1940* (Washington, DC: Superintendent of Documents, 1941), 43.

11 Marion Lyon Faegre, "Mental Health Begins at Home," White House Conference Leaflets, Series on Personality 1, 1930, box 1, folder 2, WHC, EL; "A Tentative Proposal regarding the Focus and Fact-Finding Activities of the Midcentury White House Conference on Children and Youth," p. 1, box 7, Background Material file, WHC, EL.

12 "A Tentative Proposal regarding the Focus and Fact-Finding Activities of the Midcentury White House Conference on Children and Youth," p. 1, box 7, Background Material file, WHC, EL.

13 "Minutes of Executive Committee Meeting, October 22, 1949," box 6, Midcentury White House Conference on Children and Youth file (1), WHC, EL.

14 *This Fabulous Century, 1950–1960* (New York: Time-Life Books, 1970), 25; "The 36-Hour War," *Life* 19 (November 19, 1945): 27.

15 May, *Homeward Bound*, 93; Laura McEnaney, *Civil Defense Begins at Home: Militarization Meets Everyday Life in the Fifties* (Princeton, NJ: Princeton University Press, 2000), 7; Phil Woods, "Reciprocal Paranoia: Reflections on the Atomic Era and the Cold War," in Bradley, ed., *Learning to Glow*, 63.

16 *Duck and Cover* film, 1950s exhibit, Museum, EL; Bo Jacobs, "Atomic Kids: Duck and Cover and Atomic Alert Teach American Children How to Survive Atomic Attack," *Film & History: An Interdisciplinary Journal of Film and Television Studies* 40 (Spring 2010): 25–44; National School Boards Association, *School Boards Plan for Disaster Problems*, pamphlet (Chicago: National School Boards Association, Inc., 1959), 9–10, 12.

17 Dave Webb to author, July 22, 2009; Woods, "Reciprocal Paranoia," 63; Austen Ken Kutscher, *Watching Walter Cronkite: Reflections on Growing Up in the 1950s and 1960s* (New York: Gordian Knot Books, 2009), 33.

18 May, *Homeward Bound*, 17; Kathryn Close, "Impressions of the White House Conference," *Children* 7 (May-June 1960): 86. In the preface to *Huck's Raft*, 3–4, Steven Mintz notes that the "modern ideal of a sheltered childhood" came into its own during the 1950s, but soon broke down during the postmodern era.

19 Harry S. Truman, "Address before the Midcentury White House Conference on Children and Youth, December 5, 1950," John T. Woolley and Gerhard Peters, The American Presidency Project online.

20 "History of Television," Federal Communications Commission official website; "Television Stations on the Air in 1948," and "Television, 1948–1949," in *The World Almanac and Book of Facts for 1949* (New York: New York World Telegram, 1949), 303.

21 Oettinger, "The Growth and Meaning of the White House Conference on Children and Youth," 3; Close, "Impressions of the White House Conference," 88, 90; Senate Judiciary Subcommittee Investigating Juvenile Delinquency, *Television and Juvenile Delinquency: Interim Report of the Subcommittee to Investigate Juvenile Delinquency*, 84th Cong., 1st sess. (Washington, DC: Government Printing Office, 1955), 44; "The Children's Hour," *Time* 64 (November 1, 1954): 64.

22 Close, "Impressions of the White House Conference," 88; Blanche Crippen, "Educational Television—Public Servant," *Children* 2 (January-February 1955): 22, 26.

23 *White House Conference on Children in a Democracy*, Ch. 4.

24 "Verbatim Discussion: Subcommittee on Guidelines for the 1965 Report to the Nation, October 17, 1963," pp. 9–10, box 287, Committee for Guidelines file (1), WHC, EL; Close, "Impressions of the White House Conference," 86.

25 "Mississippi Field Report," box 4, Mississippi file, and "Children and Youth: Democracy's Future—The Governor's Committee for Illinois on the Midcentury White House Conference on Children and Youth," box 2, Illinois file (1), WHC, EL; Lindenmeyer, *"A Right to Childhood,"* 256.

26 "Report on Children and Youth, 1950–1952," pp. 26–28, box 17, Publications file (2), and "Platform Recommendations and Pledge to Children," p. iv, box 9, Follow-Up Meeting file, WHC, EL; Close, "Impressions of the White House Conference," 84, 86, 90; Bess Furman, "Flemming Praises Youth Proposals," *New York Times*, April 2, 1960, p. 25.

27 Oettinger, "The Growth and Meaning of the White House Conference on Children and Youth," 3; "The 10th Year of Work: Interdepartmental Committee on Children and Youth, 1958," p. 21, box 195, Interdepartmental Committee on Children and Youth file (1), WHC, EL.

28 Close, "Impressions of the White House Conference," 90.

29 Everett M. Dirksen, "The Congressional Front," newsletter, January 29, 1946, Everett M. Dirksen Papers, Dirksen Congressional Center online; McCullough, *Truman*, 470.

30 "National Affairs," *Time* 50 (July 7, 1947): 13; May, *Homeward Bound*, 150–151; "Report of Governor's State Conference on Youth, October 18–19, 1948," p. 68, box 4, Minnesota file, WHC, EL.

31 "Moving Ahead for Children and Youth: Programs of the National Commission on Children and Youth, January 1949," pp. 9–11, box 7, Background Material file, and "Proposed Platform for Consideration by Delegates in Plenary Session, December 7, 1950," p. 7, box 7, Conference Material file, WHC, EL; McCullough, *Truman*, 468.

32 Robert J. Donovan, *Tumultuous Years: The Presidency of Harry S. Truman, 1949–1953* (New York: W. W. Norton, 1982), 127; Richard M. Flanagan, "The Housing Act of 1954: The Sea Change in National Urban Policy," *Urban Affairs Review* 33 (November 1997): 265–266; McCullough, *Truman*, 468; John Hope Franklin, *From Slavery to Freedom: A History of Negro Americans*, 3rd. ed. (New York: Vintage Books, 1967), 610.

33 "Verbatim Discussion: Subcommittee on Guidelines for the 1965 Report to the Nation," pp. 29–30, box 287, Committee for Guidelines file, WHC, EL; Edward A. Richards, ed., *Proceedings of the Midcentury Conference on Children and Youth* (Raleigh, NC: Heath Publications, 1951), 282; "Report of Governor's State Conference on Youth, October 18–19, 1948," p. 68, box 4, Minnesota file, WHC, EL; Roger Morris, *Richard Milhous Nixon: The Rise of an American Politician* (New York: Henry Holt, 1990), 650–651; Close, "Impressions of the White House Conference," 89.

34 Clifford E. Clark, Jr., "Ranch-House Suburbs: Ideals and Realities," in May, ed., *Recasting America*, 183; Frank Hobbs and Nicole Stoops, "Demographic Trends in the 20th Century," Special Reports, Series CENSR-4, U.S. Census Bureau (Washington, DC: Government Printing Office, 2002), 32–33; Margaret Mead and Frances Balgley Kaplan, eds., *American Women: The Report of the President's Commission on the Status of Women and Other Publications of the Commission* (New York: Charles Scribner's Sons, 1965), 80.

35 David Halberstam, *The Fifties* (New York: Villard Books, 1993), 135.

36 Clark, "Ranch-House Suburbs," 171, 183; Lewis Mumford, *The City in History* (New York: Harcourt, Brace, 1961), 486; William J. Levitt, "What! Live in a Levittown?" *Good Housekeeping* 147 (July 1958): 47, 175–176.

37 Cohen, *A Consumers' Republic*, 14. Chapter 5 of Cohen's book details the inequities of suburban home ownership, including lending practices. See also Franklin, *From Slavery to Freedom*, 610.

38 Stephanie Coontz, *The Way We Never Were: American Families and the Nostalgia Trap* (New York: Basic Books, 1992), 167; Louis I. Dublin, "Look on the Bright Side of Marriage: Some Facts and Figures concerning American Family Life," *Parents Magazine* 23 (December 1948): 68.

39 "Public Health, Nursing and Medical Social Work: Abstract," *Pediatrics* 1 (March 1, 1948): 429–432.

40 Stephen J. Spingarn to Clark M. Clifford, May 2, 1949, box 1578, President's Commission to Study Marriage and Divorce Law file, Official Files, Central Files, TL.

41 Robert W. Smuts, *Women and Work in America* (New York: Columbia University Press, 1959), 60; National Manpower Council, *Womanpower: A Statement by the National Manpower Council* (New York: Columbia University Press, 1957), 56, 315; Katherine G. Howard, "On Being a Woman," speech, 1957, p. 5, box 14, 1957 speech folder, Katherine G. Howard Papers, EL.

42 Florence Hollis, *Women in Marital Conflict: A Casework Study* (New York: Family Service Association of America, 1949), 86–94.

43 Joanne Meyerowitz, "Beyond *The Feminine Mystique*: A Reassessment of Post-

war Mass Culture, 1946–1958," in Meyerowitz, ed., *Not June Cleaver*, 230–232; May, *Homeward Bound*, 187.

44 Henry C. Lajewski, "Working Mothers and Their Arrangements for Care of Their Children," *Social Security Bulletin* 22 (August 1959): 1; "Remarks by the President, December 6, 1958," box 847, 156-A-7 file, Central Files, EL.

45 Close, "Impressions of the White House Conference," 88–89.

46 Dr. Benjamin Spock, *The Common Sense Book of Baby and Child Care* (New York: Duell, Sloan & Pearce, 1946), 40; Lois Wladie Hoffman, "Effects of Maternal Employment on the Child," p. 2, box 120, Effects on Children . . . Employment of the Mother Outside the Home file, WHC, EL; Governor's State Committee on Children and Youth, "Unmet Needs of Oregon's Children: A Special Report to the Staff of the 1960 White House Conference on Children and Youth, April 1959," box 229, Oregon Final State Report file (4), WHC, EL.

47 Jack Wiener, *Survey Methods for Determining the Need for Services to Children of Working Mothers* (Washington, DC: Department of Health, Education and Welfare, 1956), 3–4; S. Gray Garwood, Deborah Philips, Andrew Hartman, and Edward F. Zigler, "As the Pendulum Swings: Federal Agency Programs for Children," *American Psychologist* 44 (February 1989): 436.

48 Wiener, *Survey Methods*, 3–4; May, *Homeward Bound*, 58; "National Day Care Conference Planned," press release, November 9, 1959, box 192, Government Contributions file, and "Problems Affecting Children in Critical Defense Areas," p. 24, box 9, Federal Follow-Up file, WHC, EL; Questionnaire, cover letter, March 9, 1959, and "Joint Survey of Day Care Activities and Interest of National Organizations Announced by Children's Bureau and Women's Bureau, May 6, 1959," Records of the President's Committee on Migratory Labor, 1941–63, Bureau of Employment Security, box 12, folder 7, U.S. Children's Bureau, Record Group 102, National Archives and Records Administration, College Park, MD (hereinafter cited as Children's Bureau, RG 102, NARA).

49 "Joint Survey of Day Care Activities and Interest of National Organizations Announced by Children's Bureau and Women's Bureau, May 6, 1959," Records of the President's Committee on Migratory Labor, 1941–63, Children's Bureau, RG 102, NARA.

50 Press release, March 5, 1959, Office of Senator Jacob K. Javits, and "Day Care Assistance Act, Senate Bill 1286," box 120, folder 3, Workgroups file, WHC, EL; Lindenmeyer, *"A Right to Childhood,"* 254; Sonya Michel, *Children's Interests/Mothers' Rights: The Shaping of America's Child Care Policy* (New Haven, CT: Yale University Press, 1999), 232.

51 "President's Proclamation," 1; Dean W. Roberts, "Highlights of the Midcentury White House Conference on Children and Youth," *American Journal of Public Health* 41 (January 1951): 99; Betty Barton and Katherine D. Pringle, "Today's Children and Youth, I: As Viewed from the States," *Children* 7 (March-April 1960): 50.

52 Close, "Impressions of the White House Conference," 91; "Final Report of the Massachusetts Committee, September 1951," p. A-2, box 3, Massachusetts file (2), WHC, EL.

53 "Conference Interpretation, Report and Evaluation, 1960," box 265, Conference Interpretation History file, and Mary Ann Christoffersen to J. Douglas Knox, September 30, 1959, box 265, Celebrities file, and memo, Mrs. Joan Gaines to E. R. Gomberg and Mrs. Margaret K. Taylor, December 1, 1959, box 42, Danny Kaye's Participation at Conference file, WHC, EL.

54 Marilyn Irvin Holt, "Children as Topic No. 1," *Prologue* 42 (Summer 2010): 20; "Advisory Council on Youth Participation, Leadership Plan for Group Discussions," box 6, Advisory Council for Youth Participation file (1), and "Suggestions for Members of Youth Panels," box 42, Danny Kaye's Participation Conference file, WHC, EL; Close, "Impressions of the White House Conference," 84.

55 "National Midcentury Committee for Children and Youth, Inc.," memo, box 14, Two-Year Anniversary Conference, Dec. 1952 file, and "Project—1965 Report to the Nation, Narrative Description," 1–2, box 288, Miscellaneous file (1), and "Preliminary Summary. . . . 1965 Report. . . . March 21, 1963," box 287, Committee on Guidelines for the 1965 Report to the Nation file (2), and "The 10th Year of Work: Interdepartmental Committee on Children and Youth, 1958," box 195, Interdepartmental Committee on Children and Youth file (1), WHC, EL; Oettinger, "The Growth and Meaning of the White House Conference on Children and Youth," 7–8.

56 Close, "Impressions of the White House Conference," 91.

CHAPTER 2. EDUCATION AT MIDCENTURY

Epigraph: "Opening Address by Neil H. McElroy, Nov. 28, 1955," box 21, White House Conference Press Releases 1955 file, Hobby Papers, EL.

1 "Democratic Party Platform of 1948," "Democratic Party Platform of 1950," "Republican Party Platform of 1948," "Republican Platform of 1952," "Republican Platform of 1956," and Harry S. Truman, "Address before the Midcentury White House Conference on Children and Youth, December 5, 1950," John T. Woolley and Gerhard Peters, The American Presidency Project online; Margaret Truman, *Harry S. Truman* (New York: William Morrow, 1973), 48; Dwight D. Eisenhower, *At Ease: Stories I Tell to Friends* (New York: Doubleday, 1967), 82.

2 Clarence Hines, "Elementary Education Today," *Current History* 42 (July 1961): 32–40; Jones, *Great Expectations*, 49.

3 "To the Patrons, Students and Teachers of American Schools," box 127, Educational Matters, 25 file, President's Personal File, Central Files, TL.

4 Truman to Irvin R. Kuenzli, American Federation of Teachers, August 2, 1946, and Truman to Glenn E. Snow, National Education Association, July 8, 1948, box 127, Educational Matters, 25 file, President's Personal File, Central Files, TL; Watson B. Miller to Truman, January 9, 1947, box 1261, Message to Congress on Education file, Official Files, Central Files, TL; Harry S. Truman, *Memoirs of Harry S. Truman: Years of Trial and Hope*, vol. 2 (Garden City, NY: Doubleday, 1956), 207, 485–486; Harry S. Truman, "Message to the Special Session of the 80th Congress, July 27, 1948," John T. Woolley and Gerhard Peters, The American Presidency Project online.

5 Hope Chamberlain, *A Minority of Members: Women in the U.S. Congress* (New

York: Praeger, 1973), 201; Irving Bernstein, *Promises Kept: John F. Kennedy's New Frontier* (New York: Oxford University Press, 1991), 222–223; Ronald L. Heinemann, *Harry Byrd of Virginia* (Charlottesville: University Press of Virginia, 1996), 293; McCullough, *Truman*, 629; Anthony Champagne, *Congressman Sam Rayburn* (New Brunswick, NJ: Rutgers University Press, 1984), 142.

6 Everett M. Dirksen, "The Congressional Front," newsletter, October 31, 1942, Everett M. Dirksen Papers, Dirksen Congressional Center online; "A National Meeting on Schools Rings the Bell for Federal Aid," clipping, *Life* (July 1955), box 21, Press Releases 1955 file, Hobby Papers, EL; Committee for the White House Conference on Education, "A Report to the President, April 6, 1956," p. 131, box 547, White House Conference on Education file, Central Files, EL; Hazel Davis and Madaline Kinter Remmlein, "Teachers' Salaries, Pensions, and Retirement Pay," *Review of Educational Research* 19 (June 1949): 240; Robert M. Segal, " A New Look: the Economics of the Profession," *American Bar Association Journal* 43 (September 1957): 792.

7 Alan Grant, "The Sixth Grade," *Life* 33 (November 17, 1952): 145, 147; Charles G. Mortimer, president, General Foods, to Eisenhower, May 22 and June 5, 1958, and Eisenhower to Charles G. Mortimer, May 29, 1958, box 547, 111-Co1, 1958 file, Central Files, EL; George N. Shuster, "Goals of American Education," *Current History* 41 (July 1961): 1–4.

8 "Television Presentation," script, box 45, Television Presentation file, Hobby Papers, EL; Craig Hosmer to Homer Gruenther, February 8, 1954, and Arthur S. Flemming to Homer Gruenther, March 5, 1954, box 548, Federal Aid to Education file (1), Central Files, EL; "A National Meeting on Schools Rings the Bell for Federal Aid."

9 Eisenhower to Mrs. Clara Swinson, September 7, 1957, box 547, 111-C-1, 1957 file, Central Files, EL; Eisenhower to Governors, September 20, 1954, box 19, White House Conference on Education Agenda, December 2, 1954 file, Hobby Papers, EL.

10 Paul E. Wilson, *A Time to Lose: Representing Kansas in* Brown v. Board of Education (Lawrence: University Press of Kansas, 1995), 209, 244, notes 13–19; "Second Topic: In What Ways Can We Organize Our School System More Efficiently and Economically?" box 20, White House Conference on Education, Oct. 6, 1955, Meeting file, Hobby Papers, EL.

11 "Suggested 'Homework' for the Participants in the White House Conference on Education," box 20, Proposed Agenda/Proposed Homework file, Hobby Papers, El.

12 U.S. Department of Commerce, "1950 Census Population: Advance Reports," *Publication No. 14* (July 1953), 1, 4.

13 *Freedom of Communications: Final Report of the Committee on Commerce, United States Senate . . . , Part III: The Joint Appearances of Senator John F. Kennedy and Vice President Nixon and Other 1960 Campaign Presentations, 87th Congress, 1st Sess. Senate Report No. 994, Part 3* (Washington, DC: Government Printing Office, 1962), 2.

14 Garwood, Philips, Hartman, and Zigler, "As the Pendulum Swings: Federal

Agency Programs for Children," 436; "Editorial," *California Medicine* 78 (April 1953): 313; McCullough, *Truman*, 531.

15 Susan Levine, *School Lunch Politics: The Surprising History of America's Favorite Welfare Program* (Princeton, NJ: Princeton University Press, 2008), 46; Marilyn Irvin Holt, *Linoleum, Better Babies, and the Modern Farm Woman, 1890–1930* (Albuquerque: University of New Mexico Press, 1995; reprint, Lincoln: University of Nebraska Press, 2005), 120–122.

16 M.I. to author, October 2008; Josephine Martin and Charlotte Oakley, *Managing Child Nutrition Programs: Leadership for Excellence*, 2nd. ed. (Sudbury, MA: Jones & Bartlett Publishers, 2008), 86–87; Jean Fairfax, "Summary of Information from the U.S. Department of Agriculture Officials," box 285, National School Lunch Program file, WHC, EL.

17 Fairfax, "Summary of Information from the U.S. Department of Agriculture Officials"; Martin and Oakley, *Managing Child Nutrition Programs*, 87, 108; Memo, Betty Barton to Oveta Culp Hobby, January 6, 1955, box 25, Interdepartmental Committee on Children and Youth file, Hobby Papers, EL.

18 Eisenhower, "State of the Union Message, 1955," box 34, State of the Union Message, 1955 file, Central Files, EL; Memo, Clint Pace to Members of the White House Conference on Education Committee, April 27, 1955, box 20, Meeting file, Hobby Papers, EL.

19 "We Confer to Reach Long-Range Remedy," *Life* 39 (September 26, 1955): 36; "Television Presentation," script, box 45, Television Presentation file, Hobby Papers, EL.

20 "Citizens 'Workbook' for Educational Conferences," pamphlet, box 19, White House Conference on Education file, Hobby Papers, EL; "Suggestions for State and White House Conference on Education," p. 547, White House Conference on Education file (1), Central Files, EL; Paula S. Fass, "The Child-Centered Family? New Rules in Postwar America," in Fass and Grossberg, eds., *Reinventing Childhood after World War II*, 6–7.

21 Rudolf Flesch, *Why Johnny Can't Read: And What You Can Do about It* (New York: Harper & Brothers, 1955), 132–133; Samuel L. Blumenfeld, *N.E.A.: The Trojan Horse in American Education* (Boise, ID: Paradigm, 1984), 84, 120.

22 Roswell B. Perkins to Congressman Victor A. Know, June 24, 1955, box 19, White House Conference on Education file, Hobby Papers, EL; Memo, Charles F. Willis, Jr., to T. P. Scantlebury, November 23, 1954, box 547, White House Conference on Education file (1), Central Files, EL.

23 Eleanor Roosevelt, "My Day," December 2, 1955, Eleanor Roosevelt Papers Project online.

24 Committee for the White House Conference on Education, "A Report to the President, April 6, 1956," p. 548, box 547, White House Conference on Education file, Central Files, EL.

25 "A Report to the President, April 6, 1956," p. 548, box 547, White House Conference on Education file, Central Files, EL; "Platform Adopted by the Midcentury Conference on Children and Youth," p. 3, box 9, Follow-Up Meeting file, and "Directory of Sections and Work Groups," box 6, Midcentury White House

Conference on Children and Youth file, 1950, and Marion Lyon Faegre, "How Children Differ Mentally," leaflet, 1930, box 1, folder 1, and Marion Lyon Faegre, "Mental Health Begins at Home," leaflet, 1930, box 1, folder 3, WHC, EL; "Standards of Child Health, Education and Social Welfare," *U.S. Children's Bureau Publication 287* (1942): 17.

26 Kriste Lindenmeyer, *The Greatest Generation Grows Up: American Childhood in the 1930s* (Chicago: Ivan R. Dee, 2005), 125; "Summary of Discussion Groups of Mid-Decade Conference on Children and Youth," pp. 3–4, box 285, Closing Session file, WHC, EL.

27 Sloan Wilson, "Public Schools Are Better Than You Think," p. 3, clipping, *Harper's Magazine* (September 1955), box 21, Newsletters and Press Releases file, Hobby Papers, EL.

28 Jones, *Great Expectations*, 54; "A National Meeting on Schools Rings the Bell for Federal Aid"; Nichols, *A Matter of Justice*, 114–115; Bernstein, *Promises Kept*, 223.

29 "Federal Education Policy and the States, 1945–2009," 10, States' Impact on Federal Education Project, 2009, New York State Archives, online; Tyler Abell, ed., *Drew Pearson Diaries, 1949–1959* (New York: Holt, Rinehart and Winston, 1974), 356.

30 Sandra Adams Curry and Philip H. Hatlen, "Meeting the Unique Educational Needs of Visually Impaired Pupils through Appropriate Placement," *Journal of Visual Impairment and Blindness* 10 (April 2007): 237; "Federal Education Policy and the States, 1945–2009," 11, New York State Archives, online.

31 "A National Meeting on Schools Rings the Bell for Federal Aid"; "A Report to the President, April 6, 1956," p. 124, box 547, White House Conference on Education file, Central Files, EL.

32 "A National Meeting on Schools Rings the Bell for Federal Aid"; Daniel D. Holt, "Desegregation of the U.S. Armed Forces," 9–10, paper, Civil Rights Conference, Central Missouri State University, Kansas City, MO, March 2004.

33 Nichols, *A Matter of Justice*, 44–45.

34 Ibid; Milton S. Katz and Susan B. Tucker, "A Pioneer in Civil Rights: Ester Brown and the South Park Desegregation Case of 1948," *Kansas History* 18 (Winter 1995–1996): 240–243.

35 Nichols, *A Matter of Justice*, 56.

36 "A Message to the American People," ca. 1956, box 897, Racial Affairs file, President's Personal File, Central Files, EL; John A. Kirk, *Redefining the Color Line: Black Activism in Little Rock, Arkansas, 1940–1970* (Gainesville: University Press of Florida, 2002), 86, 87–88; J. Harvie Wilkinson, III, *Harry Byrd and the Changing Face of Virginia Politics, 1945–1966* (Charlottesville: University Press of Virginia, 1968), 113, 119.

37 Julie Nixon Eisenhower, *Pat Nixon: The Untold Story* (New York: Simon & Schuster, 1986), 170; Marilyn Irvin Holt, *Mamie Doud Eisenhower: The General's First Lady* (Lawrence: University Press of Kansas, 2007), 121. For letters to Eisenhower and newspaper clippings, see box 551, Eisenhower Children and School Integration Problem file, President's Personal File, Central Files, EL.

38 Francis Moore to Eisenhower, October 7, 1958, box 547, 111-C-1, 1958 file, and meeting memo, October 8, 1958, and Rocco C. Siciliano to Francis Moore, October 9, 1958, box 547, 111-C-1, 1958 file, Central Files, EL.

39 Kirk, *Redefining the Color Line*, 108–111.

40 Daisy Bates, *The Long Shadow of Little Rock: A Memoir* (New York: David McKay, 1962), 74–79; "Jay's Statement," p. 2, typescript, box 694, Blind file, President's Personal File, Central Files, EL.

41 Governor's Advisory Council on Children and Youth, "Minnesota Report to the White House Conference on Children and Youth, March 27–April 2, 1960," p. 3, box 78, Minnesota Reports and Publications file, WHC, EL.

42 Kenneth R. Philip, "John Collier, 1933–45," p. 276, and Patricia K. Ourada, "Dillon Seymour Myer, 1950–53," p. 296, and Patricia K. Ourada, "Glenn L. Emmons, 1953–61," p. 303, in Robert M. Kvasnicka and Herman J. Viola, eds., *The Commissioners of Indian Affairs, 1824–1977* (Lincoln: University of Nebraska Press, 1979); "Program of the Department of the Interior in the Field of Children and Youth, Bureau of Indian Affairs," p. 1, box 195, Interdepartmental Committee on Children and Youth file (6), WHC, EL.

43 "N.C. Indians Stage Sit-In at White School," clipping, box 1165, folder 147, General File, Central Files, EL.

44 "Executive Order Establishing the President's Committee on Migratory Labor," box 1234, President's Commission on Migratory Labor file, Official Files, Central Files, TL; "White House Statement Announcing the Establishment of the President's Commission on Migratory Labor, June 1950," John T. Woolley and Gerhard Peters, The American Presidency Project online; Elizabeth Sutton, "The World of the Migrant Child," p. 2, clipping, *Educational Leadership* (January 1957), and Florence M. Kelley, "Sweatshops in the Sun," p. 12, pamphlet (1952), box 196, Migrant Workers, Non-Government file (1), WHC, EL.

45 "Colorado State Department of Education . . . Understanding Children of Migrant Farm Workers," p. 1, and "Summary Statement—The Migrant and the Community," p. 1, and Mrs. I. H. Teilman, "For Migrant Families," p. 1, clipping, *The Child* (November 1953), box 196, Migrant Workers, General file, WHC, EL; Holt, *Linoleum, Better Babies, and the Modern Farm Woman*, 186–187; Dennis Nodin Valdés, "Settlers, Sojourners, and Proletarians: Social Formation in the Great Plains Sugar Beet Industry, 1890–1940," in Manuel G. Gonzales and Cynthia M. Gonzales, eds., *En Aquel Entonces: Readings in Mexican-American History* (Indianapolis: Indiana University Press, 2000), 120–121; Varden Fuller, "No Work Today! The Plight of America's Migrants," *Public Affairs Pamphlet No. 190* (January 1954): 3–4.

46 "Democratic Party Platform of 1952," John Woolley and Gerhard Peters, The American Presidency Project online.

47 "Fresno County Project—The Educational Program for Migrant Children, December 6, 1954," pp. 4–5, box 196, Migrant Workers, General file, WHC, EL; "Detailed Report of Field Visit regarding Labor in Arizona, November 1–5, 1959," p. 1, box 12, folder 7, and Cyrus H. Karraker, "A Report on the Agricultural Seasonal Laborers of Colorado and California, September 1961," p. 12, Box

42, folder 5, Records of the President's Committee on Migratory Labor, 1941–1963, Children's Bureau, RG102, NARA.

48 "Detailed Report of Field Visit regarding Labor in Arizona, November 1–5, 1959"; Records of the President's Committee on Migratory Labor, 1941–63, Children's Bureau, RG102, NARA; Kelley, "Sweatshops in the Sun," p. 12, and Sutton, "The World of the Migrant Child."

49 Gerald P. Burns, "Higher Education Today," *Current History* 41 (July 1961): 28.

50 "President's Views on Russia's Satellite," *U.S. News and World Report* 43 (October 18, 1957): 118; "How U.S. Lost Satellite Race: Charges and Countercharges Begin to Fly," *U.S. News and World Report* 43 (October 18, 1957): 18; Paul Dickson, *Sputnik: The Shock of the Century* (New York: Walker, 2001), 226; Alfred Steinberg, *Sam Johnson's Boy: A Close-Up of the President from Texas* (New York: Macmillan, 1968), 479.

51 "The Golden Youth of Communism," *Life* 40 (March 5, 1956): 36; Dickson, *Sputnik*, 225–226, 229.

52 Dickson, *Sputnik*, 226–227.

53 Randall B. Woods, *LBJ: Architect of American Ambition* (New York: Free Press, 2006), 337.

54 "Draft Text of Radio Talk by the Secretary Reviewing Administration's Proposals in Education," p. 5, box 39, Radio Addresses 1955 file, Hobby Papers, EL.

55 Woods, *LBJ: Architect of American Ambition*, 337.

56 For Rocket Boys, see Homer H. Hickam, Jr., *Rocket Boys: A Memoir* (New York: Delacorte Press, 1998).

57 Jim Wright, *Balance of Power: Presidents and Congress from the Era of McCarthy to the Age of Gingrich* (Atlanta: Turner Publishing, 1996), 64–65.

58 *Freedom of Communications: Final Report of the Committee on Commerce, United States Senate . . . , Part III*, 1–3.

CHAPTER 3. THE DELINQUENT, THE DEPENDENT,
AND THE ORPHANED

Epigraph: "Remarks by the President, December 6, 1958," box 847, Conference file, WHC, EL.

1 "Orphans in the United States: Number and Living Arrangements," *Child Welfare* (January 1951), clipping, box 142, Child Welfare League of America file, WHC, EL.

2 Gilbert Geis, "Juvenile Gangs," p. 11, box 288, President's Committee for Juvenile Delinquency and Youth Crime file, WHC, EL; "President Voices His Faith in Youth," *New York Times*, March 28, 1960, p. 23.

3 Eisenhower to Nettie Stover Jackson, February 27, 1905, in Daniel D. Holt and James W. Leyerzapf, eds., *Eisenhower: The Prewar Diaries and Selected Papers, 1905–1941* (Baltimore, MD: Johns Hopkins University Press, 1998), 4.

4 Paul Douglas, "Democracy Can't Live in These Houses," *Collier's* 9 (July 1949): 50.

5 "Juvenile Crime: Is Your Boy Safe?" *Newsweek* 42 (November 9, 1953): 28–30; Marjorie Rittwagen, "Child Criminals Are My Job," *Saturday Evening Post* 226

(March 27, 1954): 19–21; "Delinquency: Big and Bad," *Newsweek* 42 (November 30, 1953): 30. Harrison E. Salisbury wrote the May 1958 *Time* series and later used that material to write *The Shook-Up Generation* (New York: Fawcett, 1962).

6 "Statement Opening Juvenile Delinquency Conference, June 28, 1954," box 40, Juvenile Delinquency Conference file, Hobby Papers, EL; "All Our Children," *Newsweek* 42 (November 9, 1953): 28; Gilbert Geis, "Juvenile Delinquency," box 288, President's Committee on Juvenile Delinquency and Youth Crime file (1965), WHC, EL.

7 Mazie P. Rappaport, "Prostitution, Crime and Juvenile Delinquency," *Journal of Social Hygiene* 31 (December 1945): 586–589.

8 Gilbert, *A Cycle of Outrage*, 27; Edith Abbott, "The Civil War and the Crime Wave of 1865–70," *Social Services Review* 1 (June 1927): 219; Tom C. Clark to Truman, December 7, 1945, box 650, OF 117-A file, Official Files, Central Files, TL.

9 Truman to Tom C. Clark, December 17, 1945, box 650, OF 117-A file, Official Files, Central Files, TL; "Prevention and Control of Juvenile Delinquency: A Proclamation, January 27, 1948," box 650, Juvenile Delinquency (1) file, Office files, Central Files, TL; "Children's Bureau," p. SSA-27, HEW-Children's Bureau file (1), WHC, EL; Linda Mar, "Federal Youth Corrections Act: YCA Treatment Not Required during Unexpired Term of YCA Inmate Sentenced to Consecutive Adult Term," *Journal of Criminal Law and Criminology* 73 (Winter 1982): 1654.

10 Sealander, *The Failed Century of the Child*, 21–22; U.S. Department of Commerce, *1950 Census Population: Institutional Population, Special Reports* (Washington, DC: Government Printing Office, 1953), 2C-6, 2C-11; "Statement Opening Juvenile Delinquency Conference, June 28, 1954," box 40, Juvenile Delinquency Conference file, Hobby Papers, EL.

11 Gilbert, *A Cycle of Outrage*, 13, 75.

12 J. Frederick MacDonald, "'Hot Jazz,' The Jitterbug, and Misunderstandings: The Generation Gap in Swing, 1935–1945," *Popular Music and Society* 2 (Fall 1972): 43; George Lipsitz, "Land of a Thousand Dances: Youth, Minorities, and the Rise of Rock and Roll," in May, ed., *Recasting America*, 267, 274; Glenn C. Altschuler, *All Shook Up: How Rock 'n' Roll Changed America* (New York: Oxford University Press, 2003), 6, 24, 173.

13 Jack Lait and Lee Mortimer, *U.S.A. Confidential* (New York: Crown, 1952), 37–38.

14 "Introduction by Estes Kefauver" in Dale Kramer and Madeline Karr, *Teenage Gangs* (New York: Henry Holt, 1951), vii; Eisenhower to Senator Hendrickson, November 19, 1953, box 643, OF 126-A-2 file, Central Files, EL.

15 Senate Judiciary Subcommittee to Investigate Juvenile Delinquency, *Juvenile Delinquency (Indians): Hearings before the Subcommittee to Investigate Juvenile Delinquency*, 83rd Cong., 2nd sess. (Washington, DC: Government Printing Office, 1954); Senate Judiciary Subcommittee to Investigate Juvenile Delinquency, *Juvenile Delinquency (California): Hearings before the Subcommittee to Investigate Juvenile Delinquency*, 83rd Cong., 2nd sess. (Washington, DC: Government

Printing Office, 1954), 338–340; "Delinquency: Big and Bad," 30; "Statement of Oveta Culp Hobby before the Senate Judiciary Subcommittee Investigating Juvenile Delinquency," box 51, Senate Judiciary Committee file, Hobby Papers, EL.

16 Senate Judiciary Subcommittee to Investigate Juvenile Delinquency, *Juvenile Delinquency (Comic Books): Hearings before the Subcommittee on the Judiciary*, 83rd Cong., 2nd sess. (Washington, DC: Government Printing Office, 1954), 1, 75–76.

17 Senate Judiciary Subcommittee to Investigate Juvenile Delinquency, *Comic Books and Juvenile Delinquency: Interim Report of the Committee on the Judiciary, Report No. 62*, 84th Cong., 1st sess. (Washington, DC: Government Printing Office, 1955), 10–12; Marilyn Graalfs, "Violence in Comic Books," in Otto N. Larsen, ed., *Violence and the Media* (New York: Harper & Row, 1968), 91–96; Gilbert, *A Cycle of Outrage*, 103–108.

18 Mintz, *Huck's Raft*, 292; "History of Comic Book Censorship, Part I," citing David Hajdu, *The 10-Cent Plague: The Great Comic Book Scare and How It Changed America* (New York: Farrar, Straus and Giroux, 2008), Comic Book Legal Defense Fund, 2012, online.

19 "Sprawling and Largely Uncoordinated Programs," memo, Oveta Culp Hobby to Eisenhower, July 30, 1953, box 643, OF 126-A-2 file, Central Files, EL; Edward E. Schwartz, "Counting Delinquent Children," *Children* 1 (November–December 1954): 228.

20 Dwight D. Eisenhower, "State of the Union Message, 1955," p. 12, box 304, State of the Union Message file, Central Files, EL.

21 David F. Musto, "Drug Policy: The American Evolution," in Zigler, Kagan, and Klugman, eds., *Children, Families, and Government*, 373–381; Mayor LaGuardia's Committee on Marijuana, *The Marijuana Problem in the City of New York* (Lancaster PA: Jacques Cattell Press, 1944; reprint, Metuchen, NJ: Scarecrow Press, 1973); Daniel D. Holt, *Kansas Bureau of Investigation, 1939–1989* (Topeka, KS: Kansas Bureau of Investigation, 1990), 36.

22 Victor L. Anfuso to Eisenhower, March 24, 1955, box 643, OF 126-A-2 file, Central Files, EL; "Prohibition Is Not the Answer," *American Journal of Public Health* 46 (August 1956): 1027–1028. Hoover's speech, provided by NBC News Archives, can be viewed online at the C-Span Video Library.

23 "Orphans in the United States: Number and Living Arrangements," *Child Welfare* (January 1951), clipping, box 142, Child Welfare League of America file, WHC, EL; "Trends in Data of Special Interest to the Children's Bureau, January 1959," p. 14, box 194, HEW-Children's Bureau file (12), WHC, EL; "Foster Care, 1956," p. 5, box 193, HEW-Children's Bureau file (5), WHC, EL.

24 Richard B. McKenzie, "Preface," Richard B. McKenzie, ed., *Home Away from Home: The Forgotten History of Orphanages* (New York: Encounter Books, 2009), xvii–ix, xvi.

25 "Platform Recommendations and Pledge to Children," p. 4, box 9, Follow-Up Materials file, WHC, EL; "The Children's Charter of President Hoover's White House Conference on Child Health and Protection, 1930," *Journal of the History of Childhood and Youth* 3 (Fall 2008): 378, Appendix 4.

26 New Mexico Department of Public Welfare, *Annual Report, Fiscal Year Ending June 30, 1951* (Santa Fe: New Mexico Department of Public Welfare, 1952), 42–43.

27 "Children and Youth: Democracy's Future—The Governor's Committee for Illinois on the Midcentury, 1951," box 2, Illinois file (1), WHC, EL; "Delaware's Children at Midcentury, November 1950," box 10, Miscellaneous Publications file (2), WHC, EL; "Service for Children Outside Their Own Homes: A Report of the Michigan Youth Commission, November 1953," box 4, Michigan file (2), WHC, EL.

28 Duncan Lindsey and Paul H. Stuart, "Orphanages in History and the Modern Child Welfare Setting: An Overview," in McKenzie, ed., *Home Away from Home*, 8–9.

29 Burton Z. Sokoloff, "Antecedents of American Adoption," *The Future of Children* 3 (Spring 1993): 20; "Proceedings of Wisconsin's 3rd Governor's Conference on Children and Youth, April 1953," p. 14, box 5, Wisconsin file (2), WHC, EL; "Texas: A Report to the White House Conference," pp. 17–18, box 5, Texas file (1), WHC, EL; "Missouri's Children and Youth at the Midcentury, March 1951," pp. 66–67, box 10, Miscellaneous Publications file (1), WHC, EL; Harry S. Truman, "Address before the Midcentury White House Conference on Children and Youth, December 5, 1950," John T. Woolley and Gerhard Peters, The American Presidency Project online; C. O. Wright, "At Mid-Century . . . Where Stands the Child," box 3, Kansas file (2), WHC, EL; Margaret A. Thornhill, "Unprotected Adoptions," *Children* 2 (September-October 1955): 180.

30 Dianne Creagh, "Science, Social Work, and Bureaucracy: Cautious Developments in Adoption and Foster Care, 1930–1969," in Lori Askeland, ed., *Children and Youth in Adoption, Orphanages, and Foster Care* (Westport, CT: Greenwood Press, 2006), 37–39.

31 "Adoption of Children, 1953," p. 7, box 197, Individual Authors file, WHC, EL; Mary Stanton, "The Citizens Adoption Committee of Los Angeles County, 1952," pp. 5, 13, box 2, California file (10), WHC, EL.

32 "Adoption of Children, 1953," p. 7, and Clark E. Vincent, "Unwed Mothers and the Adoption Market: Part 1—Psychological and Familial Factors," pp. 1–3, box 197, Individual Authors file, WHC, EL.

33 Lindenmeyer, *"A Right to Childhood,"* 256; Sharon Skolnick and Manny Skolnick, *Where Courage Is Like a Wild Horse: The World of an Indian Orphanage* (Lincoln: University of Nebraska Press, 1997), 136.

34 "Children in a Changing World: White House Conference on Children and Youth, 1960," p. 40, pamphlet, box 195, Interdepartmental Committee on Children and Youth file (4), WHC, EL; David Fanshel, *Far from the Reservation: The Transracial Adoption of American Indian Children* (Metuchen, NJ; Scarecrow Press, 1972), ix, 24, 33–34; Marc Mannes, "Factors and Events Leading to the Passage of the Indian Child Welfare Act," *Child Welfare* 74 (January/February 1995): 267; "South Dakota Report to the 1960 White House Conference on Children and Youth," box 106, South Dakota—State Reports file, WHC, EL; "Statement by the Bureau of Indian Affairs for the 1965 Report to the Nation Being

Made by the National Committee on Children and Youth," pp. 2–3, box 288, folder 14, WHC, EL.

35 American Merchant Marine at War, website, citing excerpts from *Mast Magazine*, July, September, December 1948.

36 Secretary of State George C. Marshall, "Testimony on Admitting Displaced Persons to the United States, July 16, 1947," in *U.S. Congress, House of Representatives, Permitting Admission of 400,000 Displaced Persons into the United States: Hearing before Subcommittee on Immigration and Naturalization* (Washington, DC: Government Printing Office, 1947), 503–504.

37 Ibid.; George L. Warren, "Problems of Financing European Migration," *Department of State Bulletin* 33 (August 22, 1955): 308–310.

38 "Law Change Urged to Admit Refugees, *New York Times*, April 2, 1947, p. 11; "The Congress," *Time* 50 (July 7, 1947): 13.

39 Don F. Holiman to Truman, June 11, 1946, box 650, Juvenile Delinquency file (1), Official Files, Central Files, TL; "The Congress," 13.

40 "Statement of the President upon Signing the Displaced Persons Act, June 25, 1948," John T. Woolley and Gerhard Peters, The American Presidency Project online; Harry N. Rosenfield Oral History, typescript, 83, 94, 126, TL; Leonard Dinnerstein, "The United States and Displaced Persons," in Yisreal Gutman and Avital Saf, eds., *She'arit Hapleta 1944–1948, Rehabilitation and Political Struggle, Proceedings of the Sixth Yad Vashem International Historical Conference* (Jerusalem: Yad Vashem, 1990), 357–363.

41 Michael J. Ybarra, *Washington Gone Crazy: Senator Pat McCarran and the Great Communist Hunt* (Hanover, NH: Steerforth Press, 2004), 3, 460, 469.

42 Alma R. Bloch to Harry N. Rosenfield, February 17, 1950, and John Foster Dulles to H. J. L'Heureux, October 28, 1949, Orphan Correspondence files, Record Group 278, National Archives and Records Administration, College Park, MD (hereinafter cited as Orphan Correspondence, RG 278, NARA).

43 Interdepartmental Committee for Children and Youth, *Programs of the Federal Government Affecting Children and Youth* (Washington, DC: Government Printing Office, 1951), 68.

44 Evelyn Rauch to ___, September 10, 1951, and ___ to John Foster Dulles, October 15, 1949, and ___ to Truman, July 18, 1950, box 1, Orphan Correspondence, RG 278, NARA. The names of correspondents were redacted by the U.S. State Department during Freedom of Information request review.

45 Scott McLeod, "First Semi-Annual Report of the Administrator of the Refugee Relief Act of 1953," pp. 1–2, 21, and "Orphans," p. 14, box 578, Displaced Persons file, 1954 (1), Central Files, EL; Hugh Gibson, "Migration from Western Europe under the Intergovernmental Committee for European Migration," *Department of State Bulletin* 29 (July 27, 1953): 117; Thurston B. Morton, "The U.S. Program for Refugee Relief," *Department of State Bulletin* 33 (October 10, 1955): 562–563.

46 White House Press Release, October 26, 1956, box 843, Children and Child Welfare file (1), Central Files, EL; Scott McLeod, "Fourth Semi-Annual Report of the Administrator of the Refugee Relief Act of 1953," p. 10, box 578, Displaced Persons file, 1955, Central Files, EL.

47 Robert Frank Futrell, *The United States Air Force in Korea, 1950–1953* (New York: Duell, Sloan and Pearce, 1961), 250; "Entertaining Field Will Aid Korea," *New York Times*, July 26, 1953, p. 37; "Missouri Crew Becomes 'Papa' to a Korea Boy," *New York Times*, April 5, 1953, p. 7; "Orphan Leaves for US," *New York Times*, May 25, 1953, p. 3.

48 Creagh, "Science, Social Work, and Bureaucracy," 39, and Elizabeth Bartholet, "International Adoption," 64, in Askeland, ed., *Children and Youth in Adoption, Orphanages, and Foster Care*; "Annual Report of the Interdepartmental Committee on Children and Youth, July 1, 1954—June 30, 1955," p. 4, box 25, Interdepartmental Committee on Children and Youth file, Hobby Papers, EL; Eleana Kim, "The Origins of Korean Adoption: Cold War Geopolitics and Intimate Diplomacy," 6–7, U.S.-Korea Institute at SAIS, Working Paper Series, 2009, online.

49 Creagh, "Science, Social Work, and Bureaucracy," 39; "Pearl Buck Meets New Adopted Girl," *New York Times*, July 19, 1958, p. 16; "Harry Holt and a Heart-full of Children," *Reader's Digest* 69 (October 1955): 67–70; "Good Samaritan of Korea," *American Mercury* 84 (October 1955): 84–88; "Unwanted Find a Home," *Look* 20 (October 30, 1955): 106–108.

50 Associated Press clipping, box 12, Adoption K file, and Kansas, Frank Carlson file, and Application Letters, boxes 3, 21, 22, 23, 24, 25, Offers of Adoption files, The President's Committee for Hungarian Refugee Relief Records, EL.

51 For references to Hoover's response to child relocation to the United States, see Homer Folks to Louis Strauss, April 17, 1919, American Relief Administration, Paris office letter to Folks, April 19, 1919, and American Relief Administration, Paris Office letter to Major F. K. Heath, April 26, 1919, American Relief Administration, European Unit, Records, 1919–1923, Hoover Institution, Stanford University, Palo Alto, CA.

52 Carlos Eire, *Waiting for Snow in Havana: Confessions of a Cuban Boy* (New York: Free Press, 2003), 270.

53 Ibid., 344; Robert M. Levine and Moisés Asis, *Cuban Miami* (New Brunswick, NJ: Rutgers University Press, 2000), 22, 24–27; "A U.S.-Cuban Airlift of Precious Cargo: Children," Morning Edition, National Public Radio, December 31, 2010, typescript, online.

54 Memo, Arthur Flemming to James M. Lambie, Jr., ca. 1957, box 29, White House file (2), Arthur S. Flemming Papers, EL.

55 Ibid.; "Bureau of Old-Age and Survivors Insurance," box 192, HEW file (2), WHC, EL; "Preliminary Statement—South Dakota," box 106, South Dakota Reports file, WHC, EL.

56 Timothy A. Hacsi, "Orphanages as a National Institution: History and Its Lessons," in McKenzie, ed., *Home Away from Home*, 229.

CHAPTER 4. A HEALTHIER GENERATION

Epigraph: Truman to Dr. V. A. Getting, October 29, 1949, box 575, Department of National Health (proposed) file, Official Files, Central Files, TL.

1 Oscar R. Ewing Oral History, transcript, pp. 233–234, TL.

2 Leonard W. Mayo, "Directions in Child Welfare Progress," *Children* 2 (July–August 1955): 149; Janis, "Health Policy for Children," 355.

3 Memorandum for the President, October 1958, and press release, October 16, 1958, box 843, Children and Child Welfare file (1), Central Files, EL. For the Better Baby Movement, see Holt, *Linoleum, Better Babies, and the Modern Farm Woman*, Ch. 4. For the World War II program, see Lindenmeyer, *"A Right to Childhood,"* 237–246.

4 Mordecai Lee, *Congress vs. the Bureaucracy: Muzzling Agency Public Relations* (Norman: University of Oklahoma Press, 2011), 177; Truman, *Memoirs . . . Years of Trial and Hope*, 207; McCullough, *Truman*, 473–474, 532, 642; "Special Message to the Congress Recommending a Comprehensive Health Program, November 19, 1945," John Woolley and Gerhard Peters, The American Presidency Project online.

5 Bremmer, Robert H., ed., *Children and Youth in America: A Documentary History*, vol. 2 (Cambridge, MA: Harvard University Press, 1971), 1016–1020.

6 McCullough, *Truman*, 473–474, 532; Ewing, Oral History, p. 178, TL.

7 Dr. Channing Frothingham, Chairman, Committee for the Nation's Health, to Truman, March 21, 1946, and Truman to Dr. Frothingham, March 25, 1946, box 552, file 2506, President's Personal File, Central Files, TL; "President Truman's Health Plan," advertisement page, box 552, file 2506, President's Personal File, Central File, TL.

8 "Reorganization of Federal Programs for Health, Education and Social Security, July 4, 1945," box 575, Department of National Health (proposed) file, Official Files, Central Files, TL; Emery A. Johnson and Everett R. Rhoades, "The History and Organization of Indian Health Services and Systems," in Everett R. Rhoades, ed., *American Indian Health: Innovations in Health Care, Promotion, and Policy* (Baltimore, MD: Johns Hopkins University Press, 2000), 75–76.

9 "Modification of Federal Grants-in-Aid for Public Health Services, Draft Report, September 1960," p. 5 Appendix, box 2, Modification of Federal Grants-in-Aid for Public Health Services file, Robert E. Merriam Records, 1956–1961, EL; Woods, *LBJ: Architect of American Ambition*, 337.

10 "Summary Statement of Current Activities and Programs in Migratory Labor of the Department of Labor, September 1955," box 196, Migrant Workers, General file, WHC, EL; Kelley, "Sweatshops in the Sun," p. 9; Ruth Boring Howard, "Better Health for Colorado's Migrant Children," *Children* 3 (March-April 1956): 43–48.

11 Alan R. Hinman and Walter A. Orenstein, "A Shot at Protection: Immunizations against Infectious Disease," in John W. Ward and Christian Warren, eds., *Silent Victories: The History and Practice of Public Health in Twentieth-Century America* (New York: Oxford University Press, 2007), 73, 75; Edward R. Schlesinger, "Child-Health Services since 1935," *Children* 2 (July-August 1955): 128; National Network for Immunization Information website.

12 Joe Palca, "Salk Polio Vaccine Conquered Terrifying Disease," April 12, 2005, National Public Radio, transcript online.

13 Press release, April 22, 1955, box 601, Infantile Paralysis file, Official File, Central Files, EL; Bart Barnes, "Jonas Salk, Polio Pioneer, Dies: Breakthrough Halted Infantile Paralysis," *Washington Post*, June 24, 1995, p. 1A.

14 Cabinet minutes, box 5, April 29, 1955 file, Ann Whitman File, EL; "Remarks by Oveta Culp Hobby," 3–4, box 44, Conference on Salk Vaccine file, Hobby Papers, EL; press release, May 31, 1955, box 601, Salk Polio Vaccine file (3), Official File, Central Files, EL.

15 Eisenhower, *At Ease*, 181.

16 Memo, legislative meeting, July 26, 1955, box 2, Legislative Meetings 1955 file, Ann Whitman File, EL; David M. Oshinsky, *Polio: An American Story* (New York: Oxford University Press, 2005), 218; "Editorial," 313; Reminiscences of Dr. Leonard Scheele, 1968, pp. 16, 18, Columbia University Oral History Research Office Collection (hereinafter cited as CUOHROC), transcript also available at Eisenhower Presidential Library.

17 Reminiscences of Dr. Leonard Scheele, 1968, p. 18, CUOHROC.

18 *Congress and the Nation, 1945–1964: A Review of Government and Politics in the Postwar Years* (Washington, DC: Congressional Quarterly Review, 1965), 1136–1137.

19 "Report to the President by the Secretary of Health, Education, and Welfare on the Distribution of Salk Vaccine, May 9, 1955," pp. 11, 39, box 601, Salk Polio Vaccine file (1), Official File, Central Files, EL; Reminiscences of Dr. Leonard Scheele, pp. 7–8, CUOHROC; Jeffrey Kluger, *Splendid Solution: Jonas Salk and the Conquest of Polio* (New York: G. P. Putnam's Sons, 2004), 308.

20 Oshinsky, *Polio*, 222, 227, 237; "Prospect Bright on Polio Vaccine," *New York Times*, April 8, 1956, p. 21; Becky Tanner, "Protection, Kansas, Was First U.S. Town to Get Polio Vaccine," *Wichita [KS] Eagle*, March 30, 2009, online.

21 Anne Finger, *Elegy for a Disease: A Personal and Cultural History of Polio* (New York: St. Martin's Press, 2006), 55.

22 Friends of Betty Harner to Eisenhower, September 21, 1957, box 726B, Letters to Children file (3), President's Personal File, EL; Frederic Fox, Special Assistant, White House, to Harold E. Roberts, January 8, 1959, box 694, Infantile Paralysis file, President's Personal File, EL.

23 "Modification of Federal Grants-in-Aid for Public Health Services, Draft Report, September 1960," pp. 8, 10 Appendix, box 2, Modification of Federal Grants-in-Aid for Public Health Services file, Robert E. Merriam Records, 1956–1961, EL; Edward Davens, "Services to Crippled Children," *Children* 2 (July-August 1955): 140.

24 I. Jack Martin to Sen. Gordon Allott, October 29, 1956, box 843, Children and Child Welfare file (1), Central Files, EL.

25 Julie Sturgeon and Janice Meer, *The First Fifty Years, 1956–2006: The President's Council on Physical Fitness and Sports Revisits Its Roots and Charts Its Future* (Washington, DC: Department of Health and Human Service, Government Printing Office, 2006), 41. The names of those attending the luncheon are listed in President's Appointment Book, Monday, July 11, 1955, Central Files, EL.

26 Sturgeon and Meer, *The First Fifty Years*, 41.

27 Eisenhower to Vice President Nixon, July 11, 1955, box 643, OF 126-A-2 file, Central Files, EL.

28 Memo, Andrew J. Goodpaster to Governor Adams, August 5, 1955, box 844, President's Conference on Physical Fitness file (1), Central Files, EL.

29 Executive Order # 10673, July 16, 1956, Box 844, President's Conference on Physical Fitness file (2), Central Files, EL; Bill Armstrong, "President's Conference on American Youth," *Amateur Athlete* 27 (July 1956): 6; "About the President's Council on Youth Fitness," *Journal of Health-Physical Education-Recreation* 6 (September 1957): 35–36.

30 "The President's Message, June 19, 1956," box 844, President's Conference on Physical Fitness file (2), Central Files, EL; "About the President's Council on Youth Fitness," 35–36; Armstrong, "President's Conference on Youth," 6; Shane MacCarthy, "Enjoy Keeping Fit," *American Recreation Society Bulletin* 9 (May 1957): 6.

31 Helen Rowe to Emmy Hartman, September 23, 1955, and Earl H. Black to Robert L. King, August 20, 1956, box 844, President's Conference on Physical Fitness file (2), Central Files, EL; MacCarthy, "Enjoy Keeping Fit," 5.

32 "Remarks by Shane MacCarthy, West Point Conference, September 9–10, 1957," box 844, American Youth Fitness file, Central Files, EL; "Shane MacCarthy," *Sports Illustrated* 5 (October 1, 1956): 1.

33 "Remarks by Shane MacCarthy, West Point Conference, September 9–10, 1957," and Dr. Ernest Jokl, "Memorandum Proposing the Establishment of a Physical Fitness Laboratory at the University of Kentucky, February 15, 1957," p. 3, box 844, American Youth Fitness file, Central Files, EL.

34 "Special Message to the Congress Recommending a Comprehensive Health Program, November 19, 1945," John Woolley and Gerhard Peters, American Presidency Project online; David A. Nichols, *Eisenhower 1956: The President's Year of Crisis, Suez and the Brink of War* (New York: Simon & Schuster, 2011), 4, 64–65.

35 Edward R. Schlesinger, David E. Overton, and Helen C. Chase, "A Long-Term Medical Study of Children in a Community with a Fluoridated Water Supply," in James H. Shaw, ed., *Fluoridation as a Public Health Measure* (Washington, DC: American Association for the Advancement of Science, 1954), 132–132; Gretchen Ann Reilly, "The Task Is a Political One: The Promotion of Fluoridation," in Ward and Warren, eds., *Silent Victories*, 324.

36 Reilly, "The Task Is a Political One," 329, 335.

37 Ibid., 333; Dr. Alfred Taylor to Dr. Eva Hill, March 19, 1959, and A. S. Robinson to Eisenhower, November 12, 1959, box 1149, Cranberries file, General File, Central Files, EL.

38 "A Kodak Moment," from the U.S. Nuclear Weapons Cost Study Project, Brookings Institution, Brookings Education online.

39 Richard L. Miller, *Under the Cloud: The Decades of Nuclear Testing* (New York: Free Press, 1986), 238.

40 Press release, Arthur S. Flemming, March 16, 1959, box 535, Radiation/Radioactive file, Official File, Central Files, EL.

41 Miller, *Under the Cloud*, 230–247, 259; Robert W. Miller, "Safeguarding Children from Radiation Risks," *Children* 3 (November-December, 1956): 206–207.

42 Press release, Arthur S. Flemming, March 16, 1959, box 535, Radioactive/Radioactive file, Official File, Central Files, EL.

43 John L. Harvey, "What Can Industry Do to Help Solve Problems of Antibiotics and Insecticides," speech, box 542, Cranberries file (1), Official File, Central Files, EL.

44 "Statement by Arthur S. Flemming, December 23, 1959, box 542, Cranberries file (1), Official File, Central Files, EL; Rachel Carson, *Silent Spring* (New York: Houghton Mifflin, 1962), 136.

45 "The Pesticide Residue Problem," box 542, Cranberries file (1), Official File, Central Files, EL.

46 David D. Vail, "Kill That Thistle: Rogue Sprayers, Bootlegged Chemicals, Wicked Weeds, and the Kansas Chemical Laws, 1945–1980," *Kansas History* 35 (Summer 2012): 121–122.

47 Memo, Don Paarlberg to Maurice Stans, October 9, 1959, box 542, Cranberry file (1), Official File, Central Files, EL.

48 George B. Kistiakowsky, *A Scientist at the White House: The Private Diary of President Eisenhower's Special Assistant for Science and Technology* (Cambridge, MA: Harvard University Press, 1976), 209; UP News Release, box 524, Cranberries file (1), Official File, Central Files, EL.

49 Frank Thompson, Jr., to Eisenhower, November 12, 1959, and Hastings Keith to Eisenhower, November 12, 1959, box 1149, Cranberries file, General File, Central Files, EL; Kistiakowsky, *A Scientist at the White House*, 208–209; "The Cranberry Boggle," *Time* 74 (November 23, 1959): 25.

50 Ullman Kilgore and Joe Kilgore to Eisenhower, November 11, 1959, box 1149, Cranberries file, General File, Central Files, EL.

51 Kistiakowsky, *A Scientist at the White House*, 208–209; Arthur S. Flemming Oral History, transcript, p. 41, EL.

52 Press release, June 19, 1956, box 844, President's Conference on Physical Fitness file (2), Central Files, EL.

CONCLUSION

Epigraph: Eisenhower to Mamie Moore, July 29, 1960, box 51, Dictation, July 1960 file, Diary Series, Ann Whitman File, EL.

1 David Lawrence, "People to People," *US News and World Report* (January 17, 1958), p. 120, clipping in Eisenhower Presidential Papers, Administrative Series, box 29, People to People file, EL.

2 "Platform Recommendations and Pledge to Children," p. iii, iv, box 9, Follow-Up Meeting file, WHC, EL.

3 Marshall, "Children's Rights and Children's Action," 355–356.

4 Michael Grossberg, "Liberation and Caretaking: Fighting over Children's Rights

in Postwar America," in Fass and Grossberg, eds., *Reinventing Childhood after World War II*, 21–23; The Universal Declaration of Human Rights, UN Document A/810 at 71, December 10, 1948; Marshall, "Children's Rights and Children's Action," 355–356; "Draft Declaration of the Rights of the Child," *United Nations Review* 5 (May 1959): 45. As of this writing, a later and more comprehensive statement of rights, the 1989 UN Convention on the Rights of the Child, has not been ratified by the United States.

5 Lois Gratz, "An Exchange of Ideas and Experiences with Observers to the White House Conference from Germany, and with Others Who Share Their Concern for Children and Youth," pp. 10–14, Office of the U.S. High Commission for Germany, Office of Public Affairs, box 10, Lois Gratz—Germany Project file, WHC, EL.

6 "Federal Agencies' Follow-Up: Midcentury White House Conference on Children and Youth, December 1950–December 1951," and "Department of State: Recommendation 66—International Cooperation," box 9, Federal Follow-Up file, WHC, EL.

7 Mintz, *Huck's Raft*, 2; Charles Loring Brace, *The Dangerous Classes of New York and Twenty Years' Work among Them*, 3rd ed. (New York: Wynkoop & Hallenbeck, 1880; reprint, Montclair, NJ: Patterson Smith, 1967).

8 H. Leroy Whitney to Truman, November 11, 1948, box 127, Educational Matters, 25, file, President's Personal File, Central Files, TL.

9 Letter from editor, Knoxville, Tennessee, February 8, 1954, and letter from editor, Albuquerque, New Mexico, February 10, 1954, box 32, Health, Education, and Welfare file, Subject Series, Central Files, EL.

10 Peggy Pizzo, "Slouching toward Bethlehem: American Federal Policy Perspectives on Children and Their Families," 12, and Theodore R. Marmor, "Competing Perspectives on Social Policy," 49–50, in Zigler, Kagan, and Klugman, eds., *Children, Families, and Government: Perspectives on American Social Policy*.

11 "Verbatim Discussion: Subcommittee on Guidelines for the 1965 Report to the Nation," pp. 4–5, box 287, Committee on Guidelines for the 1965 Report file, WHC, EL.

12 Ibid., pp. 2–5; Pizzo, "Slouching toward Bethlehem, 21–22; Edward A. Richards, "Today's Children and Youth, II: As Seen by National Organizations," *Children* 7 (March-April 1960): 61; John A. Andrew III, *Lyndon Johnson and the Great Society* (Chicago: Ivan R. Dee, 1998), 112.

13 "Summary of Discussion Groups of Mid-Decade Conference on Children and Youth," p. 3, box 285, Closing Session file, WHC, EL; Andrew, *Lyndon Johnson and the Great Society*, 132.

14 "Summary of Discussion Groups of Mid-Decade Conference on Children and Youth, p. 23, box 285, Closing Session file, WHC, EL.

15 Doris Kearns, *Lyndon Johnson and the American Dream* (New York: Harper & Row, 1976), 211, 251; Andrew, *Lyndon Johnson and the Great Society*, 5–6.

16 Mintz, *Huck's Raft*, 130, 324.

17 Ibid., 330, 333; Close, "Impressions of the White House Conference," 90.

18 "2010 White House Conference on Children and Youth," *Journal of Child and*

Adolescent Psychiatric Nursing, cited on *Bay Ledger News Zone*, online; "Why Does Ronald Reagan Fear Kids?" *Nevada* [MO] *Herald*, January 10, 1982, p. 5, *Nevada* [MO] *Daily Mail*, online; Steven Mintz and Susan Kellogg, *Domestic Revolutions: A Social History of American Family Life* (New York: Free Press, 1989), 240; Levine, *School Lunch Politics*, 175.

19 Congressional bills to reinstate the White House Conference on Children and Youth with a meeting in 2010 were introduced and failed in 2008 and 2009.

BIBLIOGRAPHY

FEDERAL ARCHIVES
National Archives and Records Administration, College Park, MD
    U.S. Children's Bureau, Record Group 102
    Orphan Correspondence Files, Record Group 278
Dwight D. Eisenhower Presidential Library, Abilene, KS
    Central Files
        Arthur S. Flemming Oral History
        Arthur S. Flemming Papers
        Oveta Culp Hobby Papers
        Katherine G. Howard Papers
        Robert E. Merriam Records
        President's Committee for Hungarian Relief Records
        President's Personal File
        White House Conference on Children and Youth Records
        Ann Whitman File
Harry S. Truman Presidential Library, Independence, MO
    Central Files
    Official Files
        Oscar R. Ewing Oral History
        President's Personal File
        Harry N. Rosenfield Oral History

OTHER COLLECTIONS AND ONLINE PROJECTS
American Merchant Marine at War, *Mast Magazine* excerpts, online.
The American Presidency Project. John T. Woolley and Gerhard Peters, online.
Columbia University Oral History Research Collection. Reminiscences of Dr. Leonard Scheele.
"The Congressional Front" (newsletters). Everett M. Dirksen Papers, Dirksen Congressional Center, online.
Eleanor Roosevelt Papers Project, online.
Federal Communications Commission, online.
"Federal Education Policy and the States, 1945–2009." States' Impact on Federal Education Project. New York State Archives, 2009, online.
Herbert Hoover speech, 1960 National Republican Convention. Video, NBC News Archives, C-Span Video Library, online.
"History of Comics Censorship, Part I." Comic Book Legal Defense Fund, 2012, online.

Hoover Institution, Stanford University, Palo Alto, CA. American Relief Adminis-
tration, European Unit, Records, 1919–1923.
Kim, Eleana. "The Origins of Korean Adoption: Cold War Geopolitics and Intimate
Diplomacy." Working Paper Series, 2009. U.S.-Korea Institute at SAIS, online.
"A Kodak Moment." U.S. Nuclear Weapons Cost Study Project. Brookings Institu-
tion, Brookings Education, online.
National Network for Immunization Information, online.
Palca, Joe. "Salk Polio Vaccine Conquered Terrifying Disease." National Public Ra-
dio, April 12, 2005, transcript, online.
"2010 White House Conference on Children and Youth." *Journal of Child and Ado-
lescent Psychiatric Nursing. Bay Ledger News Zone*, online.
"A U.S.-Cuban Airlift of Precious Cargo: Children." National Public Radio, December 31, 2010, transcript, online.
"Why Does Ronald Reagan Fear Kids?" *Nevada* [MO] *Herald*, January 10, 1982.
Nevada [MO] *Daily Mail*, online.

GOVERNMENT (STATE AND FEDERAL) PUBLICATIONS
*Congress and the Nation, 1945–1964: A Review of Government and Politics in the
Postwar Years.* Washington, DC: Congressional Quarterly Review, 1965.
*Freedom of Communications: Final Report of the Committee on Commerce, United
States Senate . . . , Part III: The Joint Appearances of Senator John F. Kennedy and
Vice President Nixon and other 1960 Campaign Presentations, 87th Congress, 1st
Sess. Senate Report No. 994, Part 3.* Washington, DC: Government Printing Of-
fice, 1962.
Gibson, Hugh. "Migration from Western Europe under the Intergovernmental
Committee for European Migration." *Department of State Bulletin* 29 (July 27,
1953): 117–121.
Hobbs, Frank, and Nicole Stoops. "Demographic Trends in the 20th Century." *Spe-
cial Reports, Series CENSR-4, U.S. Census Bureau.* Washington, DC: Govern-
ment Printing Office, 2002.
Interdepartmental Committee on Children and Youth. *Programs of the Federal Gov-
ernment affecting Children and Youth.* Washington, DC: Government Printing
Office, 1951.
Lajewski, Henry C. "Working Mothers and Their Arrangements for Care of Their
Children." *Social Security Bulletin* 22 (August 1959): 8–15.
Morton, Thurston B. "The U.S. Program for Refugee Relief." *Department of State
Bulletin* 33 (October 10, 1955): 561–565.
New Mexico Department of Public Welfare. *Annual Report, Fiscal Year Ending June
30, 1951.* Santa Fe: New Mexico Department of Public Welfare, 1952.
Senate Judiciary Subcommittee Investigating Juvenile Delinquency. *Comic Books
and Juvenile Delinquency: Interim Report of the Committee on the Judiciary, Re-*

port No. 62. 84th Cong., 1st sess. Washington, DC: Government Printing Office, 1955.

———. *Juvenile Delinquency (California): Hearings before the Subcommittee to Investigate Juvenile Delinquency.* 83rd Cong., 2nd sess. Washington, DC: Government Printing Office, 1954.

———. *Juvenile Delinquency (Comic Books): Hearings before the Subcommittee to Investigate Juvenile Delinquency.* 83rd Cong., 2nd sess. Washington, DC: Government Printing Office, 1954.

———. *Juvenile Delinquency (Indians): Hearings before the Subcommittee to Investigate Juvenile Delinquency.* 83rd Cong., 2nd sess. Washington, DC: Government Printing Office, 1954.

———. *Television and Juvenile Delinquency: Interim Report of the Subcommittee to Investigate Juvenile Delinquency.* 84th Cong., 1st sess. Washington, DC: Government Printing Office, 1955.

"Standards of Child Health, Education and Social Welfare." *U.S. Children's Bureau Publication 287* (1942).

Sturgeon, Julie, and Janice Meer. *The First Fifty Years, 1956–2006: The President's Council on Physical Fitness and Sports Revisits Its Roots and Charts Its Future.* Washington, DC: Department of Health and Human Services, Government Printing Office, 2006.

U.S. Congress, House of Representatives, Permitting Admission of 400,000 Displaced Persons into the United States: Hearing before Subcommittee on Immigration and Naturalization. Washington, DC: Government Printing Office, 1947.

U.S. Department of Commerce. "1950 Census Population: Advance Reports." *Publication No. 14* (July 1953).

———. "1950 Census Population: Advance Reports." *Publication No. 16* (July 1953).

———. *1950 Census Population: Institutional Population, Special Reports.* Washington, DC: Government Printing Office, 1953.

U.S. Department of Defense. *Manual for Intercountry Adoption.* Washington, DC: Government Printing Office, 1959.

Warren, George L. "Problems of Financing European Migration." *Department of State Bulletin* 33 (August 22, 1955): 308–310.

White House Conference on Children in a Democracy, Washington, D.C., January 18–20, 1940. Washington, DC: Superintendent of Documents, 1941.

Wiener, Jack. *Survey Methods for Determining the Need for Services to Children of Working Mothers.* Washington, DC: U.S. Department of Health, Education, and Welfare, 1956.

BOOKS

Abell, Tyler, ed. *Drew Pearson Diaries, 1949–1959.* New York: Holt, Rinehart and Winston, 1974.

Altschuler, Glenn C. *All Shook Up: How Rock 'n' Roll Changed America*. New York: Oxford University Press, 2003.

Ambrose, Stephen E. *Eisenhower: The President*, vol. 2. New York: Simon & Schuster, 1984.

Andrew, John A., III. *Lyndon Johnson and the Great Society*. Chicago: Ivan R. Dee, 1998.

Askeland, Lori, ed. *Children and Youth in Adoption, Orphanages, and Foster Care*. Westport, CT: Greenwood Press, 2006.

Bates, Daisy. *The Long Shadow of Little Rock: A Memoir*. New York: David McKay, 1962.

Bernstein, Irving. *Promises Kept: John F. Kennedy's New Frontier*. New York: Oxford University Press, 1991.

Blumenfeld, Samuel L. *N.E.A.: The Trojan Horse in American Education*. Boise, ID: Paradigm, 1984.

Brace, Charles Loring. *The Dangerous Classes of New York and Twenty Years' Work among Them*, 3rd ed. New York: Wynkoop & Hallenbeck, 1880; reprint, Montclair, NJ.: Patterson Smith, 1967.

Bradley, John, ed. *Learning to Glow: A Nuclear Reader*. Tucson: University of Arizona Press, 2000.

Bremmer, Robert H., ed. *Children and Youth in America: A Documentary History*, vol. 2. Cambridge, MA: Harvard University Press, 1971.

Brokaw, Tom. *Boom!* New York: Random House, 2007.

Brooks, Victor D. *Boomers: The Cold War Generation Grows Up*. Chicago: Ivan R. Dee, 2009.

Carson, Rachel. *Silent Spring*. New York: Houghton Mifflin, 1962.

Carter, Paul A. *Another Part of the Fifties*. New York: Columbia University Press, 1983.

Chamberlain, Hope. *A Minority of Members: Women in the U.S. Congress*. New York: Praeger, 1973.

Champagne, Anthony. *Congressman Sam Rayburn*. New Brunswick, NJ: Rutgers University Press, 1984.

Cherlin, Andrew. *Marriage, Divorce, Remarriage*. Cambridge, MA: Harvard University Press, 1992.

Cohen, Lizabeth. *A Consumers' Republic: The Politics of Mass Consumption in Postwar America*. New York: Vintage Books, 2003.

Coleman, James. *The Adolescent Society*. New York: Free Press, 1961.

Coontz, Stephanie. *The Way We Never Were: American Families and the Nostalgia Trap*. New York: Basic Books, 1992.

Dickson, Paul. *Sputnik: The Shock of the Century*. New York: Walker, 2001.

Donovan, Robert J. *Tumultuous Years: The Presidency of Harry S. Truman, 1949–1953*. New York: W. W. Norton, 1982.

Eire, Carlos. *Waiting for Snow in Havana: Confessions of a Cuban Boy*. New York: Free Press, 2003.

Eisenhower, Dwight D. *At Ease: Stories I Tell to Friends*. New York: Doubleday, 1967.

Eisenhower, Julie Nixon. *Pat Nixon: The Untold Story*. New York: Simon & Schuster, 1986.

Fanshel, David. *Far from the Reservation: The Transracial Adoption of American Indian Children*. Metuchen, NJ: Scarecrow Press, 1972.

Fass, Paula S., and Michael Grossberg, eds. *Reinventing Childhood after World War II*. Philadelphia: University of Pennsylvania Press, 2012.

Finger, Anne. *Elegy for a Disease: A Personal and Cultural History of Polio*. New York: St. Martin's Press, 2006.

Flesch, Rudolf. *Why Johnny Can't Read: And What You Can Do about It*. New York: Harper & Brothers, 1955.

Franklin, John Hope. *From Slavery to Freedom: A History of Negro Americans*, 3rd. ed. New York: Vintage Books, 1976.

Futrell, Robert Frank. *The United States Air Force in Korea, 1950–1953*. New York: Duell, Sloan and Pearce, 1961.

Gilbert, James. *A Cycle of Outrage: America's Reaction to the Juvenile Delinquent in the 1950s*. New York: Oxford University Press, 1986.

Gillon, Steve. *Boomer Nation: The Largest and Richest Generation Ever and How It Changed America*. New York: Free Press, 2004.

Gonzales, Manuel G., and Cynthia M. Gonzales, eds. *En Aquel Entonces: Readings in Mexican-American History*. Indianapolis: Indiana University Press, 2000.

Grant, Julia. *Raising Baby by the Book: The Education of American Mothers*. New Haven, CT: Yale University Press, 1998.

Gutman, Yisreal, and Avital Saf, eds. *She'arit Hapleta 1944–1948, Rehabilitation and Political Struggle, Proceedings of the Sixth Yad Vashem International Historical Conference*. Jerusalem: Yad Vashem, 1990.

Hajdu, David. *The 10-Cent Plague: The Great Comic Book Scare and How It Changed America*. New York: Farrar, Straus and Giroux, 2008.

Halberstam, David. *The Fifties*. New York: Villard Books, 1993.

Heinemann, Ronald L. *Harry Byrd of Virginia*. Charlottesville: University Press of Virginia, 1996.

Hickam, Homer H., Jr. *Rocket Boys: A Memoir*. New York: Delacorte Press, 1998.

Hollis, Florence. *Women in Marital Conflict: A Casework Study*. New York: Family Service Association of America, 1949.

Holt, Daniel D. *Kansas Bureau of Investigation, 1939–1989*. Topeka: Kansas Bureau of Investigation, 1989.

Holt, Daniel D., and James W. Leyerzapf, eds. *Eisenhower: The Prewar Diaries and Selected Papers, 1905–1941*. Baltimore, MD: Johns Hopkins University Press, 1998.

Holt, Marilyn Irvin. *Linoleum, Better Babies, and the Modern Farm Woman, 1890–1930*. Albuquerque: University of New Mexico Press, 1995; reprint, Lincoln: University of Nebraska Press, 2005.

———. *Mamie Doud Eisenhower: The General's First Lady*. Lawrence: University Press of Kansas, 2007.

Humphrey, Hubert H. *The Education of a Public Man: My Life and Politics*. New York: Doubleday, 1976; reprint, Minneapolis: University of Minnesota Press, 1991.

Jones, Landon Y. *Great Expectations: America and the Baby Boom Generation*. New York: Coward, McCann & Geoghegan, 1980.

Kearns, Doris. *Lyndon Johnson and the American Dream*. New York: Harper & Row, 1976.

Kirk, John A. *Redefining the Color Line: Black Activism in Little Rock, Arkansas, 1940–1970*. Gainesville: University Press of Florida, 2002.

Kistiakowsky, George B. *A Scientist at the White House: The Private Diary of President Eisenhower's Special Assistant for Science and Technology*. Cambridge, MA: Harvard University Press, 1976.

Kluger, Jeffrey. *Splendid Solution: Jonas Salk and the Conquest of Polio*. New York: G. P. Putnam's Sons, 2004.

Kramer, Dale, and Madeline Karr. *Teenage Gangs*. New York: Henry Holt, 1953.

Kutscher, Austen Ken. *Watching Walter Cronkite: Reflections on Growing Up in the 1950s and 1960s*. New York: Gordian Knot Books, 2009.

Kvasnicka, Robert M., and Herman J. Viola, eds. *The Commissioners of Indian Affairs, 1824–1977*. Lincoln: University of Nebraska Press, 1979.

Lait, Jack, and Lee Mortimer. *U.S.A. Confidential*. New York: Crown, 1952.

Larsen, Otto N., ed. *Violence and the Media*. New York: Harper & Row, 1968.

Lee, Mordecai. *Congress vs. the Bureaucracy: Muzzling Agency Public Relations*. Norman: University of Oklahoma Press, 2011.

Levine, Robert M., and Moisés Asis. *Cuban Miami*. New Brunswick, NJ: Rutgers University Press, 2000.

Levine, Susan. *School Lunch Politics: The Surprising History of America's Favorite Welfare Program*. Princeton, NJ: Princeton University Press, 2008.

Lindenmeyer, Kriste. *The Greatest Generation Grows Up: American Childhood in the 1930s*. Chicago: Ivan R. Dee, 2005.

———. *"A Right to Childhood": The U.S. Children's Bureau and Child Welfare*. Urbana: University of Illinois Press, 1997.

McCullough, David. *Truman*. New York: Simon & Schuster, 1992.

McEnaney, Laura. *Civil Defense Begins at Home: Militarization Meets Everyday Life in the Fifties*. Princeton, NJ: Princeton University Press, 2000.

McKenzie, Richard B., ed. *Home Away from Home: The Forgotten History of Orphanages*. New York: Encounter Books, 2009.

Martin, Josephine, and Charlotte Oakley. *Managing Child Nutrition Programs: Leadership for Excellence*, 2nd ed. Sudbury, MA: Jones & Bartlett Publishers, 2008.

May, Elaine Tyler. *Homeward Bound: American Families in the Cold War Era*, rev. ed. New York: Basic Books, 1999.

May, Lary, ed. *Recasting America: Culture and Politics in the Age of the Cold War*. Chicago: University of Chicago Press, 1989.

Mayor LaGuardia's Committee on Marijuana. *The Marijuana Problem in the City of New York*. Lancaster, PA: Jacques Cattell Press, 1944; reprint, Metuchen, NJ: Scarecrow Press, 1973.

Mead, Margaret, and Frances Balgley Kaplan, eds. *American Women: The Report of the President's Commission on the Status of Women and Other Publications of the Commission*. New York: Charles Scribner's Sons, 1965.

Meyerowitz, Joanne, ed. *Not June Cleaver: Women and Gender in Postwar America, 1945–1960*. Philadelphia: Temple University Press, 1994.

Michel, Sonya. *Children's Interests/Mothers' Rights: The Shaping of America's Child Care Policy*. New Haven, CT: Yale University Press, 1999.

Mickenberg, Julia L. *Learning from the Left: Children's Literature, the Cold War, and Radical Politics in the United States*. New York: Oxford University Press, 2006.

Miller, Richard L. *Under the Cloud: The Decades of Nuclear Testing*. New York: Free Press, 1986.

Mintz, Steven. *Huck's Raft: A History of American Childhood*. Cambridge, MA: Belknap Press, Harvard University Press, 2004.

Mintz, Steven, and Susan Kellogg. *Domestic Revolutions: A Social History of American Family Life*. New York: Free Press, 1989.

Morris, Roger. *Richard Milhous Nixon: The Rise of an American Politician*. New York: Henry Holt, 1990.

Mumford, Lewis. *The City in History*. New York: Harcourt, Brace, 1961.

National Manpower Council. *Womanpower: A Statement by the National Manpower Council*. New York: Columbia University Press, 1957.

National School Boards Association. *School Boards Plan for Disaster Problems*. Chicago: National School Boards Association, Inc., 1959.

Newton, Jim. *Eisenhower: The White House Years*. New York: Doubleday, 2011.

Nichols, David A. *A Matter of Justice: Eisenhower and the Beginning of the Civil Rights Revolution*. New York: Simon & Schuster, 2007.

———. *Eisenhower 1956: The President's Year of Crisis, Suez and the Brink of War*. New York: Simon & Schuster, 2011.

Oshinsky, David M. *Polio: An American Story*. New York: Oxford University Press, 2005.

Rhoades, Everett R., ed. *American Indian Health: Innovations in Health Care, Promotion, and Policy*. Baltimore, MD: Johns Hopkins University Press, 2000.

Richards, Edward A., ed. *Proceedings of the Midcentury Conference on Children and Youth*. Raleigh, NC: Heath Publications, 1951.

Salisbury, Harrison. *The Shook-Up Generation*. New York: Fawcett, 1962.

Sammond, Nicholas. *Babes in Tomorrowland: Walt Disney and the Making of the American Child, 1930–1960*. Durham, NC: Duke University Press, 2005.

Sealander, Judith. *The Failed Century of the Child: Governing America's Young in the Twentieth Century*. New York: Cambridge University Press, 2003.

Shaw, James H., ed. *Fluoridation as a Public Health Measure*. Washington, DC: American Association for the Advancement of Science, 1954.

Skolnick, Sharon, and Manny Skolnick. *Where Courage Is Like a Wild Horse: The World of an Indian Orphanage*. Lincoln: University of Nebraska Press, 1997.

Smuts, Robert W. *Women and Work in America*. New York: Columbia University Press, 1959.

Spock, Dr. Benjamin. *The Common Sense Book of Baby and Child Care*. New York: Duell, Sloan & Pearce, 1946.

Steinberg, Alfred. *Sam Johnson's Boy: A Close-Up of the President from Texas*. New York: Macmillan, 1968.

This Fabulous Century, 1950–1960. New York: Time-Life Books, 1970.

Trattner, Walter I. *From Poor Law to Welfare State: A History of Social Welfare in America*, 4th ed. New York: Free Press, 1974.

Truman, Harry S. *Memoirs of Harry S. Truman: Years of Trial and Hope*, vol. 2. Garden City, NY: Doubleday, 1956.

Truman, Margaret. *Harry S. Truman*. New York: William Morrow, 1973.

Tuttle, William M., Jr. *"Daddy's Gone to War": The Second World War in the Lives of Children*. New York: Oxford University Press, 1993.

Ward, John W., and Christian Warren, eds. *Silent Victories: The History and Practice of Public Health in Twentieth-Century America*. New York: Oxford University Press, 2007.

Wilkinson, J. Harvie, III. *Harry Byrd and the Changing Face of Virginia Politics, 1945–1966*. Charlottesville: University Press of Virginia, 1968.

Wilson, Paul E. *A Time to Lose: Representing Kansas in* Brown v. Board of Education. Lawrence: University Press of Kansas, 1995.

Woods, Randall B. *LBJ: Architect of American Ambition*. New York: Free Press, 2006.

World Almanac and Book of Facts for 1949. New York: New York World Telegram, 1949.

Wright, Jim. *Balance of Power: Presidents and Congress from the Era of McCarthy to the Age of Gingrich*. Atlanta: Turner Publishing, 1996.

Ybarra, Michael J. *Washington Gone Crazy: Senator Pat McCarran and the Great American Communist Hunt*. Hanover, NH: Steerforth Press, 2004.

Zigler, Edward F., Sharon Lynn Kagan, and Edgar Klugman, eds. *Children, Families, and Government: Perspectives on American Social Policy.* Cambridge, UK: Cambridge University Press, 1983.

ARTICLES

Abbott, Edith. "The Civil War and the Crime Wave of 1865–70." *Social Services Review* 1 (June 1927): 219.

"About the President's Council on Youth Fitness." *Journal of Health-Physical Education-Recreation* 6 (September 1957): 35–36.

"All Our Children." *Newsweek* 42 (November 9, 1953): 28.

Armstrong, Bill. "President's Conference on American Youth." *Amateur Athlete* 27 (July 1956): 6.

Barton, Betty, and Katherine D. Pringle. "Today's Children and Youth, I: A View from the States." *Children* 7 (March-April 1960): 50–56.

Brownlee, Aleta. "The American Indian Child." *Children* 5 (March-April 1958): 55–60.

Burns, Gerald P. "Higher Education Today." *Current History* 41 (July 1961): 26–34.

"The Children's Charter of President's White House Conference on Child Health and Protection, 1930." *Journal of the History of Childhood and Youth* 3 (Fall 2008): 378, Appendix 4.

"The Children's Hour." *Time* 64 (November 1, 1954): 64.

Close, Kathryn. "Impressions of the White House Conference." *Children* 7 (May-June 1960): 83–91.

"The Congress." *Time* 50 (July 7, 1947): 13.

"The Cranberry Boggle." *Time* 74 (November 23, 1959): 25.

Crippen, Blanche. "Educational Television—Public Servant." *Children* 2 (January-February, 1955): 22–26.

Curry, Sandra Adams, and Philip H. Hatlen. "Meeting the Unique Educational Needs of Visually Impaired Pupils through Appropriate Placement." *Journal of Visual Impairment and Blindness* 10 (April 2007): 237–238.

Davens, Edward. "Services to Crippled Children." *Children* 2 (July-August 1955): 139–144.

Davis, Hazel, and Madaline Kinter Remmlein. "Teachers' Salaries, Pensions, and Retirement Pay." *Review of Educational Research* 19 (June 1949): 240–249.

"Delinquency: Big and Bad." *Newsweek* 42 (November 30, 1953): 30.

Douglas, (Sen.) Paul. "Democracy Can't Live in These Houses." *Collier's* 9 (1949): 50.

"Draft Declaration of the Rights of the Child." *United Nations Review* 5 (May 1959): 45.

Dublin, Louis I. "Look on the Bright Side of Marriage: Some Facts and Figures concerning American Family Life." *Parents Magazine* 23 (December 1948): 68–70.

"Editorial." *California Medicine* 78 (April 1953): 313–314.

Flanagan, Richard M. "The Housing Act of 1954: The Sea Change in National Urban Policy." *Urban Affairs Review* 33 (November 1997): 265–282.

Fuller, Varden. "No Work Today! The Plight of America's Migrants." *Public Affairs Pamphlet No. 190* (January 1954).

Garwood, S. Gray, Deborah Philips, Andrew Hartman, and Edward F. Zigler. "As the Pendulum Swings: Federal Agency Programs for Children." *American Psychologist* 44 (February 1989): 434–440.

"The Golden Youth of Communism." *Life* 40 (March 5, 1956): 36–38.

"Good Samaritan of Korea." *American Mercury* 84 (October 1955): 84–88.

Grant, Alan. "The Sixth Grade." *Life* 33 (November 17, 1952): 145–147.

"Harry Holt and a Heartfull of Children." *Reader's Digest* 69 (October 1955): 67–70.

Hines, Clarence. "Elementary Education Today." *Current History* 41 (July 1961): 32–40.

Holt, Marilyn Irvin. "Children as Topic No. 1." *Prologue* 42 (Summer 2010): 18–27.

"How U.S. Lost Satellite Race: Charges and Countercharges Begin to Fly." *U.S. News and World Report* 43 (October 18, 1957): 18.

Howard, Ruth Boring. "Better Health for Colorado's Migrant Children." *Children* 3 (March-April 1956): 43–48.

Jacobs, Bo. "Atomic Kids: Duck and Cover and Atomic Alert Teach American Children How to Survive Atomic Attack." *Film & History: An Interdisciplinary Journal of Film and Television Studies* 40 (Spring 2010): 25–44.

"Juvenile Crime: Is Your Boy Safe?" *Newsweek* 42 (November 9, 1953): 28–30.

Katz, Milton S., and Susan B. Tucker. "A Pioneer in Civil Rights: Ester Brown and the South Park Desegregation Case of 1948." *Kansas History* 18 (Winter 1995–1996): 234–247.

Levitt, William J. "What! Live in a Levittown?" *Good Housekeeping* 147 (July 1958): 47, 175–176.

Life, "Teen-age Boys Are Just the Same as They've Always Been." 19 (June 11, 1945): 91–97.

Life, "The 36-Hour War." 19 (November 19, 1945): 27–35.

MacCarthy, Shane. "Enjoy Keeping Fit." *American Recreation Society Bulletin* 9 (May 1957): 4–7.

MacDonald, J. Frederick. "'Hot Jazz,' The Jitterbug, and Misunderstandings: The Generation Gap in Swing, 1935–1945." *Popular Music and Society* 2 (Fall 1972): 43–49.

McDonald, Mary Jean. "The Citizen's Committee for Children of New York and the Evolution of Child Advocacy (1945–1972)." *Child Welfare* 74 (January/February 1995): 283–304.

Mannes, Marc. "Factors and Events Leading to the Passage of the Indian Child Welfare Act." *Child Welfare* 74 (January/February 1995): 264–282.

Mar, Linda. "Federal Youth Corrections Act: YCA Treatment Not Required during

Unexpired Term of YCA Inmate Sentenced to Consecutive Adult Term." *Journal of Criminal Law and Criminology* 73 (Winter 1982): 1654–1677.

Marshall, Dominique. "Children's Rights and Children's Action in International Relief and Domestic Welfare: The Work of Herbert Hoover between 1914 and 1950." *Journal of the History of Childhood and Youth* 3 (Fall 2008): 351–388.

Mayo, Leonard W. "Directions in Child Welfare Progress." *Children* 2 (July-August 1955): 149–153.

Miller, Robert W. "Safeguarding Children from Radiation Risks." *Children* 3 (November–December 1956): 203–207.

"National Affairs." *Time* 50 (July 7, 1947): 13.

Norris, Jim. "Growing Up Growing Sugar: Local Teenage Labor in the Sugar Beet Fields, 1958–1974." *Agricultural History* 79 (Summer 2005): 298–320.

Oettinger, Katherine B. "The Growth and Meaning of the White House Conference on Children and Youth." *Children* 7 (January-February 1960): 3–8.

"President's Proclamation." *Midcentury White House Conference on Children and Youth Bulletin* 5 (June 20, 1951): 1.

"President's Views on Russia's Satellite." *U.S. News and World Report* 43 (October 18, 1957): 118.

"Prohibition Is Not the Answer." *American Journal of Public Health* 46 (August 1956): 1027–1028.

"Public Health, Nursing and Medical Social Work: Abstract." *Pediatrics* 1 (March 1, 1948): 429–432.

Rappaport, Mazie P. "Prostitution, Crime and Juvenile Delinquency." *Journal of Social Hygiene* 31 (December 1945): 586–589.

Richards, Edward A. "Today's Children and Youth, II: As Seen by National Organizations." *Children* 7 (March-April 1960): 57–62.

Rittwagen, Marjorie. "Child Criminals Are My Job." *Saturday Evening Post* 226 (March 27, 1954): 19–21.

Roberts, Dean W. "Highlights of the Midcentury White House Conference on Children and Youth." *American Journal of Public Health* 41 (January 1951): 96–99.

Schlesinger, Edward R. "Child-Health Services since 1935." *Children* 2 (July-August 1955): 128–132.

Schwartz, Edward E. "Counting Delinquent Children." *Children* 1 (November–December 1954): 227–231.

Segal, Robert M. "A New Look: The Economics of the Profession." *American Bar Association Journal* 43 (September 1957): 789–792.

"Shane MacCarthy." *Sports Illustrated* 5 (October 1, 1956): 1.

Shuster, George N. "Goals of American Education." *Current History* 41 (July 1961): 1–4.

Smith, Julie. "Where Was Dorothy's Mother?" *Newsletter: Society for the History of Children and Youth* 7 (Winter 2006): 1–3.

Sokoloff, Burton Z. "Antecedents of American Adoption." *The Future of Children* 3 (Spring 1993): 17–25.

"Speaking of Pictures: Teen-age Ballet." *Life* 19 (May 28, 1945): 12.

Stearns, Peter N. "Defining Happy Childhoods: Assessing a Recent Change." *Journal of the History of Children and Youth* 3 (Spring 2010): 165–186.

Steel, F. A. "The Cult of the Child." *Littell's Living Age* 237 (April-June 1903): 761.

Thornhill, Margaret A. "Unprotected Adoptions." *Children* 2 (September-October 1955): 180–184.

"Unwanted Find a Home." *Look* 20 (October 30, 1955): 106–108.

Vail, David D. "Kill That Thistle: Rogue Sprayers, Bootlegged Chemicals, Wicked Weeds, and the Kansas Chemical Laws, 1945–1980." *Kansas History* 35 (Summer 2012): 116–133.

"We Confer to Reach Long-Range Remedy." *Life* 39 (September 26, 1955): 36.

NEWSPAPERS

New York Times, 1950–1960

Washington Post, 1995

Wichita (KS) Eagle, 2009

INDEX

adolescence, defined, 18
adoption, 98, 101, 115
    California study of, 101–102
    international, 103, 106–113, 115
    laws, 99, 100
    of Native American children, 102, 103, 160
    private, 100
    standards for, 99–100
    and U.S. Children's Bureau, 99, 102
    U.S. rates for, 100, 101
Adventures of Ozzie and Harriet (TV show), 101
Adventures of Rin Tin Tin (TV show), 29
African Americans, 31, 64
    as migrant workers, 73
    and school integration, 67–71
    and White House Conferences on Children and Youth, 31–33, 45
Agricultural Act (1954), 58
agriculture
    and cranberry scare, 144–145
    and herbicide/pesticide use, 142–145
    and migrant workers, 73–74
    and National School Lunch Program, 56–57
Aid to Dependent Children (ADC), 13, 31–32, 152, 155
Aid to Dependent Mothers, 98
Aid to Families with Dependent Children (AFDC), 13, 155, 161
Alabama, 55, 68
Alaska, 128
Albuquerque (NM), 151
Allen, Gracie, 101
Allott, Gordon, 130
Ambrose, Stephen, 9
American Bandstand (TV show), 29
American Broadcasting Company (ABC), 30
American Child Health Association, 21
American Dental Association, 136
American Farm Bureau, 61
American Hellenic Education Progressive Association, 107
American Home Economics Association, 37
American-Korean Foundation, 109

American Medical Association, 120, 127
American Mercury (magazine), 110
American Psychological Association, 32
American Public Health Association, 43
American Red Cross, 165
American Relief Association, 112
American Samoa, 128
Anderson County (TN) School Board, 69
Anfuso, Victor L., 94–95
Angels with Dirty Faces (movie), 83
Annapolis (MD), 133
Anne of Green Gables (book), 96
antibiotics, 124
Arizona, 74
[Arizona] Governor's Committee on Migratory Labor, 74
Arkansas, 68, 70–71
Arkansas National Guard, 70
Armed Forces Aid to Korea, 110
Association for the Aid for Crippled Children, 165
atomic bomb, 24, 26, 27. *See also* nuclear testing and radioactive fallout
Atomic Energy Commission (AEC), 138, 140
Atomic Kid, The (movie), 139
Atomic Man, The (movie), 139
"Atoms for Peace" (speech), 147
Austria, postwar, 83, 104, 107, 108, 112

baby boom, 3, 6, 10, 17, 50–51
Ball, Lucille, 101
Barden, Graham A., 51
Benson, Ezra Taft, 144
Better Baby Movement, 119
bilingual education, 74, 160
Bilingual Education Act (1968), 160
birth rates, 6, 17
Blackboard Jungle, The (movie), 86
Blaik, Earl H., 134
Blaisdell, Russell L., 109
Blossom, Virgil, 70
Boggs Act (1951), 94
bomb shelters, 24–26
Bondy, Robert Earl, 15
Boone, Pat, 45
Boys Clubs of America, 132